Taking the Field

Women, Men, and Sports

Michael A. Messner

Sport and Culture Series, Volume 4

University of Minnesota Press
Minneapolis • London

An earlier version of chapter 1 originally appeared as "Barbie Girls vs. Sea Monsters: Children Constructing Gender," *Gender & Society* 14 (2000): 765–84. Parts of chapter 4 originally appeared as "Silence, Sports Bras, and Wrestling Porn: The Treatment of Women in Televised Sports News and Highlights," by Michael A. Messner, Margaret Carlisle Duncan, and Cheryl Cooky, in *Journal of Sport and Social Issues* (forthcoming).

Published by the University of Minnesota Press
111 Third Avenue South, Suite 290
Minneapolis, MN 55401-2520
http://www.upress.umn.edu

Printed in the United States of America on acid-free paper

Library of Congress Cataloging-in-Publication Data

Messner, Michael A.
  Taking the field : women, men, and sports / Michael A. Messner.
    p. cm. — (Sport and culture series ; v. 4)
  Includes bibliographical references (p.   ) and index.
    ISBN 0-8166-3448-3 (HC : alk. paper) — ISBN 0-8166-3449-1 (PB : alk. paper)
    1. Sex discrimination in sports—United States. 2. Sports—United States—
  Sex differences. 3. Feminism and sports—United States. I. Title. II. Series.
  GV706.32 .M47 2003
  796'.082—dc21
                                                                  2001008548

12 11 10 09 08 07 06 05 04 03   10 9 8 7 6 5 4 3 2

Taking the Field

SPORT AND CULTURE SERIES
TOBY MILLER AND M. ANN HALL, EDITORS

For Penatzi and The Great Scattiniavich,

friends for life

Contents

Preface

This past fall, my teenaged niece Samantha took me on a tour of my old high school. I was struck initially by the similarities between the Salinas High School that Samantha inhabits today and the school I went to from 1966 to 1970. I stood in the school's beautiful new gymnasium and spoke with Joe Chappell, the boys' basketball coach. My dad had been the varsity basketball coach here at Salinas High from 1947 to 1971; Chappell had played ball for my dad and then took over as varsity boys' coach in 1971. The season of 2000–2001 would be his thirtieth. That's over half a century, I mused, with only two varsity boys' basketball coaches: impressive continuity.

But when I looked around at the new gym, the beautifully remodeled campus, and the students, it struck me that as much had changed over the past thirty years as had stayed the same. The old "boys' gym" that my dad had labored in for most of his adult life (and that I had played in for several years) had been reduced to rubble to make way for the much larger new gym. I asked the coach what had become of the old girls' gym—a tiny cracker box whose walls were so close to the edge of the court, the building seemed to dictate that nobody should ever consider running very fast in that place. He said, yes, the old girls' gym was still standing and was still in use. However, he told me, "It's not called the girls' gym anymore. It's called the old gym, and the new one is called the new gym. The boys don't own the good facilities around here anymore." To emphasize his point, he took me outside the "new gym" and pointed to the top edge of the building. "Remember the tiles that were on the face of the old boys' gym?" he asked. Indeed, I did. The old Spanish-style building had sported individual tiles, each of which depicted a different icon of classic athletic performance: a hurdler; football, basketball, and baseball players. Back in the 1920s, the 1950s, even in 1970 when I was there, I'm sure few people even thought to notice that every single one of the athletes depicted on these beautiful tiles was a *man*. But in 1999, when they were building the new gym, somebody did notice. So they lovingly removed the older tiles from the doomed old boys' gym and fashioned some new ones of the same style to include, side by side, with the old tiles on the façade of the new gym. And these new ones depicted women athletes hurdling, playing basketball and soccer.

The gender symmetry depicted on the tiles of the new gym represents a dramatic shift toward an acceptance—even a symbolic celebration—of girls' and women's presence in sports. And these changes are not simply symbolic. Salinas High School, like other high schools in the United States, now has a large number of interscholastic sports for girls. Money is now budgeted for uniforms, travel, coaches' salaries, and trophies for girls' sports. We now think about the importance of the girls having access to good practice facilities. After visiting the high school, I pulled out my old yearbook from 1970, and I now see that at that time, gender inequity appeared so natural, it was invisible to me. In the yearbook, boys' sports teams occupied forty pages of photos that were accompanied by respectful and celebratory descriptions of wins, losses, glorious championships, and individual stars' triumphs and accomplishments. The boys were all decked out in the official school athletic uniform of the Salinas Cowboys, and each photo was accompanied by a caption—"Messner scrambles for layup"—that described the action and named the boys or coaches who were depicted.

By contrast, the girls' sports—all of which were intramural—were illustrated in the 1970 yearbook with ten pages of seemingly unrelated photos of girls throwing, swimming, jogging, doing sit-ups and jumping jacks, practicing archery, and bouncing on a trampoline. None of these girls were wearing official school sports uniforms, because such things did not then exist for girls. A few of them were dressed in street clothes. Most of the photos stand alone, with no captions at all. These girls had no uniforms, teams, or leagues; indeed, they appeared to have no names. What little written text accompanied this collage of photos was mostly trivial and apologetic: on one page we read that the girls were apparently trying to "Hop, Skip, and Jump to Fitness," and on another, we learn that "participating in numerous athletic activities develops coordination while providing many amusing moments." One caption read, "In achieving physical fitness girls must prove their abilities by performing certain tasks," and was placed directly under a photo of two girls in street clothes, one of whom appears to be placing a hat on the other's head.

The 2001 Salinas High School yearbook, like the tiles on the new gym, depicts girls' sports in much more equitable, respectful, even celebratory ways. The first thing I noticed is that the yearbook staff did not cordon off two separate spaces in the book for girls' sports and boys' sports, as they had in the past. Instead, there is simply one sports section of the book, with girls' teams, boys' teams, and (another very big difference) coed teams mixed in together. Roughly the same number of pages are allotted to girls' teams as to boys' teams. And three sports (cross country, wrestling, and track and field) appear in the yearbook as mixed, or coed, teams (though there was only one girl on the wrestling team). In addition to the numerical equity, the photos of the girl athletes stand in stark contrast to those in the 1970 yearbook. These girls of 2001 are depicted competing in interscholastic sports, wearing their school uniforms. And the captions under the photos give their names and list their athletic accomplishments. When we look at this public imagery, it seems that girl athletes have fully arrived at Salinas High School.

But has full equity been achieved for girls in sports at Salinas High or anywhere else? Before I left the campus on the day of my visit, I decided to peek into the girls'—that is, the old—gym. Curiously, it seemed that a girls' basketball team was practicing there, during a time when the new gym was not being used at all. Is the new gym, I wondered, still thought of as belonging primarily to the boys? To what extent is talk of gender equity—like the tiles on the new gym—a symbolic façade that may serve to obscure stubbornly persistent inequities in people's day-to-day practices?

Institutions have changed, yes, and in some dramatic ways since 1970. But we still devote far more resources to boys' and men's sports than to girls' and women's. Our symbolic understandings of athleticism have expanded—like the tiles on the new gym—to include images of girls and women. But the mass media still spend a grossly disproportionate amount of their time covering men's sports while ignoring, marginalizing, or trivializing women's sports. Girls and women are playing sports in greater numbers than ever before. But too often they still have to fight for the kinds of access, support, and respect that boys and men take for granted. This book examines these current tensions and paradoxes in the gender dynamics of sport. After thirty years of Title IX and surging female athleticism, the sport world we know barely resembles the world many of us were born into. But it's not quite yet a whole new ball game.

Acknowledgments

I wrote most of this book during a year-long sabbatical from my teaching and administrative work at the University of Southern California. I thank my colleagues and students in the Department of Sociology and in the Gender Studies Program at USC for generously allowing me the time to write. Bits and pieces of this work are based on research I conducted in recent years with colleagues and students. Thanks go to my research collaborators Mark Stevens, Shari Dworkin, Cheryl Cooky, Darnell Hunt, Michele Dunbar, and Margaret Carlisle Duncan. Thanks go also to the Amateur Athletic Foundation of Los Angeles and Children Now for funding two media studies that are incorporated into chapter 4.

Over the past decade, I have been inspired by the activist work of several people and organizations—too many to list here—to bring about equity and fairness and to confront core issues of violence, misogyny, and homophobia in sports. My hope for positive social change that underscores this book is buoyed by these activists' brave work in schools, athletic departments, coaches and athletic directors associations, public playgrounds, sport organizations, the media, and the law. I am also indebted to a diverse array of scholars in the fields of sex and gender and sport studies for their foundational research. Though I can't list them all here, I have done my best to reference their works in my notes.

Several trusted colleagues and friends generously took the time to read all or parts of an earlier draft of this manuscript. My appreciative thanks go to Jim McKay, Shari Dworkin, Bob Dunn, Toby Miller, Ann Hall, Paula Pearlman, Don Sabo, and Mark Stevens. I took their comments seriously, especially when they challenged my assumptions and arguments. And though I did not fully incorporate all of their suggestions, their collective contribution has improved the book substantially. Thanks go to Susan Fogel and the California Women's Law Center for providing me information on gender and the use of Los Angeles City Parks athletic facilities, and to Oscar Narro for introducing me to talk radio. Thanks go also to Wayne Wilson and Cheryl Cooky for their help in securing two of the photographs that appear in the book and to Samantha Rios for the high school tour and the yearbook pages. I also thank my editor Jennifer Moore at the University of Minnesota Press for her vision and support throughout the writing stages of this project. When Jennifer left the Press to pursue other goals, Carrie Mullen and Laura Westlund provided the final editorial shepherding that brought the book home.

Authors often say that writing a book is a lonely process. It was rarely so for me. In the months during which I spent several hours each day at my computer, I was constantly plugged into e-mail and had almost daily "conversations" with my mom, Anita Messner-Voth, who shared her daily life with me and, as always, urged me on. I also exchanged daily messages with various friends—especially my e-mail group of long-term friends Jim, Mo, Donnie, and Jon (the last two to whom I have dedicated this book). Moreover, my writing time was bookended daily by the twin school-day events of the 8:00 A.M. drop-off and the 2:20 P.M. pickup of my sons.

Miles and Sasha offer me continual joy, challenges, laughs, and (as readers of this book will see) valuable insights into children's worlds. As the years go by, my love, respect, and appreciation for my partner and colleague Pierrette Hondagneu-Sotelo continue to grow. I'm most fortunate, I know, to be able to say that my family is the uncontested center of my life.

Jumping Center

Los Angeles Lakers center Shaquille O'Neal shakes hands with his opponent, Philadelphia 76er Dikembe Mutombo, before the opening center jump. The referee who will toss the ball up is dwarfed by the two centers, both over seven feet tall. The capacity Staples Center crowd roars and stomps with the exciting NBA championship series game moments away from starting. The camera zooms to a close-up of O'Neal's already sweating face, then pulls back to reveal the other nine players, who have taken up their positions for the center jump. When the referee tosses up the ball, O'Neal and Mutombo lift their combined 580 pounds off the floor. The Lakers control the tip and take the offense. For most of the game, this will entail posting up O'Neal low on the block and, as the television announcers describe it, "sending the offense to and through their big center as much as possible."

Randy Johnson, perched at the center of the diamond, pulls his six-foot-ten-inch frame into the stretch position. He glances at the runner on first base, holding him close, and turns toward home plate, as forty thousand fans begin to chant for another strikeout. The television camera zooms in on Johnson's face; he glares at the catcher, shakes off a sign, then nods. Johnson takes another quick glance at the runner and begins his delivery. The crowd noise swells, the catcher adjusts his position and opens his glove to provide a target, the umpire leans in for a good view, the batter tenses, the fielders shift their weight to the balls of their feet, ready to react instantly, the cameras pull back for a wider angle view, and millions of fans watch when Johnson unleashes what the announcers will call a "wicked ninety-six-mile-per-hour fastball."

The huddle breaks. Green Bay Packer quarterback Brett Favre follows his 305-pound center up to the line of scrimmage, and the crowd of sixty-five thousand rises to their feet, screaming for a big third-down play. The center adjusts his shoulder pads, leans over the ball, and gives it a spin to get the seams just so. Favre lines up behind him, placing both hands between the center's legs, surveys the field to the left, to the right, and begins to bark out signals. The offensive linemen get into their three-point stances, then hold still as rocks. An offensive back goes into lateral motion. Defensive linemen and linebackers dodge and feint, but cannot broach the line of scrimmage until Favre barks out the right signal for the center to snap the ball. The camera pulls back from a close-up of the quarterback's bobbing head to a wide-angle of the line of scrimmage. The crowd noise swells; most of the players are motionless, awaiting their cue. Suddenly, the ball is snapped to Favre, and all hell breaks loose as huge, armored bodies begin to slam into one another.

Sports fans take it for granted that some players, some positions, some places on the court or field represent the center of everyone's attention. The baseball pitcher and the football quarterback both operate at the geographic center of the action, and each initiates the action of every play in their respective sport. The basketball center jumps for the ball at center court to begin each half, operates as a locus for the ball's movement in the "post" on offense, and is expected to "clog the middle" of the team's defense. The center is the place where it all starts; one's teammates and opponents must respond to what is initiated at the center. It is a position occupied by the biggest, strongest, and highest-paid athletes (O'Neal signed a contract extension with the Lakers in 2000 that will pay him $88.4 million to play basketball for three years; Johnson was paid $13,350,000 in 2000 by the Arizona Diamondbacks to pitch a baseball; and in 2001, Favre signed a ten-year $100 million contract with the Green Bay Packers). The center is a position of domination. And it is the focal point of the gaze (and hopes, fantasies, and disappointments) of fans and spectators.

In the middle of the twentieth century, sport had an almost un-contested institutional "center": men's baseball, football, and basketball clearly ruled. Sport, though, has undergone fundamental challenges and changes in recent decades. Although sports were once widely thought to be a pastime that was set aside almost exclusively for boys and men, its face has shifted dramatically since the passage of Title IX in 1972. Parents increasingly see sports participation as a good thing for their daughters, and opportunities for girls to participate in youth soccer, softball, baseball, basketball, and other sports have expanded dramatically.[1] In U.S. high schools in 1971, boys playing interscholastic sports outnumbered girls by a whopping margin of 3,666,917 to 294,015. Since then, the gap has steadily shrunk. In 2000–2001, 3,921,069 boys and 2,784,154 girls played interscholastic sports in U.S. high schools.[2] Changes in U.S. colleges and universities have been equally dramatic. In 1978, the average U.S. college offered 5.61 women's sports per school; by the year 2000 that had climbed to an all-time high of 8.14 women's sports per school.[3] In the latter half of the 1990s, women's professional basketball began to take off in popularity. Meanwhile, women's soccer participation rates rose dramatically,[4] punctuated by the media frenzy that accompanied the 1999 U.S. women's world championship. And a celebratory popular literature on girls' and women's sports accomplishments is burgeoning.[5]

Once almost entirely dominated by the "big three" of men's football, basketball, and baseball (in the northeastern United States and Canada, ice hockey would surely be included), participation rates in new "alternative" and "extreme" sports (snowboarding, skateboarding, bicycling, body building, triathlons, martial arts, aerobics, etc.) have sprouted. This mostly grassroots development has shifted many people's sports participation, spectating interests, and even their definitions of what constitutes "sport" in widely divergent directions.[6]

The dramatic expansion of mass media—especially the proliferation of specialized cable television stations, Internet web sites, and print magazines that are aimed at specific market interest groups (e.g., women's sports, bodybuilding, health and fitness, and magazines devoted to specific sports)—have created a situation where people's particular sports and fitness interests can be developed within narrowly defined consumer networks or participant niche communities.[7]

These new developments have raised central questions among scholars who study sport. Can we even claim to know what the term *sport* defines anymore? Don't recent changes and developments call for a more expansive and inclusive definition of our object of study?[8] Can we even empirically locate "sport" anymore? Is there still a cultural and institutional center to sport, or have new popular practices and media developments simply spun us off into a postmodern mélange of fragmented physical practices and a smorgasbord of choices that represent an expanded realm of freedom for consumers? In this book, I argue that it is possible—indeed, crucial—for us to identify and critically examine the contested, but still powerful, "center" of sport. Despite the growth of women's sports, and alternative and gay sports, and despite the explosive expansion of fragmented sports media that correspond with specifically targeted submarkets, there still is a center to the cultural and structural gender regime of sport. We locate the center of sport, I will argue, partly by "following the money" to the most highly celebrated, rewarded, and institutionalized bodily practices that are defined largely by physical power, aggression, and violence. The center of sport is where it all starts, a place that serves as symbolic and economic reference point for alternative images and practices. The center is a position occupied by the biggest, wealthiest, and most visible sports programs and athletes. It is a site of domination and privilege. It is the major focal point of the gaze of millions of fans and spectators. We find sport's center at the core of athletic departments in schools and universities, at the locus of peer status systems among young people, and at the major nodes of sports media. And sport's center is still, by and large, a space that is actively constructed by and for men.

Why does this matter? Even if it's true that there is still a center to sport, isn't it also true that people are increasingly free to ignore this center, to play, watch, or read about a wide range of alternative physical activities? Yes and no. People today do have a wider range of participation and consumption choices with respect to sports and physical activity, but there is a danger in simply celebrating this new landscape as a realm of expanded freedom. An individual with the resources to do so can often escape to her or his preferred physical activity, specialized sports magazine, cable channel, or web site. But this does not change the fact—indeed, it may help obscure the fact—that the center of sport still has a huge impact on lives both inside and outside sport.

For example, nearly three decades after Title IX, U.S. boys' and men's sports participation opportunities, scholarships, and funding still outnumber girls' and women's by wide margins. Despite the emergence of some coed sports, boys' and girls' sports are still mostly organized as separate (and unequal) enterprises. In high school sports there has been a gradual closing of the gap between U.S. girls' and boys' athletic participation, but in 2001, boy athletes still outnumbered girls by more than a million.[9] Vast inequities persist in colleges and universities, too. A 2000 survey of 311 institutions by the *Chronicle of Higher Education* concluded that U.S. college women athletes "still lack opportunities to participate at many institutions, and they often do not receive fair shares of scholarship funds, coaching-salary budgets, recruiting budgets, and operating budgets."[10] Despite the recent arrival of the Women's National Basketball Association, far fewer women athletes than men play professional sports, and those women who do play tend to earn far less money than men. And whether we are talking about children, high school, college, or pro athletes, male participants in core sports still tend to enjoy very high social status.[11]

Also, the domination of major sports media by core men's sports provides viewers with racialized and gendered images and ideologies that continue to support views that have long since been challenged in other institutional venues. Tens of millions of children and adults consume sports media. A 1999 study by the Amateur Athletic Foundation of Los Angeles found that 94 percent of U.S. children ages eight to seventeen consume some sort of sports media; one of three did so on a daily basis, and seven in ten did so at least twice a week.[12] Sports media are thus likely to be one of the major influences on children's views of gender, race, commercialism, and other key issues.

The idea that there is a center, a core or a heart, to the increasingly wide range of physical practices, institutional arrangements, and cultural imagery that fall under the umbrella of "sport" is of course debatable. My thinking on this issue takes as a point of departure sociologist R. W. Connell's discussion of what he calls "core" and "peripheral" institutions. Connell argues that the societal gender order is made up of a cluster of "core" institutions (the military, the state, corporations) that still retain both a powerful patriarchal legacy of male power, control, and exploitation of women's labor and a heterosexual hegemony.[13] Other institutions (such as education and families), though still retaining a patriarchal legacy, are more contested by women and by sexual minorities. Through most of the twentieth century, sport was clearly one of the less contested, core institutions in which heterosexual men's embodied power was enabled and celebrated in ways that supported and naturalized patriarchal beliefs in male superiority and female frailty and dependence. Once generated within sport, these conservative ideas were then liberally transported into other core institutions such as the military and the state and used to support the "naturalness" of men's rule. As institutions like higher education and certain workplaces and professions became more contested by women, the patriarchal ideas generated by sport continued to be used as a damper on women's quest for full respect, equality, and power.[14]

However, by the last third of the twentieth century, the rate of change in sport accelerated, especially in response to girls' and women's movement into sport. Here is where Connell's concept of "gender regimes" is useful.[15] When we consider not simply the state of play between large-scale institutions within the overall gender order but also the internal state of play—the gender regimes—of institutions, then we see far more complexity. Sport, as an institution, is not fully internally consistent or coherent. Some of the terrain of sport, especially its center, is still thoroughly patriarchal and is tightly (often violently) controlled by heterosexual men (and by the corporations that profit from them). This core of the sport institution is made up of the sport-media-commercial complex that organizes, promotes, and profits from big-time college and pro football, big-time college and men's pro basketball, pro baseball, and men's pro ice hockey and boxing.[16] Its dominant principles and practices tend to filter down, though unevenly, into school-based and children's sports. Less central, though, are sport spaces that are not fully integrated into or controlled by the sport-media-commercial complex: most women's sports, extreme sports, gay and lesbian community sports, recreational sports, and "nonrevenue" school-based sports such as cross country, swimming, gymnastics, lacrosse, and golf. It's not that these sports are fully outside the commercial and bodily discipline regimes of the core of sport; in fact, there is often a tension that simultaneously pulls these sports toward and repels them away from sport's institutional center.[17] However, the very fact that these sports are not fully integrated into the center of the gender regime of sport means that there is greater space for the development of a range of (sometimes even subversive) meanings, identities, and relationships around issues of gender and sexuality.

Examining the gender regime of sport, then, becomes a complex process of exploring the different kinds of spaces within sport, how these spaces are variously occupied, given meaning, and contested. My main task in this book is to critically examine the gender dynamics at the core, or center, of sport, but I will do so with an understanding of how this center is defined in relation to the less central parts of the gender regime (e.g., women's sports, noncentral men's sports) as well as in relation to nonsport institutions (e.g., media, the economy, and schools). Scholarship of the past two decades has demonstrated that it is impossible to examine gender without simultaneously examining other group-based power dynamics, so I also attend to economic factors, race-ethnicity, and sexuality within my frame of analysis.[18]

The Purpose and Logic of the Book

In this book, I introduce a trilevel conceptual framework with which I demonstrate that the center of sport is constructed through (1) the routine day-to-day practices of sports participants, (2) the structured rules and hierarchies of sport institutions, and (3) the dominant symbols and belief systems transmitted by the major sports media. In other words, in the language of social theory, I analyze sport as a routine set of interactions and performances of social agents, variously enabled and constrained by institutional structures and by dominant cultural symbols and ideologies.[19] In chapter 1, I lay out this trilevel conceptual framework (interaction, structure, culture) by demonstrating its utility in analyzing a moment of gender construction in the lives of four- and five-year-old children at a soccer opening ceremony. In the next chapter, I focus on interaction and gender performance to analyze the problem of male athletes' "triad of violence" against women, against other men, and against their own bodies. In chapter 3, I examine sport as a structured gender regime, with a particular focus on the ways that financial interests and dominant men's interests have managed thus far to "hold" the center largely intact in the face of recent challenges. In chapter 4, I turn to an examination of the dominant cultural imagery of the core of sport, with a particular focus on gender in televised sports. In the final chapter, I examine the current historical moment in terms of how the center of sport is being challenged. I return to the issue of men's violence as a key part of the practice, structure, and cultural imagery of sport's center and assess some of the current challenges and paradoxes of the moment.

A generation ago, sport was a core, patriarchal institution in a larger, contested gender order. Now, with the dramatic growth of girls' and women's athletic participation, sport no longer simply or unambiguously plays this reactionary role in gender relations. Sport is now more internally contested. I argue in this book that despite these changes, sport largely retains and continues its conservative role in gender relations, but it does so in somewhat different ways. In the past, sport simply excluded girls and included boys, thus making the ideological equation of males with active athletic power and of females with physical weakness and passivity seem to appear natural. Now, with girls involved in sports in great numbers, a more complicated process of differentiation has replaced simple exclusion. As chapter 1 will illustrate, formal sex segregation and other more informal processes of differentiation continue to reinforce ideas of natural difference between the sexes, even in the face of dramatically increasing sports participation by girls.

Center Snap:
Children Creating the Fiction of Gender

"Men are from Mars," my six-year-old son announced to me, out of the blue, "and women are from Venus." "What's that mean?" I asked him. "Well, I guess it means that men and women are from different planets." "Where did you hear that?" I asked him. "Oh, it was on a TV commercial: 'Men are from Mars, women are from Venus, and children are from heaven.'" I took it as good news that my son could not recall what product they were trying to sell him with this enlightened message, but I also took it as just another bit of depressing evidence of how a renewed essentialism—the belief that women and men are so naturally and categorically different that we might as well be from different planets—has worked its way back into mainstream thinking in recent years. Sometimes it almost seems as though thirty years of the most recent wave of feminism, and the accompanying social scientific research on gender that tends to show greater similarities between women and men than differences, never really happened.[1]

But then I considered the fact that the snappy gender formula my son had related to me actually had a third part: "Men are from Mars, women are from Venus, *and children are from heaven*." So I asked him, "If men and women are from different planets, how is it that as children, they are all from the same place?" This stumped him, but maybe this was too complicated a question to ask of a six-year-old. Indeed, this is the key question that many scholars of gender have taken up: If boys and girls are so much alike, how do we come to see them as being so essentially different? What is the social process that creates separate and seemingly categorically different gendered beings? In this chapter, I will explore how sport provides a context in which the fiction of separate, categorically different, and unequal sexes can be constructed and made to appear natural, even in this allegedly "postfeminist" era.[2] I present a highly salient gendered moment of group life among four- and five-year-old children as a point of departure for exploring the conditions under which gender boundaries become activated and enforced. I was privy to this moment when I observed my five-year-old son's first season in organized soccer.[3] I will first describe the observation—an incident that occurred as a boys' four-to-five-year-old soccer team waited next to a girls' four-to-five-year-old team for the beginning of the season's opening ceremony of the community's American Youth Soccer Organization (AYSO). I will then examine this moment using three levels of analysis that form the basis of this book.

1. At the level of *social interaction*: How do children "do gender," and what are the contributions and limits of theories of performativity in understanding these interactions?
2. At the level of *structural context*: How does the institutional gender regime, particularly the larger organizational level of formal sex segregation of AYSO and the concrete, momentary situation of the opening ceremony, provide a context that variously constrains and enables the children's interactions?
3. At the level of *cultural symbol*: How does the children's shared immersion in popular culture (and their differently gendered locations in this immersion) provide symbolic resources for the creation, in this situation, of apparently categorical differences between the boys and the girls?

Though I will discuss these three levels of analysis separately, I hope to demonstrate that interaction, structural context, and culture are simultaneous and mutually intertwined processes, none of which supersedes the others.[4]

Barbie Girls vs. Sea Monsters

It is a warm, sunny Saturday morning. Summer is coming to a close, and schools will soon reopen. As in many communities, this time of year in this small, middle- and professional-class suburb of Los Angeles is marked by the beginning of another soccer season. This morning, 156 teams, with approximately 1,850 players ranging from four to seventeen years old, along with another two thousand to three thousand parents, siblings, friends, and community dignitaries have gathered at the local high school football and track facility for the annual AYSO opening ceremonies. Parents and children wander around the perimeter of the track to find the assigned station for their respective teams. The coaches muster their teams and chat with parents. Eventually, each team will march around the track, behind their new team banner while they are announced over the loudspeaker system and are applauded by the crowd. For now though, and for the next forty-five minutes to an hour, the kids, coaches, and parents must stand, mill around, talk, and kill time as they await the beginning of the ceremony.

The Sea Monsters is a team of four- and five-year-old boys. Later this day, they will play their first ever soccer game. A few of the boys already know each other from preschool, but most are still getting acquainted. They are wearing their new uniforms for the first time. Like other teams, they were assigned team colors—in this case, green and blue—and asked to choose their team name at their first team meeting, which occurred a week ago. Though they preferred Blue Sharks, they found that the name was already taken by another team, so they settled on Sea Monsters. A grandmother of one of the boys created the spiffy team banner, which was awarded a prize this morning. While they wait for the ceremony to begin, the boys inspect and then proudly pose for pictures in front of their new, award-winning team banner. The parents stand a few feet away, some taking pictures, some just watching. The parents are also getting to know each other, and the common currency of topics is just how darned cute our kids look, and will they start these ceremonies soon before another boy has to be escorted to the bathroom?

Queued up one group away from the Sea Monsters is a team of four- and five-year-old girls in green and white uniforms. They too will play their first game later today, but for now, they are awaiting the beginning of the opening ceremony. They have chosen the name Barbie Girls, and they too have a new team banner. But the girls are pretty much ignoring their banner, for they have created another, more powerful symbol around which to rally. In fact, they are the only team among the 156 marching today with a team float—a red Radio Flyer wagon base, on which sits a Sony boom box playing music, and a three-foot-plus tall Barbie doll on a rotating pedestal. Barbie is dressed in the team colors; indeed, she sports a custom-made green and white cheerleader-style outfit, with the Barbie Girls' names written on the skirt. Her normally all-blond hair has been streaked with Barbie Girl green and features a green bow with white polka dots. Several of the girls on the team have supplemented their uniforms with green bows in their hair as well.

The volume on the boom box nudges up, and four or five girls begin to sing a Barbie song. Barbie is now slowly rotating on her pedestal, and as the girls sing more gleefully and more loudly, some of them begin to hold hands and walk around the float, in synch with Barbie's rotation. Other same-aged girls from other teams are drawn to the celebration and, eventually, perhaps a dozen girls are singing the Barbie song. The girls are intensely focused on Barbie, on the music, and on their mutual pleasure.

While the Sea Monsters mill around their banner, some of them begin to notice and then begin to watch and listen when the Barbie Girls rally around their float. At first, the boys are watching as individuals, seemingly unaware of each other's shared interest. Some of them stand with arms at their sides, slack-jawed, as though passively watching a television show. I notice slight smiles on a couple of their faces, as though they are drawn to the Barbie Girls' celebratory fun. Then, with side glances, some of the boys begin to notice each other's attention on the Barbie Girls. Their faces begin to show signs of distaste. One of them yells out, "NO BARBIE!" Suddenly, they all begin to move, jumping up and down, nudging, and bumping one other, and join in a group chant: "NO BARBIE! NO BARBIE! NO BARBIE!" They now appear to be every bit as gleeful as the girls as they laugh, yell, and chant against the Barbie Girls.

Figure 1. The Sea Monsters pose in front of their team banner, and the Barbie Girls begin to rally around their icon.

The parents watch the whole scene with rapt attention. Smiles light up the faces of the adults while our glances sweep back and forth, from the sweetly celebrating Barbie Girls to the aggressively protesting Sea Monsters. "They are SO different!" exclaims one smiling mother approvingly. A male coach offers a more in-depth analysis: "When I was in college," he says, "I took these classes from professors who showed us research that showed that boys and girls are the same. I believed it, until I had my own kids and saw how different they are." "Yeah," another dad responds. "Just look at them! They are so different!"

The girls, meanwhile, show no evidence that they hear, see, or are even aware of the presence of the boys, who are now so loudly proclaiming their opposition to the Barbie Girls' songs and totem. The girls continue to sing, dance, laugh, and rally around the Barbie for a few more minutes, before they are called to reassemble in their groups for the beginning of the parade.

After the parade, the teams reassemble on the infield of the track, but now in a less organized manner. The Sea Monsters once again find themselves in the general vicinity of the Barbie Girls and take up the "NO BARBIE!" chant. Perhaps put out by the lack of response to their chant, they begin to dash, in twos and threes, invading the girls' space and yelling menacingly. With this, the Barbie Girls have little choice but to recognize the presence of the boys; some look puzzled and shrink back, some engage the boys and chase them off. The chasing seems only to incite more excitement among the boys. Finally, parents intervene and defuse the situation, leading their children off to their cars, homes, and eventually to their soccer games.

The Performance of Gender

In the past decade, especially since the publication of Judith Butler's highly influential book *Gender Trouble*,[5] it has become increasingly fashionable among academic feminists to think of gender not as some "thing" that one "has" (or not), but rather as situationally constructed through the performances of active agents. The idea of gender-as-performance analytically foregrounds the agency of people in the construction of gender, thus highlighting the situational fluidity of gender: here, conservative and reproductive, there, transgressive and disruptive. Surely, the Barbie Girls vs. Sea Monsters scene that I witnessed can be fruitfully analyzed as a moment of group-based, cross-cutting, and mutually constitutive gender performances: The girls, at least at first glance, appear to be performing (for each other?) a conventional version of femininity for four- and five-year-olds. At least on the surface, there appears to be nothing terribly transgressive here. They are just "being girls" together. The boys initially are unwittingly constituted as an audience for the girls' performance but quickly begin to perform (for each other? for the girls, too?) a masculinity that constructs itself in opposition to Barbie, and to the girls, as not-feminine. They aggressively confront—first through loud verbal chanting, eventually through bodily invasions—the girls' ritual space, apparently with the intention of disrupting its upsetting influence. The adults are simultaneously constituted as an adoring audience for their children's performances and as parents who perform for each other by sharing and mutually affirming their experience-based narratives concerning the natural differences between boys and girls.

In this scene, we see children performing gender in ways that constitute them as two separate, opposed groups (boys vs. girls), and we see parents performing gender in ways that give the stamp of adult approval to the children's performances of difference while constructing their own ideological narrative that naturalizes this categorical difference. In other words, the parents do not seem to read the children's performances of gender as social constructions of gender. Instead, they interpret them as the inevitable unfolding of natural, internal differences between the sexes. That this moment occurred when it did and where it did is explicable, but not entirely with a theory of performativity. Commenting on the limitations of theories of performativity, sociologist Suzanna Danuta Walters argues:

> The performance of gender is never a simple voluntary act, and is always already constituted by the rules and histories of gender.... This performance trope becomes vacuous when it is decontextualized.... Theories of

gender as play and performance need to be intimately and systematically connected with the power of gender (really, the power of male power) to constrain, control, violate, and configure. Too often, mere lip service is given to the specific historical, social, and political configurations that make certain conditions possible and others constrained.[6]

Indeed, feminist sociologists operating from the traditions of symbolic interactionism and/or Goffmanian dramaturgical analysis have anticipated the recent interest in looking at gender as a dynamic performance. As early as 1978, Suzanne Kessler and Wendy McKenna developed a sophisticated analysis of gender as an everyday, practical accomplishment of people's interactions.[7] Nearly a decade later, Candace West and Don Zimmerman argued that in people's everyday interactions, they were "doing gender," and, in so doing, they were constructing masculine dominance and feminine deference.[8] As these ideas have been taken up in sociology, their tendencies toward a celebration of the "freedom" of agents to transgress and reshape the fluid boundaries of gender have been put into play with theories of social structure.[9] In these accounts, gender is viewed as enacted or created through everyday interactions but crucially, as Walters suggested above, within "specific historical, social, and political configurations" that constrain or enable certain interactions.

The parents' response to the Barbie Girls vs. Sea Monsters performance suggests one of the main limits and dangers of theories of performativity. Lacking an analysis of structural and cultural context, performances of gender can all too easily be interpreted as free agents' acting out the inevitable surface manifestations of a natural inner essence of sex difference.[10] An examination of structural and cultural contexts, though, reveals that there was nothing inevitable about the girls' choice of Barbie as their totem or in the boys' response to it.

The Structure of Gender

In the entire subsequent season of weekly games and practices, I never once saw adults point to a moment in which boy and girl soccer players were doing the *same* thing and exclaim to each other, "Look at them! They are *so similar!*" The actual similarity of the boys and the girls, evidenced by nearly all of the kids' routine actions throughout a soccer season—playing the game, crying over a skinned knee, scrambling enthusiastically for their snacks after the games, spacing out on a bird or a flower instead of listening to the coach at practice—is a key to understanding the salience of the Barbie Girls vs. Sea Monsters moment for gender relations. In the face of a multitude of moments that speak to similarity, it was this anomalous Barbie Girls vs. Sea Monsters moment, where the boundaries of gender were so clearly enacted, that the adults seized to affirm their commitment to difference. It is the kind of moment, to use Judith Lorber's phrase, where "believing is seeing,"[11] where we selectively "see" aspects of social reality that tell us a truth that we prefer to believe, such as the belief in categorical sex difference. No matter that our eyes do not see evidence of this truth most of the rest of the time.

In fact, it was not so easy for adults actually to "see" the empirical reality of sex similarity in everyday observations of soccer throughout the season. That difficulty is due to one overdetermining factor: an institutional context that is characterized by informally structured sex segregation among the parent coaches and team managers and by formally structured sex segregation among the children. Organizations, even while appearing gender neutral, tend to reflect, re-create, and naturalize a hierarchical ordering of gender.[12] Following R. W. Connell's method of structural analysis,[13] I will examine the gender regime of the local AYSO organization by conducting a structural inventory of the formal and informal sexual divisions of labor and power.[14]

Adult Divisions of Labor and Power

There was a clear, though not absolute, sexual division of labor and power among the adult volunteers in the AYSO. The board of directors consisted of twenty-one men and nine women, with the top two positions, commissioner and assistant commissioner, held by men. Among the organization's head coaches, 133 were men and 23 were women. The division among the organization's assistant coaches was similarly skewed. Each team also had a "team manager," who was responsible for organizing snacks, making reminder calls about games and practices, organizing team parties, and the end-of-the-year present for the coach. The vast majority of team managers were women. A common slippage in the language of coaches and parents revealed the ideological assumptions underlying this position: I often noticed people describe a team manager as the "team mom." In short, as Table 1 shows, the vast majority of the time, the formal authority of the head coach and assistant coach was in the hands of a man, whereas the backup, support role of team manager was in the hands of a woman.

These data illustrate how sexual divisions of labor are interwoven with and mutually supportive of divisions of power and authority among women and men. They also suggest how people's choices to "volunteer" for certain positions are shaped and constrained by previous institutional practices. There is no formal AYSO rule that men must be the leaders; women, the supportive followers. And there are, after all, *some* women coaches and *some* men team managers.[15] So, it may appear that the division of labor among adult volunteers simply manifests an accumulation of individual choices and preferences. When analyzed structurally, though, individual men's apparently free choices to volunteer disproportionately for coaching jobs alongside individual women's apparently free choices to volunteer disproportionately for team manager jobs can be seen as a logical *collective* result of the ways that the institutional structure of sport has differentially constrained and enabled

TABLE 1. Percentage distribution of adult volunteers as coaches and team managers, by gender (N = 156 teams)

	Head coaches	Assistant coaches	Team managers
Women	15	21	86
Men	85	79	14

women's and men's previous options and experiences. Since boys and men have had far more opportunities to play organized sports and thus to gain skills and knowledge, it subsequently appears rational for adult men to serve in positions of knowledgeable authority, with women serving in a support capacity.[16] Structure—in this case, the historically constituted division of labor and power in sport—constrains current practice. In turn, structure becomes an object of practice, because the choices and actions of today's parents re-create divisions of labor and power similar to those that they experienced in their youth.

The Children: Formal Sex Segregation

As adult authority patterns are informally structured along gendered lines, the children's leagues are formally segregated by AYSO along lines of age and sex. In each age group, there are separate boys' and girls' leagues. The AYSO in this community included eighty-seven boys' teams and sixty-nine girls' teams. Though the four- and five-year-old boys often played their games on a field that was contiguous with a field where four- and five-year-old girls played theirs, there was never a formal opportunity for cross-sex play. Thus, both the girls' and the boys' teams could conceivably proceed through an entire season of games and practices in entirely homosocial contexts.[17] In the all-male contexts that I observed throughout the season, gender never appeared to be overtly salient among the children, coaches, or parents. It is against this backdrop that I might suggest a working hypothesis about structure and the variable salience of gender: The formal sex segregation of children does not, in and of itself, make gender overtly salient. In fact, when children are absolutely segregated, with no opportunity for cross-sex interactions, gender may appear to disappear as an overtly salient organizing principle. Ironically, sex segregation at times makes gender appear to disappear. By contrast, when formally sex-segregated children are placed in immediately contiguous locations, such as during the opening ceremony, highly charged gendered interactions between the groups (including invasions and other kinds of borderwork) become more possible, making gender more visible.

Though it might appear to some that formal sex segregation in children's sports is a natural fact, it has not always been so for the youngest age groups in AYSO. As recently as 1995, when my older son signed up to play as a five-year-old, I had been told that he would play in a coed league. But when he arrived to his first practice, we found that he was on an all-boys team. The coach conceded that there did not seem to be any physical reason to separate kids at this age; four- and five-year-old boys and girls appear equally able to chase and kick a ball. (Indeed, the research on children's motor skills supports the coach's observation.)[18] The coach went on to explain that AYSO had decided this year to begin sex segregating all age groups for what seem to be purely *social* reasons: "During halftimes and practices, the boys and girls tend to separate into separate groups. So the league thought it would be better for team unity if we split the boys and girls into separate leagues." I suggested to some coaches that a similar dynamic among racial-ethnic groups (say, Latino kids and white kids clustering as separate groups during halftimes) would not similarly result in a decision to create racially segregated leagues. That this comment appeared to fall on deaf ears illustrates the extent to which the belief of many adults in the need for sex segregation, at least in the context of sport, is grounded in a mutually agreed-upon notion of boys' and girls' "separate worlds," a belief perhaps based in ideologies of natural sex difference.

The gender regime of AYSO (and, for the most part, of children's sports in general) is structured by formal and informal divisions of labor and power by sex. This social structure sets ranges, limits, and possibilities for the children's and parents' interactions and performances of gender, but it does not determine them. Put another way, the formal and informal gender regime of AYSO made the Barbie Girls vs. Sea Monsters moment possible, but it did not make it inevitable. It was the agency of the children and the parents within that structure that made the moment happen. But why did this moment take on the symbolic forms that it did? How and why do the girls, boys, and parents construct and derive meanings from this moment, and how can we interpret these meanings? These questions are best grappled with in the realm of cultural analysis.

The Culture of Gender

The difference between what is structural and what is cultural is not clear-cut. For instance, the AYSO assignment of team colors and choice of team names (cultural symbols) seem to follow logically from, and in turn reinforce, the sex segregation of the leagues (social structure). These cultural symbols such as team colors, uniforms, songs, team names, and banners often carried encoded gendered meanings that were then available to be taken up by the children in ways that constructed (or, potentially, contested) gender divisions and boundaries.

Team Names

Each team was issued two team colors. It is notable that across the various age groupings, several girls' teams were issued pink uniforms, a color commonly recognized as encoding feminine meanings, but no boys' teams were issued pink uniforms. Children, in consultation with their coaches, were then asked to choose their own team names and were encouraged to use their assigned team colors as cues to the theme of the team name (e.g., among the boys, the Red Flashes, the Green Pythons, and the blue and green Sea Monsters). When I analyzed the team names of the 156 teams by age group and by sex, three categories emerged:

1. *Sweet names*: These are cutesy team names that communicate small stature, cuteness, and/or vulnerability. These kinds of names would most likely be widely read as encoded with feminine meanings (e.g., Blue Butterflies, Beanie Babes, Sunflowers, Pink Flamingos, and Barbie Girls).
2. *Neutral or paradoxical names*: Neutral names are team names that carry no obvious gendered meaning (e.g., Blue and Green Lizards, Team Flubber, Galaxy, Blue Ice). Paradoxical names are girls' team names that carry mixed (simultaneously vulnerable *and* powerful) messages (e.g., Pink Panthers, Flower Power, Little Tigers).
3. *Power names*: These are team names that invoke images of unambiguous strength, aggression, and raw power (e.g., Shooting Stars, Killer Whales, Shark Attack, Raptor Attack, and Sea Monsters).

As Table 2 illustrates, across all age groups of boys, there was only one team name coded as a sweet name—The Smurfs, in the ten-to-eleven-year-old league. Across all age categories, the boys were far more likely to choose a power name than anything else, and this was nowhere more true than in the youngest age groups, where thirty-five of forty (87 percent) of boys' teams in the four-to-five and six-to-seven age groupings took on power names. A different pattern appears in the girls' team name choices, especially among the youngest girls. Only two of the twelve four-to-five-year-old girls' teams chose power names, while five chose sweet names, and five chose neutral/paradoxical names. At age six to seven, the numbers begin to tip toward the boys' numbers but still remain different, with half of the girls' teams now choosing power names. In the middle and older girls' groups, the sweet names all but

TABLE 2. Numeric and percentage distributions of team name types, by age group and gender (N = 156 teams)

Type of name	4–5 years	6–7 years	8–13 years	14–17 years	Total
Girls					
Sweet names	5 (42%)	3 (17%)	2 (7%)	0	10 (15%)
Neutral and paradoxical names	5 (42%)	6 (33%)	7 (25%)	5 (45%)	23 (32%)
Power names	2 (17%)	9 (50%)	19 (68%)	6 (55%)	36 (52%)
Boys					
Sweet names	0	0	1 (4%)	0	1 (1%)
Neutral and paradoxical names	1 (7%)	4 (15%)	4 (12%)	4 (31%)	13 (15%)
Power names	13 (93%)	22 (85%)	29 (85%)	9 (69%)	73 (82%)

disappear, with power names dominating, but still with a higher proportion of neutral/paradoxical names than among boys in those age groups.

Barbie Narrative vs. Warrior Narrative

How do we make sense of the obviously powerful spark that Barbie provided in the opening ceremony scene described above? Barbie is likely one of the most immediately identifiable symbols of femininity in the world. More conservatively oriented parents tend to buy Barbie dolls for their daughters happily while perhaps deflecting their sons' interest in Barbie toward more sex-appropriate "action toys." Feminist parents, on the other hand, have often expressed open contempt, or at least uncomfortable ambivalence, for Barbie. This is because both conservative and feminist parents see dominant cultural meanings of femininity as condensed in Barbie and assume that these meanings will be imitated by their daughters. Recent developments in cultural studies, though, should warn us against simplistic readings of Barbie as merely conveying hegemonic "messages" about gender to unwitting children.[19] In addition to critically analyzing the cultural values (or "preferred meanings") that may be encoded in Barbie or other children's toys, feminist cultural studies scholars point to the necessity of examining "reception, pleasure, and agency," and especially "the fullness of reception contexts."[20] The Barbie Girls vs. Sea Monsters moment can be analyzed as a "reception context," in which differently situated boys, girls, and parents variously used Barbie to construct pleasurable intergroup bonds as well as boundaries between groups.

Barbie is plastic both in form and in terms of cultural meanings children and adults create around her.[21] It is not that there aren't hegemonic meanings encoded in Barbie: Since her introduction in 1959, Mattel has been successful in selling millions of this doll, who "was recognized as a model of ideal teenhood" and "an icon—perhaps *the* icon— of true white womanhood and femininity."[22] However, Erica Rand argues that "we condescend to children when we analyze Barbie's content and then presume that it passes untransformed into their minds, where, dwelling beneath the control of consciousness or counterargument, it generates self-image, feelings, and other ideological constructs."[23] In fact, people who are situated differently (by age, sex, sexual orientation, social class, race-ethnicity, and national origin) tend to consume and construct meanings around Barbie variously. For instance, some adult women (including many feminists) tell retrospective stories of having rejected (or even mutilated) their Barbies in favor of boys' toys, and some adult lesbians tell stories of transforming Barbie "into an object of dyke desire."[24]

Mattel, in fact, clearly strategizes its marketing of Barbie, not around the imposition of a singular notion of what a girl or woman should be, but around hegemonic discourse strategies that attempt to incorporate consumers' range of possible interpretations and criticisms of the limits of Barbie. For instance, the recent marketing of "multicultural Barbie" features dolls with different skin colors and culturally coded wardrobes. Erica Rand argues that this strategy broadens the Barbie market, deflects potential criticism of racism, but still "does not boot blond, white Barbie from center stage."[25] Similarly, Mattel's marketing of Barbie as a career woman (since the 1970s) raises issues concerning the feminist critique of Barbie's supposedly negative effect on girls. Lynn Spigel observes that when the Association of American University Women recently criticized Barbie, adult collectors defended Barbie, asserting that "Barbie, in fact, is a wonderful role model for women. She has been a veterinarian, an astronaut, and a soldier—and even before real women had a chance to enter such occupations."[26] And when the magazine *Barbie Bazaar* ran a cover photo of its new Gulf War Barbie, it served "as a reminder of Mattel's marketing slogan: 'We Girls Can Do Anything.'"[27] The following year, Mattel unveiled its Presidential Candidate Barbie with the statement, "It is time for a woman president, and Barbie had the credentials for the job."[28] Spigel observes that these liberal feminist messages of empowerment for girls run, apparently unambiguously, alongside a continued unspoken understanding that Barbie must be beautiful, with an ultraskinny waist and long, thin legs that taper to feet that appear deformed so that they may fit (only?) into high heels.[29] "Mattel doesn't mind equating beauty with intellect. In fact, so long as the 11½-inch Barbie body remains intact, Mattel is willing to accessorize her with a number of fashionable perspectives—including feminism itself."[30]

It is this apparently paradoxical encoding of the all-too-familiar oppressive bodily requirements of feminine beauty *alongside* the career woman role-modeling and empowering message that "we girls can do anything" that may inform how and why the Barbie Girls appropriated Barbie as their team symbol. Emphasized femininity, Connell's term for the current form of femininity that articulates with hegemonic masculinity, as many second-wave feminists have experienced and criticized it, has been characterized by girls' and women's embodiments of oppressive conceptions of feminine beauty that symbolize and reify a thoroughly disempowered stance vis-à-vis men.[31] To many second-wave feminists, Barbie seemed to symbolize all that was oppressive about this femininity: the bodily self-surveillance, accompanying eating disorders, slavery to the dictates of the fashion industry, and compulsory heterosexuality. But Rogers suggests that rather than representing an unambiguous image of emphasized femininity, perhaps Barbie represents a more paradoxical image of "emphatic femininity" that

> takes feminine appearances and demeanor to unsustainable extremes. Nothing about Barbie ever looks masculine, even when she is on the police force.... Consistently, Barbie manages impressions so as to come across as a proper feminine creature even when she crosses boundaries usually dividing women from men. Barbie the firefighter is in no danger, then, of being seen as "one of the boys." Kids know that; parents and teachers know that; Mattel designers know that too.[32]

Recent third-wave feminist theory sheds light on the different sensibilities of younger generations of girls and women concerning their willingness to display and play with this apparently paradoxical relationship between bodily experience (including "feminine" displays) and public empowerment. In third-wave feminist texts, displays of feminine physical attractiveness and empowerment are viewed not as mutually exclusive or necessarily opposed realities but as lived (if often paradoxical) aspects of the same reality.[33] This embracing of the paradoxes of post-second-wave femininity is manifested in many punk or Riot Grrrl subcultures,[34] in popular culture in the resounding late-1990s success of the Spice Girls' mantra of "Girl Power," and in the faces of pony-tailed girl fans at women's professional soccer matches and basketball games. Today's generational expression of girl power is a key element of the pleasures of girl culture. Indeed, as the Barbie Girls rallied around Barbie, their obvious pleasure did not appear to be based on a celebration of quiet passivity (as feminist parents might fear). Rather, it was a statement that they, the Barbie Girls, were here in this public space. They were not silenced by the boys' oppositional chanting. To the contrary, they ignored the boys, who seemed irrelevant to their celebration. And, when the boys later physically invaded their space, some of the girls responded by chasing the boys off. In short, when I pay attention to what the girls did (rather than imposing on the situation what I think Barbie "should" mean to the girls), I see a public moment of celebratory girl power that the girls have imported into the sport context.

And this may give us a better basis from which to analyze the boys' oppositional response. First, the boys may have been responding to the threat of displacement they may have felt while viewing the girls' moment of celebratory girl power. Second, the boys may also have been responding to the fears of feminine pollution that Barbie may have come to symbolize to them. But why might Barbie symbolize feminine pollution to little boys? A brief example from my older son is instructive. When he was about three, following a fun day of play with the five-year-old girl next door, he enthusiastically asked me to buy him a Barbie like hers. He was gleeful when I took him to the store and bought him one. When we arrived home, his feet had barely hit the pavement getting out of the car before an eight-year-old neighbor boy laughed at and ridiculed him: "A *Barbie*? Don't you know that Barbie is a *girl's toy*?" No amount of parental intervention could counter this devastating peer-induced injunction against boys playing with Barbie. My son's pleasurable desire for Barbie appeared almost overnight to transform itself into shame and rejection. The doll ended up at the bottom of a heap of toys in the closet, and my son soon became infatuated, along with other boys in his pre-school, with Ninja Turtles and Power Rangers.

Research indicates that there is widespread agreement as to which toys are appropriate for one sex and polluting, dangerous, or inappropri-ate for the other sex. When Campenni asked adults to rate the gender appropriateness of children's toys, the toys considered most appropriate to girls were those pertaining to domestic tasks, beauty enhancement, or child rearing.[35] Of the 206 toys rated, Barbie was rated second only to Makeup Kit as a female-only toy. Toys considered most appropriate to boys were those pertaining to sports gear (football gear was the most masculine-rated toy, and boxing gloves were third), vehicles, action fig-ures (G.I. Joe was rated second only to football gear), and other war-related toys. This research on parents' gender stereotyping of toys reflects similar findings in research on children's toy preferences.[36] Children tend to avoid cross-sex toys, with boys' avoidance of feminine-coded toys appearing to be stronger than girls' avoidance of masculine-coded toys.[37] Moreover, preschool-aged boys who perceive their fathers to be opposed to cross-sex-typed play are more likely than girls or other boys to think that it is bad for boys to play with toys that are labeled as appropriate for girls.[38]

By kindergarten, most boys appear to have learned—through experiences similar to my son's, where other males police the boundaries of gender-appropriate play and fantasy, and/or by watching the clearly gendered messages of television advertising—that Barbie dolls are not appropriate toys for boys.[39] To avoid ridicule, they learn to hide their desire for Barbie, either through denial and oppositional or pollution discourse or through sublimation of their desire for Barbie into play with male-appropriate action figures.[40] In a fascinating study of a kinder-garten classroom, Ellen Jordan and Angela Cowan noted that the most commonly agreed upon currency for boys' fantasy play was "warrior narratives . . . that assume that violence is legitimate and justified when it occurs within a struggle between good and evil."[41] They observed that the boys seem commonly to adapt story lines that they have seen on television. Popular culture (film, video, computer games, television, and comic books) provides boys with a seemingly endless stream of Good Guy vs. Bad Guy characters and stories (from cowboy movies, Superman, and Spiderman to Ninja Turtles, Star Wars, Pokémon, and WWF wrestlers) that they can appropriate as the raw materials for the construction of their own warrior play.

In the kindergarten that Jordan and Cowan studied, the boys initially attempted to import their warrior narratives into the domestic setting of the Doll Corner. Teachers eventually drove the boys' warrior play outdoors, while the Doll Corner was used by the girls for the "appropriate" domestic play for which it was originally intended. Jordan and Cowan argue that kindergarten teachers' outlawing of boys' warrior narratives inside the classroom contributed to boys' defining schools as a feminine environment, to which the boys responded with a resistant, underground continuation of masculine warrior play. Eventually though, boys who acquiesce and successfully sublimate warrior play into fantasy or sports are more successful in constructing what Connell calls "a masculinity organized around themes of rationality and responsibility [that are] closely connected with the 'certification' function of the upper levels of the education system and to a key form of masculinity among professionals."[42]

In contrast with the "rational or professional" masculinity constructed in schools, the institution of sport historically constructs hegemonic masculinity as *bodily superiority* over femininity and over nonathletic masculinities.[43] In sport, warrior narratives are allowed to thrive publicly—indeed, are openly celebrated (witness, for instance, the commentary of a televised NFL football game or especially the spectacle of televised professional wrestling). Preschool boys and kindergartners seem already to know this, easily adopting aggressively competitive team names and an us-versus-them attitude. By contrast, many of the youngest girls appear to take two or three years in organized soccer before they adopt, or partly accommodate themselves to, aggressively competitive discourse, indicated by the ten-year-old girls' shifting away from the use of sweet names toward more power names. In short, where the gender regime of preschool and grade school may be experienced as an environment in which mostly women leaders enforce rules that are hostile to masculine fantasy play and physicality, the gender regime of sport is experienced as a place where masculine styles and values of physicality, aggression, and competition are enforced and celebrated by mostly male coaches.

A cultural analysis suggests that the boys' and the girls' previous immersion in differently gendered cultural experiences shaped the likelihood that they would derive and construct different meanings from Barbie—the girls through pleasurable and symbolically empowering identification with "girl power" narratives; the boys through oppositional fears of feminine pollution (and fears of displacement by girl power?) and with aggressively verbal, and eventually physical, invasions of the girls' ritual space. The boys' collective response thus constituted them differently, *as boys*, in opposition to the girls' constitution of themselves *as girls*. An individual girl or boy, in this moment, who may have felt an inclination to dissent from the dominant feelings of the group (say, the Latina Barbie Girl who, her mother later told me, did not want the group to be identified with Barbie, or a boy whose immediate inner response to the Barbie Girls' joyful celebration might be to join in) is most likely silenced into complicity in this powerful moment of borderwork.

What meanings did this highly gendered moment carry for the boys' and girls' teams in the ensuing soccer season? Though I did not observe the Barbie Girls after the opening ceremony, I did continue to observe the Sea Monsters' weekly practices and games. Over the course of the boys' ensuing season, gender never reached this "magnified" level of overt and obvious salience again; indeed, gender was rarely raised verbally or performed overtly by the boys.[44] On two occasions, though, I observed the coach jokingly chiding the boys during practice, "If you don't watch out, I'm going to get the Barbie Girls here to play against you!" This warning was followed by gleeful screams of agony and fear and nervous hopping around and hugging by some of the boys. Normally, though, in this sex-segregated, all-male context, if boundaries were invoked, they were not boundaries between boys and girls but boundaries between the Sea Monsters and other boys' teams, or sometimes age boundaries between the Sea Monsters and a small group of dads and older brothers who would engage them in a mock scrimmage during practice. But it was also evident that when the coach was having trouble getting the boys to act together, as a group, his strategic and humorous invocation of the dreaded Barbie Girls once again served symbolically to affirm their group status. They were a team. They were the boys.

To some readers, the story that I focus on in this chapter may appear innocuous; after all, nearly everybody in the story appeared to derive some kind of pleasure from this magnified moment. So what's the problem? What I hope will become apparent as this book unfolds is that it is precisely this kind of everyday, taken-for-granted moment that serves to construct gender dichotomies. And this process of gender dichotomization has consequences. For instance, in her research on children's school-based sports experiences, Cynthia Hasbrook has shown how social contexts that highlight differences (rather than similarities) between boys and girls often result in girls' undervaluing their physical abilities and dropping out of sports participation, while boys come not only to value their own skills and athletic potential but also to feel free to put down girls' physical abilities. This process contributes to a widening gap between male and female sports participation rates as children go up through the school grades, eventually reinforcing ideas of male natural superiority and female frailty and inferiority.[45] Day-to-day interactions among children, as contextualized by parents, teachers, institutions, and popular culture, still tend mostly to push men and masculinity to the center of the athletic status system while marginalizing girls, women, and femininity. It is precisely the everyday, seemingly innocuous, and (perhaps especially) pleasurable aspects of such moments that make them so powerful in perpetuating and naturalizing gender hierarchy.

Interaction, Structure, Culture

This chapter introduces the multilevel (interactionist, structural, cultural) conceptual framework that I will develop in this book. In the Barbie

Girls vs. Sea Monsters moment, the children's gendered performances created and marked boundaries between the boys' and the girls' groups. The resulting binary split between the sexes occurred in the context of a situation systematically structured by sex segregation, sparked by the imposing presence of a shared cultural symbol that is saturated with gendered meanings and actively supported and applauded by adults who basked in the pleasure of difference reaffirmed.[46] The result was an apparently "natural" split based on apparently "natural" sex differences. What we already believed—that boys and girls are categorically different— became what we saw: Heaven transformed itself into Mars and Venus.

At the most general level, I base the subsequent analysis of gender and sport in this book on the following working propositions: First, *interactionist theoretical frameworks* that emphasize the ways that social agents "perform" or "do" gender are most useful in describing how groups of people actively create (or at times disrupt) the boundaries that delineate seemingly categorical differences between males and females. In this chapter, we saw how the children and the parents interactively performed gender in a way that constructed an apparently natural boundary between the two separate worlds of the girls and the boys. In chapter 2, I will examine how men and boys in core sport contexts often "do masculinity" in ways that are violently dangerous to women, to other males, and to themselves. It is, I will argue, the group-based nature of these interactions that is the key to understanding dangerous and violent actions by male athletes.

Second, *structural theoretical frameworks* that emphasize the ways that gender is built into institutions through hierarchical sexual divisions of labor are most useful in explaining under what conditions social agents mobilize variously to disrupt or to affirm gender differences and inequalities. In this chapter, we saw how the sexual division of labor among parent volunteers (grounded in their own histories in the gender regime of sport), the formal sex-segregation of the children's leagues, and the structured context of the opening ceremony created conditions for possible interactions between girls' teams and boys' teams. In chapter 3, we will see how the institutional center of the gender regime of sport both constrains and enables the choices and actions of male and female athletes as well as fans.

Third, *cultural theoretical perspectives* that examine how popular symbols that are injected into circulation by the culture industry and are variously taken up by differently situated people are most useful in analyzing how the meanings of cultural symbols, in a given institutional context, might trigger or be taken up by social agents and used as resources to reproduce, disrupt, or contest binary conceptions of sex difference and gendered relations of power. In this chapter, we saw how a girls' team appropriated a large Barbie around which to construct a pleasurable and empowering sense of group identity, and how a boys' team responded with aggressive denunciations of Barbie and invasions of the girls' space. In chapter 4, we will examine the dominant images, words, and symbols generated from the center of the powerful sport-media-commercial complex.

Utilizing any one of these three theoretical perspectives by itself will lead to a limited, even distorted, analysis of the social construction of gender. Together, they can illuminate the complex, multileveled architecture of the social construction of gender in everyday life. For heuristic reasons, in this chapter I have falsely separated interaction, structure, and culture. In fact, we need to explore their constant interrelationships.

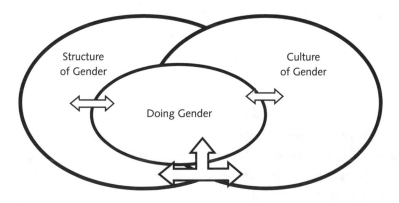

Figure 2. Gender as structure, culture, and interaction.

As Figure 2 suggests, the day-to-day doing of gender is contextualized within organized structures, including divisions of labor and power, and in a sea of cultural images and ideologies. While social structure and cultural imagery are mutually constitutive and always in flux, they also tend disproportionately to reflect the entrenched interests of groups who hold dominant class, racial, gender, and sexual positions in a matrix of domination. The doing of gender is variously constrained, enabled, and given meaning by individuals' and groups' positions within this matrix of domination.

For example, we cannot understand the boys' aggressive denunciations and invasions of the girls' space and the eventual clarification of categorical boundaries between the girls and the boys without first understanding how these boys and girls have already internalized four or five years of "gendering" experiences that have shaped their interactional tendencies and how they are already immersed in a culture of gendered symbols, including Barbie and sports media imagery. Although only preschoolers, they are already skilled in collectively taking up symbols from popular culture as resources to be utilized in their own group dynamics— building individual and group identities, sharing the pleasures of play, clarifying boundaries between in-group and out-group members, and constructing hierarchies in their worlds.

Further, we cannot understand the reason that the girls first chose Barbie Girls as their team name without our first understanding the fact that a particular institutional structure of AYSO soccer preexisted the girls' entrée into the league. The informal sexual division of labor among adults and the formal sex segregation of children's teams are part of a preexisting gender regime that constrains and enables the ways that the children enact gender relations and construct identities. One concrete manifestation of this constraining nature of sex-segregated teams is the choice of team names. It is reasonable to speculate that if the four- and five-year-old children were still sex-integrated, as in the pre-1995 era, no team would have chosen Barbie Girls as its team name, with Barbie as its symbol. In other words, the formal sex segregation created the conditions under which the girls were enabled, perhaps encouraged, to choose a sweet team name that is widely read as encoding feminine meanings. The eventual interactions between the boys and the girls were made possible, though by no means fully determined, by the structure of the gender regime and by the cultural resources that the children variously drew on.

On the other hand, the gendered division of labor in youth soccer is not seamless, static, or immune to resistance. One of the few woman head coaches, a very active athlete in her own right, told me that she is "challenging the sexism" in AYSO by becoming the head of her son's league. As post–Title IX women increasingly become mothers and as media images of competent, heroic female athletes become more a part of the cultural landscape for children, the gender regimes of children's sports may be increasingly challenged.[47] Put another way, the dramatically shifting opportunity structure and cultural imagery of post–Title IX sports have created opportunities for new kinds of interactions, which will inevitably challenge and further shift institutional structures. Social structures simultaneously constrain *and* enable, and agency is simultaneously reproductive *and* resistant.

CHAPTER 2

Playing Center:
The Triad of Violence in Men's Sports

In November 2000, newspapers reported that six high school football players in Yucca Valley, California, had been arrested on felony charges of false imprisonment, sexual battery, rape with a foreign object, and conspiracy. The crimes were allegedly perpetrated during a hazing ritual, when senior members of the football team "initiated" freshmen and sophomore members of the team.[1] These days, we seem to hear story after story describing male athletes' violent acts of ritualized hazing on athletic teams, acquaintance and gang rapes perpetrated against women, and verbal and physical abuse of girlfriends and spouses.[2] Statements of shock and surprise routinely follow these stories. School officials and coaches, backed up by psychologists and other professionals, vow to develop better means of "weeding out the bad apples" in the future. A common working assumption in these cases is that the perpetrators of these kinds of violent acts are deviating from the norms of proper behavior in the school and on the athletic teams. As the Yucca Valley principal put it in the wake of the charges against his students, "Some bad things are alleged to have happened. It's unfortunate, because these things tend to eclipse all the good things we're doing here."[3]

Are male athletes more likely than nonathletes to engage in acts of violence off the field, or when some athletes assault others are we just more likely to notice it because of their high-profile public status?[4] In this chapter, I will argue that we should not be surprised when we hear

of male athletes committing acts of off-the-field violence, whether sexual or otherwise. Far from being an aberration perpetrated by some
marginal deviants, male athletes' off-the-field violence is generated from
the normal, everyday dynamics at the center of male athletic culture.
Indeed, a number of studies of men's college athletics in recent years
have pointed to statistically significant relationships between athletic
participation and sexual aggression.[5] In what is widely considered the
most reliable study to date, sociologist Todd Crosset and his colleagues
surveyed twenty universities with Division I athletic programs and
found that male athletes, who in 1995 made up 3.7 percent of the student population, were 19 percent of those reported to campus Judicial
Affairs offices for sexual assault.[6] In a more recent article, Crosset argues
that researchers have more than likely been using far too broad a brush
in looking generally at the relationship of "men's sports" to violence
against women.[7] Studies that have involved comparisons across various
sports have found important differences: the vast majority of reported
assaults were perpetrated by athletes in revenue-producing contact sports
such as basketball, football, and ice hockey. For instance, in Crosset's
study, male football and basketball players made up 30 percent of the
student-athlete population but were responsible for 67 percent of the
reported sexual assaults. These data, according to Crosset, should warn
us of the dangers of "lumping all sport environments together under
the rubric of 'athletic affiliation.'"[8] More to the point of my argument in
this book, the research points to the conclusion that the athletes most
likely to engage in sexual and other violent assaults off the field are those
participating in the sports that I define as being at the institutional center of sport.

Some activists such as Donald McPherson, of the University of
Massachusetts Mentors in Violence program, are wary of pointing the
finger at athletes. McPherson argues that athletes are no more or less
likely than other men to be engaged in violence against women. Rather,
men's violence against women is a broad social problem that is propor-
tionately reflected, like other social problems, in sport.[9] Perhaps fearing
that pointing the finger at high-profile athletes will reinforce destructive

and oppressive stereotypes of African American males (who make up about 80 percent of the NBA, for instance) as violent sexual predators, activists like McPherson prefer instead to pull male athletes into positions of responsibility to educate peers to prevent violence against women. This is a real concern. As the media frenzy surrounding the trials of Mike Tyson and O. J. Simpson (for rape and for murder, respectively) illustrated, American culture seems especially obsessed with what Stuart Alan Clarke has called images of "black men misbehaving," especially if the alleged misbehaviors involve a combination of sex and violence.[10] Given the ways that racist stereotypes of black men as violent sexual predators have historically served as a foundation for institutional and personal violence perpetrated against African Americans, we should be wary of the various ways that these images continue to surface.[11] So, when data reveal that college athletes in revenue-producing sports have higher rates of sexual assault against women, there is a very real danger that the term *athletes in revenue-producing sports* will smuggle in racist stereotypes as a thinly veiled code word for *black male athletes*.[12]

Evidence suggests that the apparent overrepresentation of black male athletes charged with sexual assault in college is due to their dramatic overrepresentation in the central team sports of football and basketball. When we look at high schools, where white males are more evenly represented in the student athlete population, we see that white male athletes perpetrated many of the most egregious examples of sexual assault. And when we look at Canada, where the central sport, ice hockey, is dominated by white men, we see the vast majority of sexual assaults by athletes are committed by white males.[13] Following this logic, I begin with the assumption that it is not their race or ethnicity but their *positions at the center of athletics* that make certain male athletes more likely to engage in sexual assault than other men.

This is not to confuse the "center" with the "majority." In fact, a key to my analysis is the fact that the majority of male athletes do *not* commit acts of off-the-field violence against women or other men. Though in the numerical minority, the men at the center of the athletic peer group are expressing the dominant, hegemonic, most honored form of masculinity. What helps hegemonic masculinity sustain itself as the dominant form in a system of power relations is the *complicity* of other men, some (or many) of whom might be uncomfortable with some of the beliefs and practices that sustain hegemonic masculinity. Intervention strategies must confront the root causes of men's violence against women, and a key way to accomplish this confrontation is to provide a context in which the "silent majority" of men move affirmatively away from being quietly complicit with the culture of misogyny, homophobia, and violence at the center of men's sport culture.

We saw in the previous chapter how early experiences in sports commonly divide children into seemingly different and opposed groups of "the boys" and "the girls." In this chapter, I will show how, once separated into all-male homosocial groups, boys and men tend to construct a masculine, athletic center through their everyday peer group interactions. And they construct this center through what political scientist Michael Kaufman calls a "triad of men's violence," which consists of men's violence against women, against other men, and against themselves.[14] Homosocial sport offers an institutional context in which boys and men learn, largely from each other, to discipline their bodies, attitudes, and feelings within the logic of the triad of men's violence. I will look separately at the three aspects of the triad of men's violence, first examining men's violence against women, next turning to an analysis of men's violence against other men, and finally looking at men's violence against their own bodies. My goal in this chapter is to locate the key linking processes that hold this triad of men's violence together: group-based processes of misogyny, homophobia, and suppression of empathy. My level of analysis in this chapter is primarily interactional. That is, I focus mostly on the ways that boys and men perform a particular form of masculinity in their athletic peer groups.

Male Athletes' Violence against Women

In a riveting account of the infamous 1989 Glen Ridge, New Jersey, gang rape case, journalist Bernard Lefkowitz describes how thirteen white male, high-status high school athletes lured a seventeen-year-old "slightly retarded" girl into a basement.[15] The dynamics of the sexual assault that ensued are instructive for my purposes here: First, the boys set up chairs, theater style, in front of a couch. While some boys sat in the chairs to watch, others led the girl to the couch and induced her to begin to give one of the highest-status boys oral sex. When the assault began, one sophomore boy noticed "puzzlement and confusion" in the girl's eyes, turned to his friend, and said, "Let's get out of here." Another senior baseball player felt queasy, thought, "I don't belong here," and climbed the stairs to leave with another baseball player. On the way out, he told another guy, "It's wrong. C'mon with me," but the other guy stayed.[16] In all, six of the young men left the scene, while seven—six seniors and one junior—remained in the basement. While the girl was forced to continue giving oral sex to the boy, other boys laughed, yelled encouragement to their friends, and derisively shouted, "You whore!" at the girl. One boy decided it would be amusing to force a baseball bat up her vagina. When he did this (and followed it with a broomstick), the girl heard one boy's voice say, "Stop. You're hurting her," but another voice prevailed: "Do it more." Later, the girl remembered that the boys were all laughing while she was crying. When they were done, they warned her not to tell anyone and concluded with an athletic ritual of togetherness by standing in a circle and clasping "one hand on top of the other, all their hands together, like a basketball team on the sidelines at the end of a timeout."[17]

In his description of the Glen Ridge community in which the boys and their victim grew up, Lefkowitz points to a number of factors that enabled the gang rape to happen, and these are the very same factors that much of the social scientific literature on men, sexual violence, and sport has pointed to in recent years:

1. the key role of competitive, homophobic, and misogynistic talk and joking as the central, most honored form of dominance bonding in the athletic male peer group
2. the group practice of "voyeuring," whereby boys set up situations where they seduce girls into places and situations in which their

friends can watch the sex act and sometimes take an active part
in it

3. the suppression of empathy toward others—especially toward the
girls who are the objects of their competitive dominance bonding—
that the boys learn from each other

4. the enabling of some men's sexual violence against women by a
"culture of silence" among peers, in families, and in the community

As I examine these four enabling factors, I will keep in the forefront
Lefkowitz's observation that four football players and wrestlers physically perpetrated the assault. Three others apparently sat and watched,
sometimes laughing and cheering, but did not actually physically join in
the assault.[18] The other six boys left the scene when the assault was
beginning. Though these six boys felt uncomfortable enough to leave
the scene, they did not do anything at the time to stop their friends,
nor did they report the assault to parents, teachers, or the police. And
they all refused throughout the subsequent long and painful years of
litigation to "turn" on their male friends and provide incriminating
evidence. It is the *complicity* of these boys that I take as the centerpiece
of my analysis here.

Sexual Talk and Dominance Bonding

In an ethnographic study of eleven- and twelve-year-old Little League
baseball players, sociologist Gary Alan Fine found that one of the key
ways that these boys connected with each other was through sexually
aggressive banter.[19] Reading Fine's descriptions of boys' verbal sparring
brought back memories of engaging in what we called cut fights during childhood. I learned in grade school that high-status boys achieved
and maintained their centrality in the male peer group not simply
through athletic prowess but also through informal, often homophobic
and misogynist, banter on the playgrounds, streets, and playing fields.
Those who were the most ruthlessly competitive "cut fighters" seemed
always capable of one-upping another boy's insults. Following another
boy's sharp, cutting insult with silence or with a lame comment like "you

too" left one open to derision. I learned this firsthand one day while walking home from fifth grade with a group of boys. Chris, a boy well known for his verbal prowess, and I were in a cut fight. Back and forth we went. I thought I was doing pretty well until Chris hit me with one for which I had no answer: "Messner," he asserted, "blow me!" I didn't know what to say back, and so of course I lost the cut fight. But behind my lack of response was confusion. In my eleven-year-old mind, I knew a few things about sex but was unclear about others. One thing I had recently learned from friends was that there were some men who had sex with other men. They were called homosexuals, and I was told that they were sick and sinful individuals. So, my confused mind spun, if Chris was saying, "blow me," to me, he was in effect asking me to be involved in some homosexual act with him. If homosexuality is such a bad and shameful thing, why then did *he* win the cut fight?

It took me years to figure that one out. Meanwhile, in the short run, I simply added "blow me" to my own cut fight repertoire. Now I can see that insults like "you suck," "blow me," or "fuck you" smuggle into children's and preadolescent groups a powerful pedagogy about sexuality, power, and domination.[20] In short, though children obviously do not intend it, through this sort of banter they teach each other that sex, whether of the homosexual or heterosexual kind, is a relational act of domination and subordination. The "men" are the ones who are on top, in control, doing the penetrating and fucking. Women, or penetrated men, are subordinate, degraded, and dehumanized objects of sexual aggression. This kind of sexual domination is played out most clearly in cases of rape in men's prisons, where those being raped are symbolically defined as either women or fags.[21] The actual sexual orientation of these men matters little in these cases; it is their vulnerable, subordinate, and degraded status that makes them "women" or "fags." By contrast, those who are doing the raping are not defined as gay. They are "men" who are powerful, in control, and dominant over the symbolically debased "women" or "fags."

A key to the importance of this verbal sparring is the central role it plays in *groups*. Rarely will two boys, alone, engage in a cut fight. But put the same two boys in a group, they will often be compelled to insult each other or to turn on another boy in the group. A cut fight is a group phenomenon that requires an audience. On center stage are the higher-status boys; around the periphery are the lower-status boys, constituted as an admiring audience who, by their very presence, attention, and laughter, validate the higher status of the boys at the center. This dynamic starts early. In their study of first graders, sport scholars Cynthia Hasbrook and Othello Harris observed that "Martin," the highest-status boy in the class, was both athletically tough and socially aggressive. When he refused to hold hands during a relay race, this had an impact on the other boys:

> Other boys fell over themselves trying to be friends with Martin. They mimicked his speech, gestures, and postures; they covered for him so that he would not get in trouble; sought him out as a partner; and wrote stories portraying him as their friend. Martin constantly negotiated a masculine identity that was physically aggressive, tough, distant, and cool, and his refusal to join hands both consolidated his ascendant position and constricted other expressions of masculinity.[22]

These same tendencies are evident among preadolescent children. Patricia Adler and Peter Adler point to patterns of high-status grade school children picking on lower-status kids as well as teasing and "ingroup subjugation" as key elements that "served to solidify the group and to assert the power of the strong over the vulnerability of the weak."[23] Similarly, in their study of high school basketball players, Scott Eveslage and Kevin Delaney found that the boys' "trash talking" on the court and their "insult talk" among teammates off the field have common traits: they establish hierarchies, they "involve personal insults or put-downs, often as calls to defend masculinity and honor, and they often degrade objects defined as 'feminine.'"[24] These processes continue into the worlds of young adult men. In a revealing study of talk in a college men's athletic locker room, sociologist Tim Curry observed that there is a dominant mode of conversation that is inclined toward the dual themes of competition and boasting of sexual conquests of women.[25] This dominant conversation is characterized by its high volume—it is clearly intended as a performance for the group—and by its geographic and cultural centrality in the locker room.

But Curry's study also revealed a less obvious dynamic. On the margins of the locker room, other young men were engaged in conversations that were very different from the dominant conversation at the center of the group. These men were speaking in hushed tones, usually in dyads, and were clearly not projecting a performance that was intended to be public. And the topics of their talks were not of competition and sexual conquest of women; rather, they were speaking to each other about personal issues, problems, even insecurities about dating or relationships with girlfriends. These conversations remain marginal, quiet, and private—in contrast with the loud, public, central conversation—partly because boys and young men have had the experience of being (or seeing other boys) humiliated in male groups for expressing vulnerability or for expressing care for a particular girl.[26] The main policing mechanisms used to enforce consent with the dominant conversation are misogyny and homophobia: boys and men who reveal themselves as vulnerable are subsequently targeted as the symbolic "women," "pussies," and "faggots" on athletic teams (and, indeed, in many other male groups). In fact, it is a key part of the group process of dominance bonding that one or more members of the male group are made into the symbolic debased and degraded feminized "other" through which the group members bond and feel that their status as "men" is safely ensured. Most boys learn early to avoid at all costs offering one's self up as a target for this kind of abuse.[27] The power of this group dynamic was illustrated in an interview I conducted with a former world-class athlete who, during his athletic career, had been a closeted gay man. One of the best ways that he found to keep his sexual identity secret within this aggressively homophobic world was to participate in what he called "locker room garbage" talk about sexual conquests of women.[28]

Curry's descriptions of the dominant, central conversation and the marginal, quiet conversations in the locker room are remarkably similar to Lefkowitz's description of how the Glen Ridge boys set up their gang rape. In both cases, a small minority of high-status young men staged an aggressive, violently misogynist performance at the center of the room. I sketch out this internal dynamic of the athletic male peer group in Figure 3.

1. *Leaders*: At the center of the athletic male peer group are the highest-status boys and young men. They are the members of the group who most actively conform to and directly benefit from hegemonic masculinity. Their performances (from homophobic and misogynist verbal sparring, teasing, or bullying vulnerable boys, to hazing younger athletes, to actual sexual assaults of girls or other boys) involve directing their aggression toward debased feminized objects of sexual conquest.

2. *Audience*: Closely connected to the center, another group of boys constitutes itself as an adoring, cheering audience that directly supports and validates the hegemony of the central performance of the leaders. The gaze of these boys is directed inward, toward the group's center, to which they are erotically attached. They are

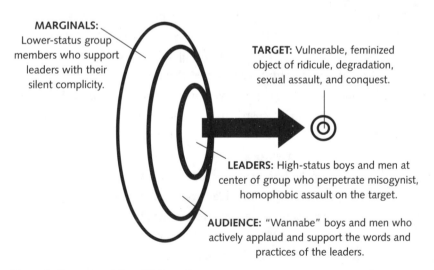

MARGINALS: Lower-status group members who support leaders with their silent complicity.

TARGET: Vulnerable, feminized object of ridicule, degradation, sexual assault, and conquest.

LEADERS: High-status boys and men at center of group who perpetrate misogynist, homophobic assault on the target.

AUDIENCE: "Wannabe" boys and men who actively applaud and support the words and practices of the leaders.

Figure 3. Dynamics of the athletic male peer group.

similar to what Adler and Adler call "wannabes":[29] though not central in the group's status hierarchy, these boys hope desperately to belong, to share in the benefits and pleasures of hegemonic masculinity, and to avoid the pain of becoming the object of the group's put-downs.

3. *Marginals*: Further out, at the margins of the group, are other boys and young men, whispering to each other in quiet dyads. They are perhaps not fully comfortable with the words and actions at the center of the group. They may experience empathy with the victims of the group's jokes and assaults. And they may at times, out of discomfort, opt out of some of the group's more cruel activities. However, they may also feel a powerful, magnetic pull toward the erotic dominance bonding at the group's center. After all, this is the place where these boys have experienced some acceptance and belonging. And their association with this group brings a certain level of respect from outsiders. Moreover, they know that silence will keep them safely in the group.

The active support of the audience and the compliant silence of the marginals make these two groups complicit in constituting the center as a high-status site of homophobic and misogynist domination. Indeed, the center would not be the center without the active support of the audience and the silent complicity of the outer circle of marginals.

What keeps those at the margins of the peer group silent? Partly, it's fear. One fifth-grade boy told Adler and Adler that he compliantly goes with the flow when high-status kids pick on his friends: "It's a real risk if you want to try to stick up for someone because you could get rejected from the group or whatever."[30] According to Katherine Farr, sexually aggressive banter in groups provides a means of "dominance bonding" for young males.[31] Internal hierarchies are constructed and contested as the boys and young men simultaneously mark the boundaries where the in-group ends and the realm of "outsiders" (women, gay men, non-athlete men, etc.) begins. I speculated in chapter 1 how a member of the boys' Sea Monsters team might have felt compelled to ignore his inner desire to join the Barbie Girls' celebration and instead joined in his peers' denunciation of the girls. Similarly, when a marginal young man does not feel comfortable with the dominant locker room conversation or with his teammates' gang rape of a girl or young woman, he knows that to speak out against these actions would be to risk severing his already tenuous connection to the group's center, a social location of power and status.

But it's not simply fear that keeps marginal boys in silent complicity with the group's practices. It's also pleasure. The bonds of the male peer group often have a decidedly erotic base, as Peter Lyman's research on sexual joking among fraternity members illustrates.[32] To say that male groups' dominance bonding is erotic is not to say necessarily that men's bonds in sports are simply a means of sublimating a desire to have sex with each other. Undoubtedly, that is true with some boys and men, for whom sports are experienced as a "heterosexualization process," in which same-sex desire is repressed, perhaps sublimated into aggression, and eventually converted to sexual desire for women.[33] Some might speculate that this same-sex desire remains submerged in the unconscious of young men who self-define as "100 percent heterosexual." Whether it does or not, the erotic bond among male athletes tends to be overtly coded as fiercely heterosexual. Boys and men learn to bond with each other through sexually aggressive, erotically exciting talk that serves to forge an aggressive, even violent, hierarchical ordering of bodies, both inside the male peer group and between the male peer group and any other group. To thwart the dominant modes of one's peer group, then, is not simply to risk ridicule and ostracism; it also threatens to undermine the major way that a young male has learned to experience erotic excitement and pleasure with his peers.

"Voyeuring": Women as Objects of Conquest

By the time they were teens, the "jocks" of Glen Ridge used more than talk for their erotic dominance bonding. When parents were away, they would sometimes gather together in a home to watch pornographic films and masturbate together. The next step was the development of a group form of entertainment that they called voyeuring, whereby a plan would be made for one guy at a party to "convince a girl to go upstairs to a bedroom for a sexual encounter." But first, "his buddies would go up and hide in a closet, under the bed, or behind a door," where they could watch. Sex with a girl, for these guys, was less an intimate encounter with a valued human being than it was the use of a woman's body as a sexual performance for one's male buddies. It was, in Lefkowitz's words, "a way for these guys to create their own porn movie."[34] Voyeuring was not invented in Glen Ridge. An informant told Tim Curry, in his study of a sports bar frequented by college athletes, that

> an athlete who succeeded in picking up a date would escort her back to the apartment, where some of his teammates would be sitting on the couch waiting to see if anyone scored. If the young woman were a stranger rather than the athlete's regular girlfriend, they would head upstairs at the first opportunity. They would hide in the athlete's room or go to the roof, where they could look into the bedroom through a skylight. The "game" was to get the woman into the upstairs bedroom and into bed and let the other athletes watch the sexual activity take place.[35]

Similarly, the California white high school footballers known as the Spur Posse had multiple sexual encounters with girls and young women as a competition among the boys to see who could "score" the most times. Significantly, it was the competitive talk and recapitulation of the conquest among the boys, not sex with the girls, that seemed to be the major driving force in their pursuit of this scoring.[36] In 2001, a case of voyeuring by male athletes came to light in a Maryland high school. While having sex with a fifteen-year-old girl, a sixteen-year-old lacrosse player secretly filmed the sex act and then later showed the film to his teammates.[37]

Men's use of female bodies to bond with each other is central to the dynamic of gang rape. Anthropologist Peggy Sanday and others who have studied gang rape are careful to argue that, from the point of view of the woman, the rape is not a sexual experience; rather, it is a violent, degrading, and painful assault against one's body. However, from the point of view of perpetrators, there certainly *is* a sexual dynamic at work in gang rapes. But it is not sex with a woman happening here; rather, the male group uses the debased, violated woman's body as an object through which to have sex with each other.[38] In short, the dynamic underlying gang rapes is a statement of group-based male power, expressed through a dual process of misogynist denigration of women and erotic bonding among men, and this process has its roots in the erotic bonding of the misogynist joking culture of athletic teams.

A key to understanding male groups' use of women's bodies through which to erotically bond with each other is that most heterosexual boys and young men go through a period of intense insecurity and even discomfort in learning to establish sexual relations with girls and women. Men who were former athletes reported to me retrospectively that in high school, and even for some in college, talking with girls and women raised intense anxieties and feelings of inadequacy.[39] These young men dealt with their feelings of "lameness" with young women primarily by listening to and watching their male peers deliver a "rap" to women. As the men immersed themselves in this peer pedagogy of heterosexual relations, they learned to put on a performance for girls that, surprisingly for some of them, seemed to "work." The successful utilization of this learned dramaturgy of the heterosexual come-on allowed a young man to mask, even overcome, his sense of insecurity and lameness in his own eyes and, just as important, in the eyes of his male teammates. It also intensified, at a deep psychological level, his adherence to the group process of erotic dominance bonding with other members of his male peer group through collectively constructing women as objects of conquest.

When I was a freshman in college, as a "marginal" member of my community college basketball team, I experienced this peer group dynamic directly.[40] After having been a reasonably good high school player, I found myself at the bottom of the totem pole, thirteenth on a thirteen-player college team. Moreover, off the court, I could not hold my own in the competitive sexual banter. Early in the season, on a road trip, the guys lounged around in a motel room, talking and joking about sex. Drew, our starting center and one of the highest-status guys on the team, noticed that Rob (another marginal player) and I had not been contributing anything to the raucous chronicling of the team's sexual exploits. "Hey, Robby T., hey Mess," Drew asked, "you guys ever had a piece of ass?" A virgin with little to brag about, I tensed up. I knew that Kess, another reserve player on the team, had recently been labeled the team fag after he had refused to jump into the middle of a brawl we had had against another team. I wanted to avoid becoming such a target of joking put-downs, so I employed what I thought was a subtle strategy. "Naw," I replied, but with diverted eyes and a knowing smile that I hoped would suggest that I was simply too cool to brag about sex with my girlfriend, a high school girl. Rob followed the same strategy. Drew, missing the subtleties, clobbered us: "Wow! We got two virgins on this team! We can't have that! Mess, Robby T., we gotta get you laid, and soon! We can't go having any virgins on this team. Havin' Kess is bad enough!"

A couple of weeks later, Drew invited us to a party. Robby T. and I showed up together, with our six-packs of beer. Soon, Drew announced to Rob and me loudly, "Hey, you two virgins ain't gonna be virgins after tonight, eh?" Not knowing what he was talking about, we just agreed and laughed, "Sure, Drew. We're just trying to figure out who we're going to lay tonight." Drew replied, "Man, you don't have to worry about that, because me and the guys have that taken care of. We got a lady comin' over here in a couple of hours. She's real special, and since you guys are the only two virgins on the team, you get to go first." As I felt my palms get sweaty, I knew I was supposed to act grateful. "Wow, Drew. Like, is she some kind of prostitute or something?" Drew smiled. "You could say that. She's kind of a friend of mine, you know?" He laughed loud and hard, and so did we. I took some long pulls on my beer, drained it, and opened another one. I whispered to Robby T., "Let's get the hell out of here," and we escaped out the back door.

Rob and I never did find out whether Drew was serious about his plan to get us laid, or if the guys were just pulling a joke on the two lower-status guys on the team. We felt a bit ashamed of ourselves for leaving the party, and we knew that doing so did nothing to enhance our already marginal status on the team. So we decided that the only way to handle the guys when we next saw them was to tell them a lie: We were now laying our girlfriends and just couldn't do it with someone else because we wanted to be faithful. That's how we escaped being put in the "fag bag" with Kess. We were accepted now; we had learned how to bullshit with the best of them.

But the story did not end there. After this embarrassing incident, I began to step up the pressure on my girlfriend to "put out." Like many young men, I wanted to have sex. But the urgency of my desire was not driven simply by my attraction to my girlfriend. I genuinely and desperately wanted access to the sexual experience and knowledge that would put me on a par with the guys on the team. Fortunately, my girlfriend had a mind of her own and asserted her own timetable on what we would do and when we would do it. However, I can see in retrospect how my experiences with my teammates had created fear, embarrassment, and frustration over my "virgin status" and that this in turn had encouraged a tendency to see and treat my girlfriend more as an object of conquest than as a person with feelings, fears, and desires of her own. More generally, this experience eventually helped me to understand how the athletic male peer groups' voyeuring—their tendencies to bond by watching each other have sex or by listening to each other talk about sex—don't end up only in gang rapes. This group dynamic can also feed the seemingly more private, one-on-one dynamic of date and acquaintance rape, even among young men who are marginal to the athletic peer group.[41]

Women's Sexual Agency

As my story suggests, the idea that male peer-group dynamics create women as objects of sexual conquest oversimplifies a more complex relational dynamic between women and men. After all, though I had begun to pressure my girlfriend in order to gain status with my male peers, she did not become a passive object of my actions and desires. She retained, expressed, and asserted her subjectivity in this situation. And in fact, when I talk with college male athletes these days, their descriptions of their relations with women are anything but descriptions of passive objects. Jeffrey Benedict, in his book *Athletes and Acquaintance Rape*, argues that high-status male college and professional athletes learn to take for granted that some women will seek out sex with them. This interactional dynamic, which Benedict calls the "jock-groupie tango," tends to socialize many male athletes to "an image of women as sexually compliant. The sex-for-fame commerce that exists between athletes and groupies undermines and trivializes the fundamental component of consent."[42]

Rather than simply seeing acquaintance rape by athletes as a result of objectification dynamics emanating from within the male peer group, Benedict paints a more complex picture. He argues that there is a sub-culture of sexually assertive and active women and men in sports, and he points to women's agency in this sexual dynamic. Some antirape activists and feminists may blanch at Benedict's discussion of the ways that women's "complicity reinforces the athletes' attitude of sexual license,"[43] fearing that this perspective will fuel the blame-the-victim mentality that is so common in discussions of the women who are raped by male athletes. There is a fine line to be navigated here: On the one hand, acknowledging women's agency in a relational sexual dynamic with men athletes risks letting men off the hook and, once again, blaming women for men's acts of sexual violence. On the other hand, ignoring women's agency risks academic complicity in the construction of women as passive sexual objects. A key, I think, to understanding the complexity of this situation lies in viewing both women's and men's sexual agencies as embedded in unequal power relations.

Anybody who does any work with male athletes around issues of sexuality and rape knows that some men athletes do objectify women as targets of sexual conquest and often uncritically internalize rape myths. When once conducting a workshop on sex for a college football team with my colleague Mark Stevens, we asked the players, "When you are in the early stages of sex with a woman, how do you know when you have her consent to move ahead?" After a moment or two of nervous giggling, one man, apparently quite seriously, offered this answer: "If she's wet, then she wants it." The room erupted in raucous laughter and agreement. Mark Stevens went on to challenge this belief, explaining that there can be an important distinction between bodily responses to physical stimulation and agreement to proceed to other forms or levels of sexual involvement. Heavy breathing, enthusiastic kissing, or even apparent genital lubrication on the woman's part do not necessarily imply consent to go further.

That some of these guys apparently saw sexual encounters with women as moments of physical manipulation of women's bodies to achieve a goal lends credence to the notion that they have learned to treat women as objects.[44] But when we listen to what these young men have to say, we also find that they often experience some women as sexually aggressive and even powerful. Women, they say, have tremendous control over sexual situations through their ability to manipulate men with their sexual attractiveness and their ability to say no or, more commonly, to give ambiguous sexual messages. In his workshops with college athletes, Mark Stevens introduces the metaphor of a traffic light to begin a discussion of consent. He first asks the men how they respond as drivers to red, yellow, and green lights. The men respond that they always know what to do with a red or a green light, but when approaching a yellow light, there is often a moment of confusion, usually followed by their speeding up rather than slowing down. Sexual encounters with women, the men say, are far too often experienced as yellow lights, with mixed messages abounding. Stevens extends the metaphor by explaining that a sexual encounter is also very much like an intersection, ripe with both excitement and danger, so a "yellow light" should be a sign that danger looms and that one should slow down, show caution.

When these men get a yellow light from a woman, they are not experiencing a passive female sexual object; rather, they are grappling with the active sexual agency of a woman (albeit agency that might be every bit as confused and as poorly communicated as his). These men are operating from an assumption that they, as men, should be *in control*—of their sexual partners, of the situation, of themselves. However, their sexual experiences are likely to be confusing, raising anxieties about their own lack of control and leading to an exaggerated sense of women's sexual power over them.[45] One response to this confusion during a sexual encounter is for the man to revert to an internalized sexual script, which often contains elements of rape myths ("If she's wet, she wants it"). Tim Beneke, in his book *Proving Manhood*, offers the insight that rather than simply defining women as passive objects, men more often tend to project a sexual subjectivity onto women—a subjectivity of desire and lust for "me."[46]

Sometimes, though, male athletes don't have to project an imagined sexual subjectivity onto women. Gail McKabe studied the dynamic between Canadian male Major Junior Hockey players (fifteen- to twenty-year-old elite athletes) and the women who self-identify as "puck bunnies" and aggressively seek out sexual liaisons with the jocks.[47] McKabe says that the puck bunnies are "relentless in their pursuit of the jock." These young women say they are "'proud as punch' to have sex with the jock," because this will "entitle the puck bunny to 'bragging rights'" through their affiliation with the high-status jocks. The male jocks are often happy to have sex with the puck bunnies and even see it as "tangible evidence of their celebrity status." However, in a crude derivation of the madonna/whore dichotomy, the jocks tend to define the puck bunnies as "the dirties" and place them in opposition to girlfriends, with whom they expect to have broader and longer-term relationships. McKabe's research suggests a complex dynamic. Both the male jocks and the female puck bunnies are active agents in what McKabe describes as a group-based "cultural negotiation." Put another way, both the young men and the young women are simultaneously objects (of each other's desires and actions) *and* active subjects. However, this negotiation takes place in a decidedly asymmetrical context with respect to gender and social status. The puck bunnies' agency—their active attempts to gain status through sexual affiliation with the high-status males—may be viewed as a way of resisting the gender and age constraints they face in their communities. However, the jocks have direct access to their own social status as respected and revered male ice hockey players, and this asymmetry serves ultimately to advantage them and to disadvantage the degraded "dirties" whose "bragging rights" are short lived. The agency of both groups ultimately, then, reproduces the asymmetrically gendered context.

Suppression of Empathy

A key part of the process of learning to treat a person of a particular group as an object of conquest is the suppression of empathy for such a person. But boys and men have mothers, sisters, female cousins, and friends whom they know as people and whom they are taught to "protect" and care for. How then can they conjure up the emotional distance to be able to sexually assault women? Cross-cultural research on rape has pointed to the importance of the degree and type of contact that boys and men have with girls and women as a variable that correlates with varying rates of rape. Rape rates tend to be higher in societies with rigid divisions of labor and spatial separation between the sexes, especially where these divisions are marked by male dominance and female subordination.[48] Homosocial bonding among men, especially when the bond is of the sort of sexualized dominance bonding that I discussed above, is a very poor environment for the development of empathy (or respect) for women.

Consistent with this, Lefkowitz notes that the boys who were most central in the actual assault in the Glen Ridge rape grew up without sisters, in families that were headed by domineering male figures. Moreover, their peer group, family, and community experiences taught them that boys' and men's activities were most valued, and girls' and women's were of secondary importance. "The immediate environment," Lefkowitz argues, "did not cultivate great empathy for women."[49] Contrarily, some of the boys who left the scene and felt "uncomfortable" with the assault seemed more open to seeing the pain in the victim's eyes and were thus less able to suppress their empathy for the victim. Most of these boys, Lefkowitz observes, grew up in homes with sisters.

Male Athletes' Culture of Silence

A question that plagued Lefkowitz in his description of the Glen Ridge rape was why the six boys who left the scene remained complicit in their silence, both the day of the rape and during the subsequent years of litigation. At least some of these young men were very uncomfortable with what happened, even thought it was wrong, but nobody in the group raised a hand or voice to stop it. Two other young men did, however. The case broke when another male athlete, who had not been at the scene of the assault, reported to teachers that he had overheard other guys laughing and bragging about the rape. Significantly, this African American young man who blew the whistle had always felt himself to be excluded from the tightly knit, high-status clique of white athletes. The second boy, who became an activist in the school and community in his quest to see that the jocks did not get away with their crime, was a long-haired "Gigger" (a term used to identify the small minority of radical, artsy, antijock students at the school). Both of these boys—one an athlete, one not—were outsiders to the dominant athletic male peer group. Those inside, even those who were marginal within the group, maintained a complicit silence that enabled the minority to assault their victim.

This culture of silence is built into the dynamics of the group's spoken and unspoken codes and rituals. The eroticized dominance bond has already established that "the guys" are part of a high-status, privileged in-group (and very little during adolescence can solidify this sort of feeling as much as being part of an athletic team). Others— nonathlete boys, racial and ethnic minority boys, girls, parents, teachers, police, and so on—are outsiders. Years of experience within the group have taught these boys that they will be rewarded for remaining complicit with the code of silence and punished for betraying the group. They know that a whistle-blower might be banished from the group and possibly also beaten up. Or he might remain in the group, but now with the status of the degraded, feminized "faggot" who betrayed the "men" in the group.

Men's Violence against Other Men

In February 2000, a professional basketball player with the San Antonio Spurs, Sean Elliott, announced his impending return to play following a life-threatening illness that resulted in a kidney transplant. Elliott's return was met with considerable media discussion and debate about whether it was appropriate for him to return to play at all, given the grave risks he might face should he receive a blow to his kidney. Lakers star Kobe Bryant, when asked how he would respond to playing against Elliott, said, "As soon as he steps on the court, that means he's healthy. I'll have no problem putting an elbow in his gut."[50] This statement spoke to the routine nature of bodily contact and aggression in basketball. Players and coaches know that in order to be competitive enough to win, they will need to "put their bodies on" opposing players in ways that could cause bodily harm. In football and ice hockey, the overt aggression against other players is even more intense. One former National Football League player told me that before a playoff game, his coach implored his defensive players to hurt the opposing star running back if they had an opportunity to do it. This is apparently not that unusual. A 1998 *Sports Illustrated* cover story on "the NFL's dirtiest players" admiringly described San Francisco 49ers guard Kevin Gogan's tendencies, sometimes even after a play has been whistled dead, to "punch, kick, trip, cut-block, sit on or attempt to neuter the man lined up across from him." Gogan's coach, Steve Mariuchi, expressed his approval: "Coaches want tough guys, players who love to hit and fly around and do things that are mean and nasty. Not everyone can be like that, but if you can have one or two players who are a little overaggressive, that's great."[51]

Bodily aggression toward opponents on the field or court, whether of the "routine" kind that takes place within the rules or of the "dirty" illegal kind that aims to injure an opponent, is often assumed to end when the players cross the boundaries back into the "real world." The story of the "gentle giant" football player who growls, curses, and tears opponents limb-from-limb on the field but is a kind and caring teddy bear off the field is part of our national lore. But is aggression on the field against other men related to aggression off the field? Former Dallas

Cowboy football star John Niland now says that he and many of his former teammates were involved in drugs, alcohol, and spouse abuse:

> I'm not going to name names, but my wife at the time knew of other wives who were abused.... We're paid to be violent. We're paid to beat up on the guy across from you. When you're in the game and your emotions are so high and the aura of the whole environment is so unbelievable. When the game's over, technically, it's to be turned off. But you can't.... Quite frankly, if you got every player who did drugs or alcohol or played stoned or who was a spousal abuser, you couldn't field an NFL team. It's still going on.[52]

And consider a comment by NBA coach Pat Riley, of the Miami Heat. Bemoaning an unusually long break between his team's playoff games, Riley said, "Several days between games allows a player to become a person. During the playoffs, you don't want players to be people."[53] If it is acknowledged that the supposedly civilizing influences of a player's life outside sports can (negatively!) humanize him, then doesn't it follow that it might also work the other way—that dehumanizing attitudes and experiences within sports might spill over into life outside sports? Indeed, sport studies scholars have found evidence that points to this conclusion. Jeffrey Segrave and his colleagues found that Canadian minor league (fifteen- and sixteen-year-old) ice hockey players were more likely than nonathletes to engage in physically violent acts of delinquency.[54] And sociologist Howard Nixon found that male athletes in team contact sports, especially if they reported having intentionally hurt other athletes on the field, were more likely to hurt others outside sports.[55] To understand this connection, it is necessary to look more closely at the ways that boys and men develop their identities and relationships within the culture of sport.

Boys' Embodiments of Toughness

In an earlier book, *Power at Play*, I explored the meanings of athletic participation through life-history interviews with male former athletes.

One man, a former NFL defensive back who had been known and re-warded for his fierce and violent "hits," had injured many opposing play-ers in his career, some seriously. I asked him to describe how he felt the first times he had hurt someone on a football field, and he said that hitting and hurting people had bothered him at first:

> When I first started playing, if I would hit a guy hard and he wouldn't get up, it would bother me. [But] when I was a sophomore in high school, first game, I knocked out two quarterbacks, and people loved it. The coach loved it. Everybody loved it. You never stop feeling sorry for [your injured opponent]. If somebody doesn't get up, you want him to get up. You hope the wind's just knocked out of him or something. The more you play, though, the more you realize that it is just a part of the game—somebody's gonna get hurt. It could be you, it could be him—most of the time it's better if it's him. So, you know, you just go out and play your game.[56]

This statement describes a contextual normalization of violence: "you realize it is just a part of the game." It also illustrates an emotional process, a group-based suppression of empathy for the pain and injury that one might cause one's opponent. Most children are taught that it is unacceptable to hurt other people. In order to get athletes (or soldiers) to be willing and able to inflict harm on others, the opponent must be objectified as the enemy, and the situation must be defined as "either him or me": "somebody's gonna get hurt. It could be you, it could be him— most of the time it's better if it's him." The most obvious force behind this suppression of empathy is the rewards one gets for the successful utilization of violence: "The coach loved it. Everybody loved it." And it's not just this sort of immediate positive reinforcement. The man quoted above, for instance, received a college scholarship, all-America honors, and eventually all-pro status in the NFL.

But rewards do not tell the whole story behind athletes' suppres-sion of empathy for their opponents. In fact, when I probed athletes' early experiences and motivations in sports, I found stories not of victo-ries, trophies, and public adulation. Instead, these men were more likely to drop into stories of early connection with others, especially fathers, older brothers, uncles, and eventually same-aged male peers. Some found sports to be the primary, sometimes the *only*, site in which they experienced connection with their otherwise emotionally or physically absent fathers. Many also said that they felt alone, unsure of themselves, cut off from others and that it was through sports participation, especially for those who had some early successes and received attention for these successes, that they found acceptance.

Why sports? An important part of the answer is that most boys' early experiences teach them to appear to be invulnerable. This means, don't show any fear or weakness. And little boys begin to learn this at a very young age. Learning to embody and display toughness, even if it is a veneer that covers up a quivering insecurity inside, can be a survival skill that helps boys stay safe in a hostile environment. In his eloquent description of street life for African American boys in poor communities, Geoffrey Canada describes how learning to fight, or at least displaying an attitude that you are ready and willing to fight, was necessary. Losing a fight, and "taking it like a man," was far better (and ultimately *safer*) than being labeled a coward.[57] Learning early to mask one's vulnerability behind displays of toughness may help boys survive on the street, but it can also contribute to boys (and, later, men) having difficulties in developing and maintaining emotional connection with others. Though in an emotional straitjacket, boys and men retain a human need to connect with others. And for those who have some early athletic successes, sports can become an especially salient context in which to receive a certain kind of closeness with others.[58]

A key, then, to understanding male athletes' commitment to athletic careers lies in understanding their underlying need for connection with other people and the ways that society thwarts emotional connection for boys. And there is often an additional layer of emotional salience to sports participation for boys and men from poor and ethnic minority backgrounds. African American men, in particular, when asked about their early motivations in sports, were far more likely to drop into a discussion of "respect" than other men were. Early sports successes, for them, offered the discovery of a group context in which they could earn the respect of family members, friends, schoolmates, and communities. White middle-class men in my study did not talk about the importance of respect in the same way. This is because African American boys and young men are far more likely to face a daily experience of being *suspected* (of a potential crime of violence, of shoplifting in a store, of cheating on an exam, etc.) than of being *respected*. Schools are a major source of African American boys' experience of disrespect. Sociologist Ann Arnett Ferguson observes that elementary school teachers and administrators often treat African American boys as "troublemakers" who are already "beyond redemption."[59] By contrast, most white middle-class boys and men begin each day and enter each situation with a certain baseline, taken-for-granted level of respect that includes an assumption of our competence and trustworthiness, which is then ours to lose. To receive the benefits of this baseline of respect, we simply have to show up. This respect is not earned; rather, it is an unacknowledged but very real benefit that Peggy MacIntosh has called "the invisible Knapsack of White Privilege."[60]

In short, boys' relational capacities and opportunities for expressions of emotional vulnerability tend to be thwarted and suppressed. Some boys find in their early athletic experiences that sports offer them a context in which they can connect emotionally and gain the respect of others. Ironically though, as one moves further away from the playful experiences of childhood into the competitive, routinized institutional context of athletic careers, one learns that in order to continue to receive approval and respect, one must be a winner. And to be a winner, you must be ready and willing to suppress your empathy for other athletes. In the context of sports careers, you do not experience your body as a means of connecting intimately with others; rather, your body becomes a weapon, which you train to defeat an objectified, dehumanized opponent.[61] It's a dog-eat-dog world out there; you gotta have that killer instinct.

Booze, Bonding, and Fighting

The lessons learned on the field are important, but athletes also spend large amounts of time not playing sports—in classrooms, at parties, and at other social events with friends. And the kinds of relational patterns that boys and men learn on athletic teams sometimes spill over into these nonsport contexts. Timothy Curry found that college male athletes described life at the campus bar as one of "drinking, picking up women, and getting into fights":

> ... the athletes would try to "own" every bar they frequented. Often, this meant staging bar fights to demonstrate their power. Several of the athletes were good fighters, and they were typically the ones to start the fight. Often, these fighters would pick out a particular victim based on the fact that he looked "queer." The victim need not do anything provocative— sometimes victims were chosen because "they didn't want to fight." After the first punch was thrown, others in the group would enter in, either throwing punches of their own or attempting to break up the fight. The team always backed up its most aggressive members, so that the victim seldom had much of a chance.[62]

Since the athletes were of such high status, Curry explains, they rarely got into any trouble from this fighting. Instead, most often the victim was thrown out of the bar by the bouncer, and the players would be given free drinks from the bartender and would celebrate their "victory" as "a way of building team cohesion and expressing masculine courage."[63] Alcohol consumption is obviously a key part of this process.[64] The athletes would compete among themselves to see who could consume the most free (or nearly free) drinks at the bar. The heavy drinking, an athlete told Curry, is "to prove you're not a pussy."[65]

Curry's description of the sports bar scene mirrors the interactional dynamics of male peer groups that I described earlier concerning violence against women. In the sports bar, we see a premeditated incident of violence, staged to build in-group cohesion (albeit this time in a public place, with a male victim). The victim is a vulnerable-looking man, who is degraded by the group as looking "queer." As a result, the line between "the men," who are inside the group, and others outside the group, be they "queers" or women who are marked for later sexual conquest, is created and reinforced both by the collective act of violence and by the public approval it receives.

This sort of homophobic bullying of nonathlete boys is also a common occurrence on high school and college campuses. A window was opened on this dynamic in 1999, when Eric Harris and Dylan Klebold, armed to the teeth, entered Columbine High School, in Littleton, Colorado, and proceeded to kill thirteen and wound twenty-one of their schoolmates and teachers. "All jocks stand up," the killers yelled when they began their slaughter. "Anybody with a white hat or a shirt with a sports emblem on it is dead."[66] Much of the aftermath of this tragedy consisted of media and experts discussing the origins of the anger and violence expressed by the two boys, dubbed "the trenchcoat mafia," and how in the future to predict and prevent such individuals from violently "going off." Very little discussion centered on the ways that such outsider boys are so commonly targeted as the "nerds" and symbolic "pussies" that serve as the foil for high-status athletes' construction of their own in-group status. Indeed, Columbine High School was like many other high schools in this regard. There was a "tough little group" of about seven guys, mostly football players and wrestlers, who were known for leading painfully degrading hazing rites among younger male athletes, for harassing and physically abusing girls, for destroying property, and basically getting away with it all. They also abused the outsider boys in the "trenchcoat mafia," one of whom was shoved into a locker by three football players who taunted him, "Fag, what are you looking at?"

Homophobic taunting and bullying does not always result in such serious physical violence.[67] But it is a common part of the central dynamic of male peer groups. The role homophobia plays within male peer groups is akin to Elmer's glue being used to bond two pieces of wood. Once the white glue is dried, it becomes clear, nearly invisible, and it acts simultaneously (and paradoxically) as a bond that holds the two pieces of wood together and as an invisible barrier, or shield, that keeps the two pieces of wood from actually touching each other. Homophobia works the same way. While it bonds boys together as part of the in-group (we are men, they are faggots), it also places clear limits on the extent to which boys and men can make themselves vulnerable to one another (don't get too close, emotionally or physically, or you will make yourself vulnerable). And this, again, is where alcohol often comes in. While it is part of the system of competitive status-enhancement to drink a lot of alcohol, young men also find that one of the short-term benefits of drinking with the guys is that it loosens the constraints on verbal and emotional expression.[68] The key desires underlying boys' and men's affiliations with each other—acceptance, emotional connection, respect—seem more accessible after a few drinks. The constraints normally placed around expressions of physical closeness among men are often relaxed after a few drinks; the arms draped around a teammate's shoulders and the "I love you, man" expression can be conveniently forgotten in the fog of tomorrow's hangover.

In sum, boys in central, aggressive team sports learn early to use their bodies as weapons against an objectified opponent. The empathy that one might be expected to feel for the victim of one's punches, hits, or tackles is suppressed by the experience of being rewarded (with status and prestige, and also with connection and respect) for the successful utilization of one's body against other men. Empathy for one's opponent is also suppressed through the shared contextual ethic that injury is an expected part of the game. These on-the-field values and practices are mutually constitutive of the off-the-field peer group dynamics, whereby the boundaries of the in-group are constructed through homophobia and violence directed (verbally and sometimes physically) against boys and men who are outside the group.

Male Athletes' Violence against Themselves

In June 2000, future Hall of Fame quarterback Steve Young ended several months of speculation by announcing his retirement after fifteen years of professional football. Actually, he had played his last down of football ten months earlier, when a "knock out" hit by an opposing player caused Young's fourth concussion in three years. "I'll miss many things," said Young. "What I won't miss are the hits that made my body tingle."[69] Young's announcement was not surprising. In fact, many had wondered why it took him so long to retire, given the mounting evidence concerning the dangerous cumulative effects of head injuries.[70] But Young's desire to continue playing must be seen in the context of an entire career in which he was rewarded for taking tremendous risks on the football field, playing hurt and with reckless abandon. Steve Young is not unusual in this respect. In November 2000, Denver Broncos quarterback Brian Griese suffered a shoulder separation in the first half of the game. Told by team doctors that he had a third-degree separation, the most severe type, he took a painkilling injection and returned to the game to lead his team to victory.

Football players live with the knowledge that small and moderate injuries are an expected outcome of the game and that a serious, career-ending or even life-threatening injury is always a possibility. Indeed, during the 1999 NFL season, 364 injuries were serious enough for a player to miss at least one game. Knee injuries (122) and ankle injuries (52) were the most common. Eleven were concussions.[71] In U.S. high schools, by far the greatest number of fatal, disabling, and serious sports injuries are suffered by football players (though the injury rates per hundred thousand participants are actually higher in ice hockey and gymnastics).[72] Among children, falls and sports-related injuries are now the leading causes of hospital stays and emergency room visits.[73] A survey of hospital emergency rooms and medical clinics in 1997 found a staggering number of sports injuries among U.S. children fourteen years old and under, led by bicycling (901,716 injuries), basketball (574,434), football (448,244), baseball (252,665), and soccer (227,157).[74] In Canada, injuries—a substantial proportion of which are head, neck, and cervical spinal injuries—among children ice hockey players are also escalating.[75]

The Body as Machine

Several years ago, I was watching a football game on television with a friend at his house. A big fan, he knew that his team had to win this game to secure home field advantage for the playoffs. Suddenly, the announcer observed that a key player on my friend's team was hurt. The camera focused on the player, slowly walking off the field and looking at his hand with a puzzled look on his face. His index finger, it turned out, was dislocated and sticking out sideways at a ninety-degree angle. "Oh, good," my friend sighed in relief. "It's only his finger—he can still play." Indeed, a few plays later, the player was back on the field, his hand taped up (and presumably popped back into place by the trainer, and perhaps injected with painkiller). What struck me about this moment was how normal it seemed within the context of football. Announcers, coaches, other players, and fans like my friend all fully expected this man to "suck it up" and get back out there and play. We all have incredibly high expectations of football players' (and indeed, of other professional, college, and even high school athletes') willingness and ability to cope with pain, to play hurt, often risking their long-term health. Injuries and pain levels that in other contexts would result in emergency-room visits, home bed rest, and time off work or school are considered a normal part of the workday for many athletes.

I was struck by the depth to which athletes internalize these cultural standards to endure pain when I interviewed former athletes for *Power at Play*. One man, a former major league baseball player, described an incredible litany of injuries and rehabilitations that spanned not only the everyday aches and bruises that one would expect a catcher to endure but also year after year of ankle, knee, shoulder, neck, and spinal injuries that required several surgeries. In particular, he played out the second half of one season with daily injections of painkillers and cortisone in a shoulder that he knew would require surgery. Players routinely decide to "play hurt," to "give their bodies up for the team" in this way, even with the full knowledge that they are doing so at the risk of long-term disability. But when this man's eleven-year pro baseball career finally came to an end, he described it as a "shock.... I had felt that the way I had conditioned myself and taken care of myself that I would play until I was thirty-seven, thirty-eight."[76] Nobody could listen to this man's story and not agree that he had worked very hard and been very dedicated to his craft. But to describe the way he had lived his life as taking care of himself seemed to me to express a particularly alienated relationship to his own body. He, like many other athletes, had a wide range of knowledge about his body. However, this self-knowledge was in some ways shallow; it was not an expansive sense of his body as a living organism, as a self that connects in healthy ways with others and with one's environment.[77] Rather, it was a self-knowledge firmly bounded within an instrumental view of one's body as a machine, or a tool, to be built, disciplined, used (and, if necessary, used up) to get a job done.

This kind of self-knowledge—what psychologist William Pollack calls the "hardening of boys"—starts early in life, especially for athletes.[78] Boys learn that to show pain and vulnerability risks their being seen as "soft," and they know from the media, from coaches, and from their peers that this is a very bad thing. Instead, they learn that they can hope to gain access to high status, privilege, respect, and connection with others if they conform to what sociologist Don Sabo calls "the pain principle," a cultural ideal that demands a suppression of self-empathy and a willingness to take pain and take risks.[79]

Why are so many boys and men willing to take such risks? Again, we must look to the young male's embeddedness in social groups, and again, homophobia and misogyny are key enforcement mechanisms for conformity. The boy who whines about his pain and appears not to be willing to play hurt risks being positioned by the group as the symbolic "sissy" or "faggot" who won't "suck it up and take it like a man for the good of the team." One man I interviewed, for instance, told me that in high school, when he decided not to play in a big game because of an injury, his coach accused him of faking it. And as he sat in the whirlpool nursing his injury, a teammate came in and yelled at him, "You fucking pussy!"[80] Canadian sport studies scholar Philip White and his colleagues cite a similar example of an ice hockey player who, returning to play after a serious knee injury, was told by teammates "not to ice the swelling and not to 'be a pussy.'"[81]

The fear of being seen by the team as less than a man is not the only reason an athlete will play hurt, though. As pro football player Tim Green wrote in his illuminating book:

Doctors don't coerce players into going out on the field. They don't have to. Players have been conveniently conditioned their entire lives to take the pain and put bodies at risk. Players beg doctors for needles that numb and drugs that reduce swelling and pain.... Taking the needle is something NFL players are proud to have done. It is a badge of honor, not unlike the military's Purple Heart. It means you were in the middle of the action and you took a hit. Taking the needle in the NFL also lets everyone know that you'd do anything to play the game. It demonstrates a complete disregard for one's well-being that is admired in the NFL between players.[82]

Green's statement—that demonstrating a complete disregard for one's well-being is so admired in the NFL among players—speaks volumes not just about the normalization of pain and injury in pro football but also about ways that bodily risk and endurance of pain serve as masculine performances that bring acceptance and respect among one's peers. Indeed, writing more generally about men's (often dangerous) health behaviors, Will Courtenay has argued that "health behaviors are used in daily interactions in the social structuring of gender and power.... The social practices that undermine men's health are often the signifiers of masculinity and the instruments that men use in the negotiation of social power and status."[83] In short, in the context of the athletic team, risking one's health by playing hurt is more than a way to avoid misogynist or homophobic ridicule; it is also a way of "performing" a highly honored form of masculinity.

There are concrete rewards—status, prestige, public adulation, scholarships, and even money—for men who are willing to pay the price. But we must also remember that underlying men's performances for each other is a powerful need to belong, to connect, to be respected. In refusing to play hurt, especially in the context of a team sport, a player risks losing the tenuous but powerful connection he has with the male group. Given both the negative enforcement mechanisms and the positive rewards a player might expect from choosing to play hurt, it should surprise us more when a player decides *not* to risk his long-term health, by refusing the needle, sitting down, and saying "no más."[84]

Performing the Triad of Men's Violence

In this chapter, I have outlined the group-based, interactional processes underlying the triad of men's violence in sports: violence against women, against other men, and against their own bodies. All three are explicable outcomes of the common peer interactions and performances that emanate from the center of male athletic groups. A small group of high-status males at the center of these groups set the tone with misogynist and homophobic banter, teasing, and actions. Less central boys and men within the group, some of whom may feel uncomfortable with the group's dominant values and actions, still tend to actively support or passively go along with the group. The performances of hegemonic masculinity from the center, actively supported by the applause of the less central "audience" and passively supported by the complicit "marginals," go a long way toward explaining the routine production of the triad of men's violence in sports.

But how are these three kinds of violence connected? My analysis suggests two mutually intertwined clusters of group-based interactions that are powerful linking processes between these three otherwise seemingly separate phenomena: The first is *misogynist and homophobic talk and actions*. The athletic male peer group defines, enforces, and attempts to solidify its boundaries through aggressive misogynist and homophobic talk and actions. Boys and men learn to associate the group's sexual aggression paradoxically—as an exciting and pleasurable erotic bond that holds the group together (and places it above other groups) and as an ever-present threat of demasculinization, humiliation, ostracism, and even violence that may be perpetrated against a boy or man who fails to conform with the dominant group values and practices.

The second is *suppression of empathy*. Through athletic peer groups, boys and men learn to suppress their empathy toward women as objects of the group's humorous discourse and (at times) aggressive actions. One's own body becomes a sexual machine or weapon to be used in the conquest of a woman and as a display of heterosexual masculinity for one's male peers. Men also learn to suppress their empathy toward other men, both on and off the field, as "outsiders" and as enemies to be defeated—through violence, if necessary. One's body is experienced as a weapon to be used to defeat an objectified opponent. And ultimately, the body-as-weapon comes back on the male athlete as an alien force: As the man learns to suppress his own self-empathy, to endure pain and injury to get a job done, his body is experienced not as a human self to be nurtured and cared for but as a machine or a tool to be used to get a job done.

Group-based interactions and performances are a powerful force in the day-to-day making and remaking of gender. However, as I noted in chapter 1, performances and group interactions are not free-floating. Rather, they take place in social contexts that are characterized by institutional rules, relations, and hierarchies as well as by cultural symbols. It is to an analysis of these institutional and cultural contexts that I turn in the next two chapters.

CHAPTER 3

Center of the Diamond:
The Institutional Core of Sport

Joanie Smith wanted to play softball.[1] She and her friends and teammates in the West Valley Girls' Softball League in Los Angeles had grown up with the benefits of Title IX. They assumed that if they wanted to play sports, they had the right to. But here it was 1998, and they were told that there was nowhere for them to play. It made no sense to them: there were obviously acres and acres of grassy green baseball and softball fields in their neighborhood parks. But when they and their parents tried to get access to these fields for the girls' league, they were told by the City of Los Angeles Parks and Recreation Department that the fields were already taken—mostly by boys' and men's teams. It was nothing personal, the girls were told; it had nothing to do with the fact that they were girls. It was just that access to field use had always been allotted on the basis of past use. It just so happened that the teams with long-standing seniority tended to be boys' and men's teams. The girls would have to queue up on a waiting list, until one of the existing leagues no longer needed the field.

Jerryme Negrete wanted to shower and change.[2] But he and his cross-country teammates at Huntington Beach High School, in California, found the locker room door blocked by a football player, who aggressively shoved one of the runners and proclaimed, "This is our locker room. You guys can't use it." Eric Anderson, the runners' openly gay coach, was enraged. Sophomore football players, who threatened them with homophobic taunts, had already pushed his runners out of one of the school's locker rooms. Now, the varsity football team, apparently acting on the instructions of their coach, was barring the runners from the only other available locker room. When Coach Anderson appealed to the school principal, nothing was done. The next day, football players were heard bragging to their friends that they had pushed the "fags" out of the locker room. Indeed, Coach Anderson was given the keys to a bathroom and was told that his athletes could change their clothes there. "What's next?" the coach pondered. "A closet?"

Coach Marianne Stanley wanted pay equity with her male counterpart. Fresh off an impressive 22–7 season, having won the 1993 PAC-10 Coach of the Year award, Stanley had reason to believe that University of Southern California athletic director Mike Garrett would give her a sizable salary increase. After all, they had previously discussed Garrett's bringing her salary more into line with that of George Raveling, USC's men's basketball coach, whose base salary of one hundred thirty thousand dollars per year was over twice Stanley's sixty-two thousand dollars.[3] When Garrett offered a pay increase that fell far short of Raveling's pay, Stanley decided to hold out for an offer that was closer to parity and was quickly replaced. She brought a Title IX suit against USC and sought to get her job back. USC argued that market forces justified Raveling's higher salary. But as economist Andrew Zimbalist has observed, during the first five or six years of Raveling's eight-year tenure as USC coach, game attendance had dropped 25.7 percent, and "Raveling's contribution to team revenues was most probably negative."[4] This drop-off was due to the dismal win-loss record of the team during those years. And though things picked up for the team over the next couple of seasons, Raveling's overall record at USC was a ho-hum 115–118, and his career coaching record was 326–292, with no national championships. By contrast, Stanley's USC record was 71–46, and her career record was an impressive 347–146, with three national championships.[5] Stanley eventually landed other high-profile college coaching jobs.[6] But in 1999 the 9th U.S. Circuit Court of Appeals, in a two-to-one ruling, said it wasn't necessary to decide whether the job duties of the men's coach were more demanding, because the evidence showed that former USC men's coach George Raveling was more experienced and qualified than Stanley.[7] Stanley had lost her suit.

The Gender Regime of Sport

Joanie Smith and her teammates wanted a place to play softball. Jerryme Negrete and his teammates wanted access to the boys' locker room. Marianne Stanley wanted her pay to reflect her tremendous success in college coaching. Despite these seemingly modest wishes for equal access, opportunities, and fairness, Smith, Negrete, and Stanley ran head-on into barriers. Most obviously, it was people—coaches, athletic directors, principals, athletes—who appeared to be blocking their way. But on closer examination, we can see that the people who told Joanie Smith that she had no field to play on, who told Jerryme Negrete that his team had to dress in a bathroom, who told Marianne Stanley that she had no right to pay equity were all acting in accordance with the routine practices of sports. Smith, Negrete, and Stanley were not simply up against individual people. They were bumping up against *institutional structures*— historically formed, entrenched systems of rules, conventions, allocations of resources and opportunities, and hierarchical authority and status systems. Joanie Smith was up against the decades-long inertia of rules that ensured that public athletic fields routinely "belonged" to boys' and men's teams.[8] Jerryme Negrete was up against the conventions that grant football players and coaches a sense of entitlement as the undisputed kings of the high school status system, with first claim on athletic resources. Marianne Stanley was up against a deeply entrenched system of institutional arrangements between and among athletic departments, universities, mass media, corporate sponsors, and the law that create and reinforce as "common sense" the idea that coaches of men's teams deserve higher pay than coaches of women's teams, even if their records are poorer.

Gender is most commonly thought of as an individual attribute: a person is said to "have" or to "display" masculinity, femininity, or some combination of the two. But individuals do not simply import their gendered selves into neutral organizations. Rather, organizations and institutions are themselves "gendered"; that is, gender is "present in [an institution's] processes, practices, images, ideologies, and distributions of power."[9] Modern sport has clearly been among the most masculine of institutions.[10] Extreme sexual divisions of labor have characterized sport's gender regime. From young children's sports organizations through the pros, sport remains one of the most sex-segregated institutions today. Sport's gender regime is also characterized by vastly unequal distributions of power, authority, prestige, and resources between women and men (and, indeed, between different social classes and racial groupings of men).[11] Because of their historical persistence, the masculine institutional patterns of sport have appeared to many to be natural and immutable. So, even in the late 1990s, it probably still seemed to kids in Los Angeles that boys had *always* had first crack at the baseball fields. Football players at Huntington Beach High had *always* been the highest-status boys who "owned" the locker rooms. Coaches in big-time college men's sports had *always* earned far more money than had the coaches of women's teams.[12]

People who are operating at the center of the gender regime of sport—athletic directors, men's basketball and football coaches, and male athletes in high-status sports—are enabled and privileged by virtue of their positions in this institutional structure. Boys' and men's "rights" to access fields to play on and locker rooms to change in and to higher pay for coaching rarely appear as privileges to them, though. By contrast, people are most likely to become aware of the constraining nature of institutional structures—become aware that they are up against something—when, like Smith, Negrete, and Stanley, they are operating from the institutional margins, striving to get access to the resources, opportunities, and respect that is clustered and controlled at the institution's center.

Despite their apparent immutability, institutional structures are not static.[13] They are constantly being re-created by the day-to-day interactions of people. Institutional structures do not determine what people do, but they do set the conditions and parameters within which people interact. Many, perhaps most, of these interactions tend to re-create the institution's historical pattern of unequal gender relations. Some, though, like those of Marianne Stanley, actively contest the central institutional power relations of sport. This "state of play"—the day-to-day interactions among people operating within the patterned social relations of the institution—make up the gender regime of sport. In the previous chapter, I demonstrated the importance of understanding these dominant gender dynamics in sport as being group-based rather than simply individual. The central outcome of these patterned interactions in sport is a dominant form of heterosexual masculinity that is both a product and an advocate of the triad of men's violence. This masculinity is marked by a sense of entitlement—to athletic opportunities, control of locker rooms, prestige, and resources. In this chapter, I hope to extend that argument to show how patterned group dynamics and actions—what sociologists often call *social agency*—mediate between individuals and structured institutional contexts.

In recent years, the center of sport has increasingly been contested by girls and women demanding equal opportunities and sometimes by marginalized boys and men who do not accept or support the unquestioned authority and entitlement of those at the center of the institution. When so challenged, the dominant athletic masculinity at the center of sport can turn violently defensive. Jerryme Negrete found this out the hard way at Huntington Beach High. Unfettered by the school administration or by the football coach, the football players' harassment of the cross-country runners finally escalated into a frightening assault. Jerryme was held down by a much larger football player, who pummeled Jerryme's face, breaking his jaw, while screaming, "I'm going to kill you, you fucking cross-country faggot!" Coach Anderson expressed outrage to the school authorities, and eventually to the press, at this homophobic assault on one of his players. But the school principal told the *Los Angeles Times*, "This doesn't look like an assault. I think what we have is a fight." The principal defended the football player as an "excellent student who scored 1300 on his SAT test" and wondered whether perhaps Coach Anderson had an "agenda" and was inappropriately describing the incident as homophobic.[14] In this incident, we can see how the structured context of the school-based athletic gender regime simultaneously constrained the marginal cross-country boys (and their gay coach) and enabled the aggressive masculinity of the football players who occupied (and violently defended) the institutional center.

But sport's center also is vulnerable to change, in part because the gender regime of sport is intertwined with other institutional gender regimes, such as schools and universities, the mass media, the economy, and the law. Sport is also influenced by societal shifts in cultural values, brought about by social movements (most notably, those for civil rights, feminism, and gay-lesbian liberation). These influences from outside sport tend to alter the terms of the internal dynamics of the gender regime of sport. The women's movement, for instance, has led to a broad rethinking of the value of physical activity for girls and women. It has also led directly to changes in the political and legal spheres: most important, the passage of Title IX and other equity laws has continued to have a profound influence on the internal gender regime of school- and community-based sports.[15] Marianne Stanley turned to Title IX (unsuccessfully, in the end) to contest her inequitable pay. And the girls of Los Angeles, with the support of the California Women's Law Center, successfully pressed the city of Los Angeles in 1999 to agree to create a new program that promised increased access to athletic facilities for girls and women in city parks. This agreement included a commitment to provide a permanent home for the West Valley Girls' Softball League.[16]

Though not as directly influential, the gay-lesbian liberation movement has also had an impact on sport. For instance, Eric Anderson's decision to "come out" as an openly gay high school coach was enabled by the existence of a supportive gay community. Moreover, when his (mostly heterosexually identified) high school track athletes were bullied, beaten up, and barred from full access to school facilities, the story did not stop there. The students organized a gay-straight alliance at their school and, with some notable successes, pushed to change the homophobic attitudes and practices that high-status male athletes and others routinely took for granted.

In other words, sport's gender regime, like that of other institutions, is dynamic. A large part of that dynamism comes from the fact that even when constrained by the conservative sexual and gender dynamics of sport, people's agency is fueled, in large part, by progressive shifts that are taking place outside sport. In this chapter, I consider these dynamics of structural constraint and human agency in sport.[17] First, I examine school-based sports, with a special emphasis on how Title IX has destabilized sport's gender regime. I will consider both the opportunities and the relations between the school-based sports of girls/women and those of boys/men as well as the role of marginal boys' and men's sports in the dynamics of school sports. Next, I will discuss the impact of commercialization in the gender regime of sport, with a particular focus on professional sports and big-time college sports. And finally, I will examine the increasingly central role played by the mass media and their commercial sponsors in the current gender dynamics of sport.

School Sports, Sex Equity, and the Football Lobby

Women's professional sports may draw a bit more media buzz, but for the most part schools and universities have been ground zero in sport equity battles for the past thirty years. Part of the reason for this is that schools are institutions that have been directly affected by sex equity laws. In particular, when Title IX passed Congress in 1972, it placed a powerful tool in the hands of equity activists in schools and universities.[18] Immediate compliance with neither the spirit nor the letter of the law, however, was automatic. In fact, what resulted could be described as a continuing, thirty-year legal wrestling match, the result of which has been a grudging movement toward the goal of equity. By the late 1970s, some hard-fought victories had been won: budgets for girls' and women's teams increased, some girls' and women's sports were added, coaches' salaries in women's sports rose, and girls and women surged into sports participation in greater and greater numbers. But entrenched interests, both within schools and universities and within powerful organizations like the National Collegiate Athletic Association,[19] tended to resist movements toward equity for girls and women's sports, and in many places progress for women was largely relegated to tokenism. The original compliance date of 1978—the year by which all schools receiving federal funds were to be in full compliance with Title IX—came and went with nearly all institutions in the United States still far from compliance with the law.[20] The Reagan administration managed to take the legal enforcement teeth out of Title IX during much of the 1980s; as a result, schools' and universities' movement toward equity slowed during this period. In 1988, though, Congress passed the Civil Rights Restoration Act (over a presidential veto), and this put enforcement teeth back into Title IX. The 1990s saw the continued growth of girls' and women's sports, sometimes stimulated and punctuated by battles fought in the courts over Title IX compliance.[21] Indeed, from grade school through high school and college, girls and women now enjoy an unprecedented range of opportunities to play sports. Linda Jean Carpenter, an educator, researcher, and attorney who has spent much of her adult life fighting for girls' and women's rights to play sports, triumphantly wrote in 2000:

> By the turn of the century, Title IX's remaining controversies have been settled and the vast majority of the population approves of its provisions and enforcement. The court of public opinion is very supportive of gender equity in sport.... The nation's judicial courts have also seemed supportive of full enforcement and their decisions have clarified many aspects of Title IX, usually in favor of increased equity.... It is unlikely that any significant legislative change will weaken Title IX. Although lobbyists pro and con are always walking the halls of Congress, there are too many people who now have the vision of equity who value it for themselves and their children to permit Congress to weaken legislation such as Title IX.

Carpenter's point concerning support of equity in the court of public opinion does appear well-founded.[22] Millions of girls and women play sports now, and they tend to take for granted the fact that schools have programs in place to serve them. But we should recognize too that Carpenter's statement was written during a time when Bill Clinton, a known friend of the ideals of sex equity, still sat in the White House. As the new century began, Republican president George W. Bush and a conservative Congress held the keys to stalling or reversing the apparent legal and legislative solidity of Title IX. To be sure, the equity victories won over the past thirty years are not absolute, and their outcomes are still up for grabs. Undoubtedly, in the coming years battles will continue to be fought to defend and extend the movement toward equity, a goal that is still far from fully realized. Where will the leadership to fight these battles come from? Surely, some local parents, PTA members, and attorneys will be ready to stand up to protect girls' hard-fought right to athletic opportunities. Organizations such as the Women's Sports Foundation, the National Association for Girls and Women in Sport, and the Association for Gender Equity Leadership in Education will continue to educate and agitate for equity. And organizations like the National Women's Law Center, the National Organization for Women's Legal Defense League, and the California Women's Law Center stand ready to defend the gains of the past and press for future gains. But to what extent will advocacy leadership for sex equity come from *within* the institution of sport?

An ironic outcome of the relative success of Title IX has been the dramatic erosion of women's leadership and control of college women's sports. After Title IX, most women's athletic departments were folded into men's departments, under male leadership. In 1972, over 90 percent of women's programs were headed by a female administrator; by 2000, that had dropped to 17.4 percent. And as coaching salaries and status rose in women's sports, men became more attracted to these jobs and were more and more likely to be hired (by predominantly male administrators). In 1972, women were the head coaches of over 90 percent of college women's teams. By 2000, that had dropped to 45.6 percent, an all-time low. Meanwhile, male coaches continued to head over 98 percent of men's college teams.[23] These data illustrate a common dynamic identified by sociologists who study sex segregation in work and occupations: when the status and pay of an occupation rises, men tend to be pulled into the occupation, and women are squeezed out. This demographic shift has the reciprocal effect of further raising the status of the occupation (if men do it, it *must* be important!).[24] Though many men have shown that they can be effective, competent, and even inspiring coaches for girls and women, it is a curious "gender equity" process that pushes women out of leadership positions. And it is a clear sign of the continued structural asymmetries in sport that women coaches are almost never given the opportunity to break the sex bar that keeps coaching in boys' and men's sports an almost entirely male occupation.

The male-headed football lobby continues to be one of the most powerful structural forces to mobilize against sex equity in American sport. High school and college football programs have successfully labeled themselves as revenue-generating sports and have thus created a mostly false image of themselves as geese that lay golden eggs. The successful imposition of an image of the football team as the beneficent supporter of the rest of the athletic department has given the football lobby the leverage it needs to attempt to position itself outside the sex equity debates. In effect, members of this lobby argue that sex equity calculus should consider three categories of sport: girls' sports, boys' sports, and football. Their strategic definition of the situation goes something like this: "Football is different; we generate income that supports all other sports, including girls'/women's sports; thus, if you cut us, you are cutting off your nose to spite your face." The reality, for the vast majority of schools, is the opposite. Most football programs, even many of the college football programs that are tied in to the big television bucks, *lose* money.[25] And the existence of a big-time college football program seems to create conditions that make sex equity less rather than more likely: a study commissioned by the Women's Sports Foundation to assess U.S. colleges' and universities' levels of compliance with Title IX found that, after twenty-five years of Title IX, institutions with big-time football programs were on average the least likely to be in compliance with sex equity laws.[26] Indeed, sociologist D. Stanley Eitzen notes that "it is not uncommon for a school with a big-time football program to spend *twice as much on its football program as it spent on all women's sports*."[27] A 2001 study in the Chronicle of Higher Education reported that the Division I-A schools that are members of the national Bowl Championship Series (BCS) have average annual budgets of $6.4 million. Meanwhile, "only 15 Division I-A schools spent more on women's sports in their entirety than they did on football."[28]

Key players in current sex equity struggles are the less visible "nonrevenue" men's sports (especially wrestling and gymnastics) that have taken substantial cuts in recent years. Are these "marginal" men's sports threatened by Title IX? Some recent cases seem to suggest that they are. In 2000, the University of Miami announced that it was discontinuing its men's swimming and rowing programs, and in 2001, the University of Kansas announced that it intends to drop its men's swimming and tennis programs.[29] Both schools cited the need to cut spiraling costs of athletic departments but also noted that, in deciding what to cut, they were constrained by Title IX. In effect, they said, if we need to cut something, it can't be a women's sport. Current interpretations of the law seem to support this strategy by universities. When Illinois State University cut men's soccer and wrestling teams (and added women's soccer) in 1995, the male students took their case to the courts, claiming sex discrimination. But the U.S. Court of Appeals ruled that cutting men's sports to satisfy the requirements of Title IX did not violate any of the plaintiffs' rights.[30] Federal appeals courts similarly ruled in favor of California State University at Bakersfield and Illinois State University when the schools cut men's wrestling to move toward legal proportionality under Title IX.[31]

These high-profile cases have led critics to claim that Title IX hurts men while failing to really help women, who don't want to play sports as much as men do anyway. "You can't force women to play sports," said Curt A. Levey of the Center for Individual Rights, which helped represent male athletes at Illinois State University. "A lot of times the only practical way to meet the [Title IX] proportionality is to cut men's teams."[32] But how widespread is this practice? Evidence suggests that over the past twenty years, while the number of college women athletes and women's teams has grown substantially, the number of college men athletes and men's teams has still managed to grow slightly. Yes, men's gymnastics and wrestling teams have declined in number, but so has the number of women's gymnastics and women's field hockey teams. On the plus side, while many college women's sports have grown in number, men's participation in college sports has increased in baseball, crew, football, lacrosse, squash, track, and volleyball. A 2001 study by the U.S. General Accounting Office concluded that over the past decade, most colleges and universities added women's sports without cutting men's sports.[33] In fact, the National Women's Law Center insisted on looking at the big picture and did so by drawing from a wide range of empirical studies, concluding:

> The increase in spending for men's sports has not tapered off in recent years. From 1992–1997, men's athletic operating budgets have increased by 139%. The increase in expenditures for women's sports during this time period, 89%, pales in comparison.
>
> The problem is not that Title IX has deprived men of needed athletic resources, but that the lion's share of resources that male athletes receive are inequitably distributed among men's sports. Football and men's basketball consume 69% of the total men's athletic operating budget at Division I-A institutions, leaving other men's sports to compete for remaining funds. Of the $1.38 million average increase in expenditures for men's Division I-A sports programs during the past five years, sixty-three percent of this increase, $872,000, went to football. This increase in Division I-A football spending during the past five years exceeds the entire average operating budget for all women sports in 1997 by over $200,000.[34]

Despite these facts, the periodic high-profile cuts of men's programs tend to fuel perceptions that sex equity works against the overall interests of men. In fact, it is possible to hold this view only if one accepts the logic of the football lobby and refuses to include football in calculations of sex equity. Football's enormous financial drain on resources—a lion's share of scholarships, skyrocketing salaries for coaches, huge equipment, travel, and recruiting budgets—are often safely hidden behind the nickel-and-diming debates over which "nonrevenue" men's sports should be eliminated to ensure compliance with Title IX proportionality measures. The football lobby shields its own interests by backing the claims that marginal men's sports are being victimized by Title IX. And any claims that football should be brought into the sex equity equation are likely to evoke hysterical responses. For instance, the head of the American Football Coaches Association claimed that overzealous advocates of sex equity are "the enemy" who are "out to get" football.[35] Sociologist Don Sabo calls this defensiveness expressed by the most powerful sports figures "wounded giant sexism."[36] Given their control of resources and their massive budgets, football programs can hardly claim hardship with a straight face. To do that, they have needed to seek support for the anti-equity cause from the more vulnerable "minor" men's sports. Just as the men at the center of sport culture, as I described in chapter 2, need the active support and complicity of marginal groups of men, so too the football lobby, to retain its privileged position at the institutional center of sport, seeks the support and complicity of the coaches and athletes in marginal (often called minor) men's sports.

But is it really in the interests of marginal men to join with the football lobby to resist the historic move toward sex equity? In fact, most men athletes are supportive of the growth of women's sports. Jerryme Negrete and his cross-country teammates found that the main obstacle to their receiving respect as athletes and having simple access to athletic facilities was their school's football players, not women athletes. Similarly, Don Sabo has observed that many men are discovering that "football is the major structural obstacle to reform." As such, a large part of the answer to the current dilemma of how to move toward equitable resources for women's sports while not hurting men's sports is to insist on putting football programs and budgets into the equation. This would mean insisting on a roughly equitable expenditure of resources across different sports, per athlete, and per coach.[37] When this is done, "equity" will appear to be a process that benefits women *and* the vast majority of men who have been pushed to the margins of sport. For this to happen, though, it will take a shift in consciousness among most men— away from identifying their interests with those at the institutional center and toward identifying their interests with women and advocates of equity and fairness. It will also mean challenging the market mentality that the institutional center of men's sports uses to justify its inequitable practices.[38]

The Sport-Media-Commercial Complex

It has become clichéd to point out that sport is a multibillion dollar industry. Indeed, for decades, scholars of sport have scrambled to describe and analyze the increasingly complex and high-stakes economic dynamics of sport.[39] From grade school through high school, sports occupy a significant portion of school budgets. And economist Andrew Zimbalist has described "an elaborate nexus of corporate connections that sustains big-time college athletics."[40] Indeed, corporate investment in and control of college sports have continued to increase at an astronomical rate. In 2000, in the wake of the NCAA's having signed a six-billion-dollar contract with CBS-TV, sport scholar Murray Sperber wrote: "Ten years ago, the big-time college sports entertainment industry could be termed College Sports, Inc. Since that time, its revenue has exploded, and it has become College Sports MegaInc."[41] The economic resources involved in professional sports are even greater. Multibillion-dollar stadium deals and the multimillion-dollar salaries and product endorsement deals of athletes are as much a part of the daily discussion and debate surrounding pro sports as are speculations about which team will win the championship this year.[42]

But missing from much of the discussion of the economics of sport is an analysis of the extent to which corporate sport—from schools, to universities, to the pros—is an institution with wildly distorted spending priorities. The vast, *vast* majority of funds are spent on creating, supporting, and promoting a very small number of sports: in the United States, sport's economic center is boys' and men's basketball, baseball, football, and (to a lesser extent) ice hockey. Women's sports and men's marginal sports receive far less economic support than these "big four" do, and this fact as much as anything else helps to explain the continued hegemony of these central men's sports.

Though the public outcries against the commercialization of sport have increased in recent years, modern sport has long been intertwined with commercial interests and with the mass media. In the 1980s, media scholar Sut Jhally coined the term *sport-media complex* to describe the institutionally symbiotic relationship of sport and the mass media, and Canadian scholar Richard Gruneau pointed to the elective affinity that had historically developed between sport, media, and commercial interests.[43] More recently, my colleagues Darnell Hunt and Michele Dunbar and I expanded Jhally's sport-media complex concept in order to capture the complex institutional dynamics at the nexus of sport, media, and corporate promoters and advertisers. Examining what we call the sport-media-commercial complex helps us begin to understand sport not as a separate and autonomous "sports world" but as part of a larger, increasingly global economic nexus that utilizes mediated sports to advertise a huge range of consumer products.[44]

Describing the structural dynamics at play in the sport-media-commercial complex is a large task that goes beyond the scope of this book.[45] But I do want to provide some insight into the gendered nature of the institutional dynamics within the sport-media-commercial complex, and in particular I want to reflect on some of the gender paradoxes currently at work today. How do sport, mass media, and commercial institutions often combine to support a powerful reaffirmation of masculine privilege? What are the economic processes that sometimes pull or push a new or previously marginal sport toward the center? Are corporate promoters of women's sports now among the vanguard of feminist social change? I will address these questions by briefly considering three contemporary sites within the sport-media-commercial complex: the beer industry as a key institutional nexus; extreme sports as a recently ascendant sport form; and the paradigmatic role of Nike as a promoter of sports.

The Beer Industry as Institutional Nexus

A few weeks ago, my family purchased a new digital camcorder and my sons asked me to shoot them while they played handball, so they could later show me how to edit movies on my computer. As soon as I turned on the camera, they broke spontaneously into an unscripted dialogue: "What are you *doing*?" one of them asked. The other responded, "What are *you* doing?" Back and forth it went. Seconds later, they both turned to the camera and, with tongues wagging, obnoxiously asked, "*Whazzzup?!*" This was not the first time I was struck by how quickly and easily the dialogue from televised beer ads (in this case, two highly successful Anheuser-Busch ads) was taken up in the daily parlance of children. Beer ads don't run on Nickelodeon, Disney, or on afternoon or Saturday morning children's programming, so where do kids see these ads? Mostly, they see them running with their favorite sports programs. The "What are *you* doing?" ad had its debut with the 2001 Super Bowl, and it was only a few days before I heard it being repeated among ten- and eleven-year-old boys.[46]

Beer companies have a long history of promoting professional sports; beer seems to go along with a baseball game, for instance, as much as peanuts and Cracker Jack do. Beer is served at games, and beer ads have long adorned stadium walls and have been a key part of the promotional package of radio and televised sports. But in recent years, beer companies' promotions of sporting events, especially at the college level, have really stepped up. Murray Sperber describes how, after the 1978 success of the film *Animal House*, college admissions offices jumped on the "beer and circus" bandwagon with big beer companies to promote their campuses as fun places to be. Miller Brewing Company and Anheuser-Busch's "lite beer wars" were fought out during popular televised sports shows. The strategies for these advertising wars were developed on college campuses and at college sporting events, because the beer companies saw colleges as key sites from which to expand their highly valued younger male market. Ad campaigns such as the 1980s "Spuds McKenzie" (and undoubtedly today's "Whazzzup?" and "What are *you* doing?" ads too) are shaped in response to alcohol industry market surveys, which show that "10 per cent of the U.S. population bought almost 60 per cent of their products, and that the largest segment of purchasers were young men." This same market research showed that during their college-age years, drinkers developed brand loyalty and tended to stay with their favorites for many years. Thus, alcohol producers decided to spend a disproportionate amount of their advertising budgets on campaigns aimed at college-age drinkers and, more specifically, sports fans. *The goal was to turn the major characteristic of college sports fans—personal loyalty to their teams—into similar allegiance to their favorite alcohol brands.*"[47]

Little seemed to dampen the relationship among colleges, sports, and beer companies in the 1990s. The 2000 NCAA championship football game in the New Orleans Superdome was, according to Murray Sperber, "a triumph of beer and circus," complete with fans "staggering and soused with spirits" and "a rock band on a huge stage between a pair of giant Budweiser cans."[48]

If beer promotions keep college sports afloat, they continue to put a frothy and profitable head on professional sports. The beer promoters benefit from the best marketing research available. They know that pitching suds to young men is profitable, and they know where to find these young guys. Take, for instance, the National Football League's annual Super Bowl, which is nothing less than an annual masculinity rite, sponsored by the sport-media-commercial complex.[49] Many men who don't even normally watch much football feel compelled to watch the Super Bowl. The ritualized nature of the Super Bowl is played upon and hyped by the commercial promoters of the event, who pay top dollar to pitch their products to tens of millions of viewers. To reach the audience watching the 2001 Super Bowl, advertisers paid a record $2.2 million for each thirty-second television slot. The single biggest advertiser was Anheuser-Busch, which purchased five minutes to pitch Budweiser and Bud Light.[50] That's twenty-two million dollars just for the airtime; who knows how much money the company spent to create the seven different ads it ran (including the "What are *you* doing?" ad that had such an impact on my children)? Similarly when my colleagues and I did our study of the televised sports that boys watch most, alcohol ads (mostly for beer) appeared prominently among them.[51] The beer industry literally helps to pay the bills for the sports to be on television.

Televised sports, in turn, promise to deliver the young male audience to the beer companies. As such, the beer industry is a key institutional player that promotes, facilitates, and profits from the sport-media-commercial complex. From this institutional location, the beer industry helps to construct, and in turn profits from, a certain kind of athletic-consumer masculinity.[52]

The Super Bowl continues to be the single most important commercial sporting event for the U.S. sport-media-commercial complex. But despite a continued solid fan base for football (and men's basketball, baseball, and ice hockey), commercial advertisers know that the highly valued young male fan base is shifting, perhaps splintering in different directions. What happens if significant numbers of young males decide not to stay home or go to a sports bar to watch corporate sports on television? What if they decide they'd rather create their own non-institutionalized games, physical activities, and sports? Will the sport-media-commercial complex collapse if too many boys and young men turn off their televisions and instead take to their bicycles, in-line skates, or skateboards?

From "Extreme" Margins to Center

Not long ago, while in the company of my eleven-year-old son and a few of his friends, I asked if Shaquille O'Neal was a favorite athlete of theirs. "Dad," Miles told me as though lecturing to someone who didn't have a clue, "Shaquille O'Neal is *nothing* compared to Tony Hawk!" It turned out I really *didn't* have a clue: "Who's Tony Hawk?" I asked. Tony Hawk, I learned, is only the best and most popular skateboarder in the world. Kids have his posters on their walls, read about him in magazines, visit his dynamic web site in droves, play the Tony Hawk Proskater game on their handheld Nintendo Gameboys, and watch him perform on ESPN2.[53] A few short years ago, Tony Hawk may have been legendary among a few insiders in the subculture of skateboarding, but outside that small world, he was relatively unknown. What happened?

Alternative sports, lifestyle sports, and extreme sports such as skateboarding, snowboarding, BMX biking, and windsurfing expanded dramatically in the late 1980s and through the 1990s. And the initial interest in these sports and their growth was not initiated by institutions like schools or sports organizations. Indeed, for many participants, this was the point: Their sports were *not* part of the school or corporate sport establishment. They were different. Snowboarding created a space for "alternative youth" to articulate values of cooperation, creative individuality, fun, and freedom that ran counter to the controlled, competitive, and rule-bound star system of mainstream sports.[54] Windsurfing provided a separate space, outside mainstream youth and sport culture, for a wider range of play for gender relations.[55] And skateboarding provided a realm of autonomous performativity and play for urban and suburban youth who may otherwise have been alienated from mainstream school and sport cultures.[56]

Who were these "alternative" athletes who seemed to revel in doing sports differently and autonomously, in the relative obscurity of sport's "extreme" margins? Researchers note that these sports were disproportionately created by young white males. But, at first glance, doesn't this seem a bit odd? If white males tend to "own" and "control" the center of sport, as a simple race and gender analysis would suggest, then why are young white males so much in the forefront of alternative sports forms that are self-consciously created to be outside, even counter to, sport's center?

Perhaps many young white boys have been attracted to peripheral sports like skateboarding and BMX biking not because they fully reject or resist sports at the center but, rather, because these sports (especially basketball, but also football, baseball, and track) are now so thoroughly racialized as "black sports." While a constricted race-class context has encouraged athletic African American boys to pursue this narrow range of sports, white middle-class boys face a much wider range of sports and nonsports opportunities and choices.[57] Added to this structural reality is a group psychological dynamic: white boys and young men have commonly internalized a visceral fear of African American males.[58] This fear is based, in part, on a contemporary myth of black physical superiority (and "natural" orientations toward physical violence), played out most publicly in men's sports. Thus, for some of these young white males, skateboarding or BMX biking becomes their niche for the development, embodiment, and performance of white athletic masculinity. Extreme sports, argues sport scholar Kyle Kusz, has become a cultural "site of whiteness."[59] Interestingly, though, just as in the realm of popular music, these young white male "rebels" often appropriate African American male cultural styles—in this case, hip-hop music and clothing styles—when they engage in their sports.[60]

How do we characterize, then, the group agency of the young people who created alternative or extreme sports? On one level, extreme sports can be seen as resistant to the dominant culture of school-based sports—a relatively autonomous space carved out by young people, governed only by the informal rules and relations that these young people impose upon themselves. On the other hand, especially when race and gender dynamics are taken into account, these new sports spaces can be viewed also as a reassertion of white male identity, in response to a perceived displacement from "their" space by black males (and perhaps also in response to challenges by women's sports?). Viewed this way, the eventual commercial impulse that pulled some extreme sports into the media eye and closer to the center of corporate sport becomes more understandable. When television and corporate sponsors recognized the potential to tap into the coveted young male market segment with exciting, risky, action-packed sports that are culturally coded as sites of individual rebellion and creativity, skateboarding and BMX biking were rapidly commercialized. Once pulled toward the center by television and corporate sport promoters, skateboard and BMX bike competitions developed rationalized systems of rules and hierarchical star systems, just like other institutional sports.[61] Tony Hawk—formerly a rebel individualist in a marginal sport, idolized only by the few insiders who knew of his talents—rapidly became a skateboarding icon, a wealthy star, and a household name, courtesy of ESPN, MTV, Nintendo, sports magazines, and his own web site, a nexus of access to an array of corporate products.[62] He also became, at least for some suburban white boys, a new white athletic hero who is "more important than Shaq."

Tony Hawk did not naturally gravitate toward the center of sport simply because of his athletic talents or self-promotional savvy. There was also a powerful force—exerted from the nexus of the institutions of sport, the mass media, and corporations—that pulled Hawk and skateboarding closer to the limelight. The general lesson we can draw from this is that when the powers that be within the sport-media-commercial complex decide that a marginal sport has the potential to capture a significant market demographic, especially young white males, then major sports media and commercial sponsors are capable of rather quickly lining up their resources and successfully packaging a new sport for consumers. Similarly, as commercial sponsors and the media sense a growing potential market for women's sports, are they now beginning to pull certain women's sports toward the institutional center of the sport-media-commercial complex?

Nike and Corporate Feminism

A couple of years ago at a sport sociology conference, an unusually large group of scholars assembled to listen to a session on the role of Nike in contemporary sport culture. In two separate presentations, younger women scholars discussed the then-recent and very popular "If you let me play" Nike television ads that enthusiastically touted both the rights of girls to play sports and the positive benefits that accrue to girls when they do play. The presenters discussed the ways that these ads spoke to their own and other young women's passion and enthusiasm for sports. For the first time, they said, a major corporation was affirming what they and millions of other post–Title IX girls and women knew but had never yet seen portrayed on national television: sports are good for girls, and girls are good for sports. They were deeply moved by these ads and were appreciative of Nike for running them. What's more, they argued that the Nike ads had broken with the traditional masculinist tone and tenor of most ads we see on televised sports shows. These ads, they said, expressed a feminine, perhaps even *feminist*, sensibility.

Following these mostly celebratory presentations, audience members began to take the two presenters to task for their "uncritical," even "naive," celebration of Nike. Didn't they know (and hadn't they read the literature, some of it written by the very people in that audience!) that Nike was the ultimate institutional expression of everything that is wrong with our corporate-dominated society? Didn't they know that Nike shoes are created by near-slave labor? that, compared with Reebok, Nike was a relative latecomer to promoting and supporting women's sports? that, rather than being feminists, Nike marketing people are slick appropriators and manipulators of the signs and symbols of individualist and consumerist feminism? In short, it may be explicable how millions of girls and women have been duped into Nike's seductive realm, but it's unacceptable for a sport scholar to be so uncritically sucked in!

These opposing perspectives—Nike as corporate vanguard of athletic feminism versus Nike as powerful exploiter and manipulator of women—reveal one of the main paradoxes of gender in today's sport-media-commercial complex. The passionately oppositional interpretations of Nike's relationship to women's sports also reveal a tension between different contemporary feminisms: one, a radical and collectivist feminism that sees institutional transformation as a fundamental goal; the other, a liberal feminism that sees individual equal opportunity as the fundamental goal. In the remainder of this chapter, I will reflect on the institutional dynamics of these paradoxes and tensions, and in chapter 5, I will return to these issues to discuss current tensions in feminist activism around gender and sport issues.[63]

Why does Nike, rather than the scores of other corporations who are involved in promoting women's sports, draw so much contemporary praise, criticism, and scholarly scrutiny? Economist Andrew Zimbalist has argued that

> Nike's failings notwithstanding, the company has been unfairly singled out among multinational sneaker and apparel companies. There is little evidence that Adidas or Reebok factories in Asia pay higher wages or offer better working conditions than those of Nike. Indeed, it seems that the production of Adidas World Cup soccer balls in China has been performed in part by prison labor.[64]

Zimbalist's point is well taken. Nike is not singled out for scrutiny because it is doing something unique or different with its production and marketing. Rather, it is being singled out because it is doing what other corporations do, but *better*. Nike is merely the biggest tree in a large forest; as such, it is paradigmatic of what many other corporations strive to do. For instance, other corporations would love to emulate the omnipresence of the Nike "swoosh."[65] So we should never let our scrutiny of Nike obscure the fact that it does not stand alone. It is a key player within and among the various institutions that make up the sport-media-commercial complex. Indeed, in recent years, significant segments of corporate America have begun to awaken to the vast and lucrative potential markets that might be developed within and subsidiary to women's sports. The 1996 Olympics and their aftermath saw unprecedented amounts of money spent on television and magazine ads featuring women athletes. Two new women's professional basketball leagues were begun in 1996–1997, and one of them, the Women's National Basketball Association (WNBA), began with a substantial television contract—a factor that today is the best predictor of financial success in pro sports. Along with ESPN2 and *Sports Illustrated for Women*, Nike and Sears appear prominently on the WNBA web site. The other women's pro league, the American Basketball League (ABL), did not have much television support or exposure, and it subsequently folded in 1999 after only two full seasons, its top players moving to the WNBA. Many see these developments as merely the next steps in the successful accomplishment of sex equity for women in sports, but these developments also illustrate how crucial the support of the mass media (especially television) and corporate sponsorships are to the success of big-time women's sports.

In recent years, athletic footwear advertisements by Reebok and Nike have exemplified the ways that corporations have made themselves champions of women's athletic participation. In the late 1980s, Reebok held the lion's share of the athletic shoe market, with a 30.1 percent market share to Nike's 18.2 percent. During this period, Nike's internal corporate culture was dubbed by some as "the men's club," and their lack of interest in women's sports was reflected in its masculinist approach to sports advertising and promotion. But by 1997, Nike had seized 43.6 percent of the athletic footwear market, leaving second-ranked Reebok in the dust with only a 15.9 percent market share.[66] An important part of the impetus behind Nike's mid-1990s market surge was its aggressive turn to the women's market, highlighted by a successful advertising campaign that positioned the corporation as the champion of girls' and women's rights inside and outside sport. The influential 1995 "If you let me play" ad included images of athletically active girls with various girls' voice-overs touting the social and health benefits of playing sports:

> If you let me play; If you let me play sports; I will like myself more; I will have more self-confidence; If you let me play sports; If you let me play; If you let me play; I will be 60% less likely to get breast cancer; I will suffer less depression; If you let me play sports; I will be more likely to leave a man who beats me; If you let me play; I will be less likely to get pregnant before I want to; I will learn; I will learn what it means to be strong; To be strong; If you let me play; Play sports; If you let me play sports.[67]

The commercial ended with the Nike slogan, Just Do It, and the Nike swoosh symbol on the screen. The Nike ads made use of research findings from organizations such as the Women's Sports Foundation, documenting the positive, healthy, and empowering aspects of athletic participation for girls. Couching this information in a language of individual empowerment and addressing issues such as breast cancer, spousal and domestic violence, and teen pregnancy, Nike sold feminism back to girls and women in the form of athletic shoes and other athletic apparel.

To be sure, the power of these commercials lies partly in their rare mention of shoes or even the Nike name. The message is that individual girls will be happier, healthier, and more in charge of their lives if we let them play. The Nike swoosh logo is subtly displayed in the corner of the ads so that the viewer knows who is the source of these liberating ideas. It is through this kind of campaign that Nike has positioned itself as a "celebrity feminist," in the words of cultural studies scholars C. L. Cole and Amy Hribar; its corporate liberals have successfully appropriated and co-opted the language of individual empowerment that underlies the dominant discourse of opportunity for girls and women in sports. Aspiring athletes are then encouraged by slick advertising campaigns to identify their own individual empowerment—in essence, their relationship to feminism—with that of the corporate entity that acts as a celebrity feminist.[68] If "feminist identity" can be displayed most readily by wearing the Nike logo on shoes and other athletic apparel, then displaying the Nike swoosh on one's body becomes a statement to the world that one is an independent, empowered individual—a successful young turn-of-the-century woman.[69] "The alliance between Nike and women," Cole and Hribar write, "is undoubtedly about the commodification of feminism."[70]

Of course, co-optation is not an entirely one-way process; advocates of women's sports are becoming increasingly adept at using the media, supportive celebrities, and corporate advertisers to launch, build, and sustain women's sports.[71] But there are fundamental limitations to the kind of "empowerment" that can result from this kind of agency. If radical feminists are correct in claiming that patriarchy reproduces itself largely through men's ability to dominate and exploit women's bodies, we might consider a corollary: corporations have found peace and profit with liberal feminism by co-opting a genuine collective quest by women for bodily agency and empowerment and channeling it toward a goal of individual physical achievement that is severely limited by its consumerist context. The kind of collective women's agency that fought for legal changes such as Title IX and for the building of institutions such as rape crisis centers, domestic violence shelters, and community women's athletic leagues is a *resistant agency* through which women have empowered themselves to fight against and change the institutions that oppress them. In contrast, individual women's agency expressed as identification with corporate consumerism is a *reproductive agency* that firmly situates women's actions and bodies within the power relations of the current gender order.

In addition, Nike's commitment to women's liberation is contradicted by its own corporate practices. In 1996, when it posted its largest profits and its CEO Phillip Knight's stock was estimated to be worth $5 billion, the mostly women Indonesian workers who manufactured the shoes were paid about $2.25 a day. Workers who attempted to organize for higher pay and better working conditions were fired.[72] Reporting on conditions in 1998, when Indonesia experienced an economic crisis and currency devaluation, Zimbalist states: "Eighty per cent of Nike's Asian workers are female and most between 17 and 22; some are younger. The typical work week during busy season seems to be 6 or 7 days and 10 hours or more per day.... the value of a day's pay in Indonesia is under $1."[73] Meanwhile, U.S. women's eager consumption of corporate "celebrity feminism" makes it almost impossible for them to see, much less to act upon, the exploitation of women workers halfway around the globe. In fact, it is likely that the kinds of individual empowerment that can be purchased through consumerism seriously reduce women's abilities even to identify their collective interests in changing institutions within their own societies.

With Nike's co-optation of feminist symbols of empowerment, feminism in sport has come full circle: First, equity activists collectively organized to push, with some impressive but limited success, for equal opportunities for women in sports. As these successes mounted, a key ideological support for hegemonic masculinity—the naturalized equation of male bodies with athletic ability and physical strength—was destabilized. But as corporations like Nike began to seize upon the individualist impulse of female empowerment that underlies liberal feminism, they have sold it back to women as an ideology and bodily practice that largely precludes any actual mobilizing around the *collective* concept of "women." Individual women are now implored by Nike to "Just Do It"—just as individual men do it. Given the paucity of positive and empowering images of athletic women in the media, it is easy to see why so many women strongly approve of, and feel good about, the Nike ads. But does identification with the messages of the Nike ads connect these women to a politicized feminist movement that aims to bring about institutional transformations? Or does such identification create an individualized and depoliticized feminism that locks women into a consumer lifestyle and simultaneously encourages them to ignore how individuals who "do it" with Nike are implicated in an international system of racial, gender, and class exploitation of women workers in less-developed nations?

As my brief discussion of Nike suggests, gender analysis alone is not enough in examining the current dynamics of the sport-media-commercial complex. Economic, racial-ethnic, and even global analyses are also crucial. Such a broad institutional analysis suggests that it is not just muscular or athletic or "fit" girls' and women's bodies that must be considered in women's liberation; it is laboring bodies as well. Sport, the mass media, and corporations like Nike are not simply symbolic realms for the play and display of women's empowerment. They are also *workplaces*—for coaches, referees, sports reporters, announcers, hot dog salespeople, professional cheerleaders, beer producers and distributors, Indonesian shoe assembly workers, and many others. Yet, the corporate individualist appropriation of feminist empowerment as synonymous with the development of one's athletic body tends to deflect awareness of institutional arrangements. Instead, women's "feminist" agency, especially among women privileged by class and race, is diverted toward mass consumption aimed at individual development and away from collective organizing to change institutions that disadvantage all women, but especially those who are poor, working-class, and racially disadvantaged.

Community sports organizations, the law, school sports, college athletics, professional sports, and the sport-media-commercial complex are all structured, institutional contexts that constrain and enable people's choices and actions. And, as we have seen, collective actions such as legal moves to bring about sex equity in school sports and the creation of new "extreme" sports tend to destabilize sport's institutional center. Reactions to these challenges by those at the institutional center (the football lobby, the sport-media-commercial complex) tend to result in a restabi-lized, but somewhat shifted, institutional context. But my brief discussion of Nike has also hinted at the limits of a structural analysis of institu-tional change and stability. We must also consider the power and impor-tance of signs, symbols, and ideologies,[74] especially those promoted by the central sports media and their sponsors. It is to an analysis of the gendered nature of mediated sports that I turn next.

CHAPTER 4

Center of Attention:
The Gender of Sports Media

More than ninety thousand fans at the Rose Bowl, in Pasadena, California, were on their feet cheering. Millions more were enjoying the dramatic moment in front of their television sets. It was July 10, 1999, and soccer star Brandi Chastain had just blasted the game-winning kick past the Chinese goalie. The U.S. team had won the World Cup, culminating several weeks of intense excitement that included print and electronic media saturation, the extent of which was unprecedented in the history of U.S. women's sports. The day after the championship match, a newspaper reporter called me and asked, "Do you think that the tremendous attention that these women are getting will spill over into greater media coverage of women's sports in general?" My answer was simple: "Well, that depends on you, doesn't it?"

In fact, during that exciting moment for women's sports in the United States, my colleagues Margaret Carlisle Duncan and Cheryl Cooky and I were collecting data for a study on gender in televised sports that, among other things, compared the quantity and quality of televised news coverage of women's and men's sports. We had conducted this study previously, first in 1989 and then again in 1993, so we had baseline data with which to compare our 1999 data.[1] What we found— that over the course of the decade of the 1990s very little had changed in the ways televised sports news covered women's and men's sports—ran counter to the common belief that there has been a recent explosion of media attention given to women's sports. After all, wasn't the news coverage of the women's soccer team's World Cup victory amazing? And didn't it seem during the weeks leading up to the 2000 Olympic Games in Sydney that everywhere one turned, one saw magazine covers, commercial advertisements, television images, and commentary that trumpeted the arrival of U.S. women athletes such as track star Marion Jones, soccer teammates Mia Hamm and Brandi Chastain, and swimming champion Jenny Thompson? Where women athletes used to be simply ignored (what George Gerbner in 1978 referred to more generally as the "symbolic annihilation" of women in the media), weren't we now witnessing an exploding array of images and celebratory commentary about women athletes?[2]

We have indeed entered a new era in media coverage and cultural imagery of women's sports. Women athletes are no longer simply "symbolically annihilated." There is, in fact, a larger and more varied array of images and commentary of athletic women than ever before. Electronic entertainment, in particular, has grown dramatically. However, the proliferation of cable television, the Internet, specialized sports magazines, and sports radio talk shows has not launched a feminist revolution in sport. To the contrary, it has set the stage for the creation and exploitation of new, ever more precisely defined marketing niches. What this means is that respectful coverage of women's sports can easily be relegated to small, marginal cable channels, web sites, or specialized magazines.[3] While this may be good for a few fans of women's sports, it leaves largely intact the masculinist cultural center of the sport-media-commercial complex. To begin with but one example, in its December 2000 issue, *Sports Illustrated for Women*, a magazine that began publishing in 1997, featured a triumphant cover photo of tennis player Venus Williams, with the caption "Venus! Sportswoman of the Year," along with "We Salute the Women Who Ruled in 2000." The existence of this magazine and its celebration of Williams and other women athletes surely can be viewed as a sign of progress for women's sports and as a new source of positive imagery for girls and women. However, and ironically, the very existence of *Sports Illustrated for Women* (which issues bimonthly to 400,000 readers) may leave the parent (father?) magazine, *Sports Illustrated* (a weekly with 3.15 million readers), off the hook in terms of any obligation its publishers and editors might otherwise have felt to incorporate more and better women's sports reporting. With Venus and the other "women who ruled in 2000" safely in the ghetto of *SI for Women*, the magazine that represents the cultural center for print sports media can present itself as standing above gender (notice, it's not called *Sports Illustrated for Men*),[4] representing all of sports and naming Tiger Woods as sportsman of the year.

Much of the emergent cultural imagery of women's sports is relegated to the margins of the mass media, thus leaving the masculinist center mostly intact. But still, the enthusiasm for women's sports is expanding too quickly for the imagery of women athletes to be totally and continually ghettoized. The proliferation of images of women athletes is (increasingly, I think) making sports media a contested ideological terrain, where meanings of sexuality, gender, and race are being contested and reconstructed.[5] In this chapter, I will look at how the cultural center, what I called in the previous chapter the sport-media-commercial complex, has responded to the explosion of women's sports participation. Next, I will describe the dominant images that come out of the masculinist cultural center of sport. After discussing the ways that the media deal with the common problems and contradictions that are generated at the institutional center of sports, I will end the chapter by raising questions about audiences and consumers of sports media.

Silence, Sports Bras, and Wrestling Porn

Girls' and women's increased sports participation rates and the rapid closing of the muscle and performance gaps between women and men are far too dramatic to be entirely ignored by the mass media.[6] How has the sport-media-commercial complex responded to the explosion of female athleticism? There are four patterned ways that the dominant sports media deal with women's sports: silence, humorous sexualization, backlash, and selective incorporation of standout women athletes.

Figure 4. The existence of the bimonthly *Sports Illustrated for Women* represents an expansion of media coverage of women's sports, but it may let the much larger weekly "father" magazine off the hook in terms of adequate coverage of women's sports, thus allowing it to remain implicitly *Sports Illustrated (for Men)*.

Silence

When my colleagues and I looked at the coverage of women's sports in three network affiliates' televised news broadcasts, the most striking finding of our analysis was the lack of change over the past decade. In the 1990 and 1994 studies, we noted that female athletes rarely received coverage on the televised sports news. As Table 3 shows, the latest study revealed only a slight increase in the proportion of sports news devoted to coverage of women's sports and women athletes over the ten-year time period.

Even worse was ESPN's popular sports highlights show *Sports-Center*, which earned its name as "sport's *center*" by devoting only 2.2 percent of its coverage to women's sports.[7] *SportsCenter*'s ironic, often snidely humorous style, described by sport scholar Grant Farred as "cool as the other side of the pillow,"[8] has successfully set the tone for the growth of other sports highlights shows that also appear to offer up a standard staple of men's baseball, men's basketball, men's football, with occasional smidgens of men's ice hockey, auto racing, and some golf and tennis.

Humorous Sexualization

To simply point out that the network affiliates devoted 8.2 percent and *SportsCenter* 2.2 percent of their air time to women's sports actually *overstates* the extent to which women's sports were given fair and respectful coverage on these shows. A qualitative analysis of the ways that

TABLE 3. Percentage distribution of network sports news, by sex

	1989	1993	1999
Men	92.0	93.8	88.2
Women	5.0	5.1	8.7
Neutral or both men and women	3.0	1.1	3.1

women and men are presented on the sports news reveals further gender asymmetries. Two themes that persisted from the previous studies were (1) the choice to devote a considerable proportion of the already-thin coverage of women's sports to humorous feature stories on nonserious women's sports, and (2) the (often humorous) sexualization of athlete women and nonathlete women.

As in the earlier studies, we found in 1999 that while most of the few reports on serious women's sports (such as basketball, tennis, golf, and soccer) were fairly brief, the occasional, more in-depth women's sports story was often a gag feature or a story on a marginal, but visually entertaining, pseudosport. For instance, two stations did long features on a "nude bungee jumping" story, including a film clip of the nude woman, strategically painted with St. Patrick's Day green shamrocks, leaping from a bridge while the commentator asked, "Do we have to slow that down?" When interviewed, the bungee jumper said, "That was amazing. I will remember it forever," to which the commentator replied, "And so will we," as co-anchors laughed along with him. Similarly, two stations offered up lengthy feature stories on the wrestler-model Sable. Sable was aiming to promote World Wrestling Federation (WWF) wrestling, but reporters emphasized her scanty, dominatrix-style attire and her appearance in *Playboy* magazine. One station devoted twenty-seven seconds at 6:00 P.M. and twenty-one seconds at 11:00 P.M. to Sable and reported on no other women's sports during those shows. Sable was shown at a photo shoot (not wrestling), with a commentator noting, "As you can see, Sable doesn't keep much behind the scenes herself." Another station's coverage of Sable was even more in-depth: at two minutes and forty-eight seconds, this was the longest single news story on women's sports in our 1999 sample. The news commentator invited viewers into this story by stating, "We're your source for wrestling porn." He then described Sable as a "sexy villainess" and insulted her in an interview by asking if she could count to ten. When, with a disgusted look on her face, she did so, the commentator countered, "Ah, yes: beauty and brains." He went on to joke approvingly about Sable's appearance in *Playboy*, and after a film clip of her wrestling (in slow motion in a bikini), he concluded by saluting and saying, "Sable, a champion of women's rights. We salute her." This station then managed to squeeze a ten-second report on women's tennis into its 11:00 P.M. show, but the Sable story otherwise represented all the coverage of "women's sports" that day.

The wrestling porn comment about Sable seems to express an unstated policy among many sports news commentators: part of the entertainment of sports news shows is the opportunity they present for viewers to engage in sexual voyeurism. The producers supply the images, and the commentators supply the locker-room humor. For instance, a commentator discussed the NFL's decision to allow referees once again to use an instant replay to review on-field decisions: "The problem," he deadpanned as viewers were shown a clip of referees huddled around a monitor, "[is] what will the referees actually be looking at: the play, or as we found out, something else?" Next, viewers got a peek at what the referees were supposedly watching on the monitor: a Victoria's Secret fashion show and a clip of the movie *Eyes Wide Shut*, with Tom Cruise kissing Nicole Kidman while both appear naked.

If women athletes in sexy pseudosports fail to supply television news commentators with enough material for sexual titillation, there is a supporting cast of nonathlete women who are available for humorous voyeurism. Two of the three network affiliates continually offered viewers visual shots of young bikini-clad women in the sun-drenched stands of baseball games, often adding their own tongue-in-cheek comments about the women's attractiveness. For instance, a commentator enthusiastically said, "Helloooooo Pittsburgh!" while viewers were treated to a shot of a woman in the stands. The next day, when viewers were presented an image of a blond woman in a crop-top, the same commentator said, "Speaking of perfect, it was a perfect day today in Anaheim." Sexually humorous stories and references to other women in supportive nonathlete roles were sprinkled throughout the news reports. One station took up nearly three minutes of combined broadcast time on its two July 25, 1999, broadcasts reporting on "Laker Girl" (cheerleader) tryouts: among other things, viewers learned that it was the job of these "sizzling beauties" to "sex it up" on TV.

The sports news' humorous focus on scantily clad women spectators, cheerleaders, and nude or nearly nude women in pseudosports makes a conventionally conservative statement about women's "place"—on the sidelines, in support roles, and as objects of sexualized humor—in a cultural realm that is still defined, at least in these TV programs, as a man's world. But it is the humorous sexualization of actual women athletes that brings into sharpest focus some of the current paradoxes of gender and sexuality swirling around women's sports. In the aftermath of the World Cup championship by the U.S. soccer team, two television stations focused little on the accomplishments of the team and instead continued to reintroduce the story about soccer star Brandi Chastain's having, at the moment of victory, stripped off her jersey, revealing her sports bra. One commentator seemed unable to resist the Chastain sports bra story. Three days in a row, he made joking references to this story. First, he reported, "Today, the ponytail express stopped in midtown Manhattan, where it was announced that Nike will exploit Brandi Chastain's striptease by fashioning her to a line of sports bras." The next day, he noted that the women soccer players' "ponytail express" appeared in a golf tournament and that Chastain managed to keep her shirt on but "took off her sweater during warm-ups." And then on the next day, in a humorous spoof on the film *Eyes Wide Shut*, the sports news included a clip of Chastain in her sports bra as part of a collage of half-clothed people. Said the commentator, "It seems like Hollywood is really influencing the sports world. Everybody's getting naked. I'm not complaining. That's just the way it is."[9]

Sports news commentators' penchant for sexual humor about women athletes has not been confined to soccer players. A story on a tennis match between Mary Pierce and Anna Kournikova focused typically on Kournikova's image as a sexually attractive young woman. Noting her boyfriend in the crowd, the commentator said, "That's what it takes to date Anna Kournikova: you have to be willing to go watch her play in the afternoon and then fly across the country and play yourself at night.... And it's well worth it, I think most would agree." He and the anchorperson then shared a knowing laugh. As I write this, Kournikova has still never won a major tournament. Nevertheless, she garners about ten million dollars a year in corporate endorsements (fifty-eighth on the *Forbes* worldwide celebrity power list), has appeared on the covers of *Esquire*, *Forbes*, *Vogue*, and *Cosmopolitan*,[10] and has scores of official and unofficial web sites devoted to her.[11] Simply put, Anna Kournikova is a major icon in popular culture, and her quick rise to such prominence, at least as much for her physical appearance as for her on-court tennis accomplishments, has made her a lightning rod for debates about media sexualization of women athletes. In its June 5, 2000, issue, *Sports Illustrated* ran a cover story on Kournikova that made no pretenses that it was focusing not on her tennis abilities but on her sexual attractiveness.[12] In response, the Women's Sports Foundation slammed *SI*:

> We see a 19-year-old, #15 ranked tennis player primarily illustrated by photographs of her in short skirts, slit skirts, off-the-shoulder gypsy blouses or with eligible men with only two tennis action shots out of 11 photos. *This is not about journalistic integrity. This is about selling magazines.* When circulation declines, put sex on the cover.... Female athletes should be portrayed as athletes in athletic uniforms displaying their sports skills. When have we ever seen major sports periodicals depicting Michael Jordan or other male athletes stuffed into tight-fitting uniforms that display their genitalia as a way of getting more women to buy magazines?[13]

This sort of response to *SI*'s (and other media's) unabashed celebratory sexploitation of the image of Kournikova has been criticized by sport historian Allen Guttmann as typical of feminists' tendency to deny the obviously erotic nature of sports:

> Many feminist sport sociologists continue, however, to deny the erotic attraction of the female athlete and to blame the mass media for what they—the feminists—call "sexualization," a term that implicitly denies the sexuality inherent in the athletic performance and the athletic body upon which that performance is inscribed.[14]

Guttmann is correct to be wary of the antisex neo-Victorianism present in a strand of Western feminism. And he is certainly correct in asserting that many people find erotic pleasure in sports spectating. However, his argument that "the athletic body" is inherently "erotic" ignores the *profoundly social* dynamic that underlies not only what is defined as "sexual" but also how mass media displays of sexuality are *contextualized* in cultural discourses that are defined by, and in turn help to define, group power relations. Former tennis star and feminist activist Billie Jean King understands this context. In her response to the Kournikova *SI* issue, King underlined that pro tennis is a sexualized commercial enterprise that is characterized by an asymmetrical gender dynamic:

> It doesn't bother me at all if some of the guys come out to watch women's tennis because they want to see a beautiful woman. Who could hold that against Anna? Still, it's unfortunate when others with a high skill factor don't win the endorsements. Sure, the good-looking guys get more endorsements, but the difference in men's sports is that the ugly ones get their share, too.[15]

King, of course, knows from her own experience that on the women's tour, "others" fail to win the big endorsement money not always because they are "ugly" but because they are not (or are suspected of not being) heterosexual.[16] Heterosexually attractive women athletes are actively used by professional women's leagues like the LPGA and the WNBA to promote their sport with consumers.[17] In the words of sports media scholar Pamela Creedon, promoters know that "little girls and sweethearts sell.... Homosexuality doesn't sell."[18] And media people who are friendly to women's sports will often play along with this strategy, thinking that they are helping to promote women's sports by dispelling the myth that all women athletes must be masculine dykes. But even when it is a well-meaning strategy to promote sports for girls and women, the practice of foregrounding the heterosexually attractive women in order to promote a sport tends symbolically to erase lesbian, bisexual, queer, and unfeminine-appearing women. It also costs these

Figure 5. *Sports Illustrated* rarely depicts women athletes on its cover, but the magazine did find room for tennis player Anna Kournikova on one and for model Daniela Pestova on its annual, highly lucrative swimwear issue.

"other" women thousands, sometimes millions, of dollars in lost endorsement money. And it contributes to a restabilization of narrow cultural codes of heterosexual femininity that have been restrictive for girls and women.

The racial context of Kournikova's meteoric rise to (hetero)sex-goddess celebrity status is equally important. The blond, tanned, long-limbed, and lightly muscled Kournikova clearly conforms to dominant cultural standards of white feminine beauty. Her form of beauty stands in stark contrast to the highly muscular and very black bodies of ascendant young stars Serena and Venus Williams. The Williams sisters appear to be challenging dominant cultural definitions of feminine beauty and expanding these definitions to include both muscularity and blackness; by contrast, the elevation of Kournikova to celebrity status can be read as a market-driven reassertion of conventional and culturally dominant white definitions of feminine beauty.[19]

Surely, as a *Sports Illustrated* marketing ploy, the Kournikova issue was a smashing success, following in the footsteps of the magazine's highly lucrative swimwear issue, which has become a huge, multimedia, annual cultural event.[20] But the cultural significance of these sexploitation issues of a popular national sports magazine must be read against the backdrop of what the magazine normally does, which is to cover the central *men's* sports, week after week, year after year. In the 123 issues of the magazine from 1998 until the Kournikova issue came out, *Sports Illustrated* published only five covers featuring women athletes: basketball coach Pat Summit, figure skater Michelle Kwan, tennis player Serena Williams, soccer player Brandi Chastain (in her sports bra), and the U.S. women's World Cup team—that's 4 percent of the covers devoted to women's sports. It is against the backdrop of the near absence of respectful stories of women athletes in mainstream magazines such as *Sports Illustrated* that the cultural meanings of sexualized features like the Kournikova issue or the annual swimwear issue must be read and interpreted. The mass media, it seems, are much more likely to pull women athletes to the center of cultural discourse when they are athletes who can be appreciated and exploited for their sexual appeal. Otherwise, they are relegated to the margins of the cultural radar screen.

However, this notion of the culture industry pulling certain women to the center while pushing others out to the margins of cultural discourse is still less than adequate to explain the "sexualization" of some women athletes. After all, many will argue that nobody "forces" Anna Kournikova, swimmer Jenny Thompson, or high jumper Amy Acuff to pose nearly nude or in sexy clothes that suggest heterosexual access for national magazines or calendars. It's a mistake simply to view these athletes as disempowered dupes who have allowed themselves to be "objectified" by a powerful cultural system. We must also take into account the agency of the women doing the posing. These are strong and talented young women who believe that they are making choices about their lives and their bodies. What's more, they often see no contradiction between projecting an aesthetic of desirable heterosexual femininity *and* an athletic habitus of physical strength, power, and competence. This thinking, scholars like Susan Bordo argue, is explained by an emergent breakdown in the cultural codings of masculinity and femininity as bipolar dominant-subordinate opposites.[21] And this change is especially evident among younger women, many of whom are forging new conceptions of feminine attractiveness that include muscular power. For example, when *Sports Illustrated* ran a pre-Olympics photo of swimmer Jenny Thompson, standing in a powerful pose, wearing only red boots and Wonder Woman shorts, with her fists covering her bare breasts, debate raged over the photo's meanings. Donna Lopiano of the Women's Sports Foundation told *Sports Illustrated for Women*, "It's incongruous to take that body you've worked so hard for and use it for sex."

But to Jenny Thompson, there was nothing incongruous in her pose. She disagreed vehemently with the contention that *Sports Illustrated* had turned her into a disempowered sexualized object:

My stance in the picture was one of strength and power and *girls rule!* It's nothing sexual. I wasn't pouting or giving a sexual look. I was like, here I

Figure 6. Some women's sports advocates and feminists cried foul when *Sports Illustrated* posed champion swimmer Jenny Thompson topless, but she saw nothing oppressive about it: "This idea of being proud of who you are and willing to show it off [is] a new feminism!"

am. I'm strong. The body is something to be celebrated, and Olympians have amazing bodies. So I think it's a work of art.... Someone called this— this idea of being proud of who you are and willing to show it off—a new feminism. I think that's pretty cool: I've started a new feminism.[22]

Indeed, cultural studies scholar Leslie Heywood argues that it is a mistake to employ second-wave feminist concepts of sexual objectification to interpret the meanings of some women athletes' willingness to pose nearly naked. Heywood observes that the Thompson photo in *SI* "expresses neither seductiveness nor vulnerability" and is thus not so easily seen as business-as-usual passive feminine objectification:

> Contemporary gender codes cannot be so easily polarized as they once were, though images like the Kournikova spread seek to reinforce them.... Female athletes in the generations post–Title IX have come to redeem the erasure of individual women that the old *Playboy* model sexualization performs, rewriting the symbology of the female body from empty signifiers of ready access, blank canvases or holes on which to write one's desires, to the active, self-present sexuality of a body that signifies achievement and power. The athletic body, when coded as athletic, redeems female sexuality and makes it visible as an assertion of female presence.[23]

This assertion that female athletes are active agents whose actions and images are rewriting the cultural symbology of women's bodies in ways that incorporate sexuality as part of the project of empowerment accurately reflects an emergent sensibility that Heywood and others have called "third wave feminism."[24] However, Heywood's optimistic conclusion that we are now witnessing a "new iconography that redeems sexuality from objectification and women from codes of easy access and vulnerability" needs to be considered cautiously, within a broad, institutional analysis. If the powerful-sexy shots of women continue mostly to be relegated to the sports ghettos of *ESPN2* or *Sports Illustrated for Women*, this leaves the larger, more central institutions like *Sports Illustrated* and *SportsCenter* off the hook, still at the center, and able to continue to spew out an almost unabated stream of reporting and imagery that largely erases women or sexualizes them in trivial ways. Given this institutional pattern, we must temper our optimism concerning the growing gender fluidity and sexual symmetries in popular imagery of males and females. These images exist, but they are mostly out there in market niches that are peripheral with respect to the cultural center of sport imagery, where a male-as-subject, female-as-object asymmetry still largely prevails.

Backlash against Women's Sports

After the Amateur Athletic Foundation released the televised sports study I previously referred to, I was treated to a nearly two-hour-long lambasting on a popular, syndicated shock jock radio show. The *Tom Leykis Show* deals primarily with sexuality and gender issues and features an antifeminist backlash tendency, which appears to have found fertile ground among men who feel threatened, displaced, disoriented, or disenfranchised by assertive women. Leykis reasserts a 1950s "*Playboy* philosophy" view of relations between women and men, with a postfeminist twist. He resuscitates the 1950s view of women as sexually manipulative gold diggers out to trap a male provider, and he also employs misogynist and homophobic put-downs to undercut the legitimacy of the emergent cultural counterimage of women as independent and powerful.

The AAF study on women and sport proved to be a perfect foil for Leykis's popular form of backlash; he and most of his adoring callers were no less than outraged that anybody would suggest that women athletes deserve more and better media coverage. Leykis gave no credit to women athletes, and he resorted to lowest-common-denominator misogyny and homophobia (either directly targeted at women or displaced onto the faggoty, pussywhipped male professor who apparently wants to take all of our boys, "surrender their manhood before they are even thirteen, just cut off their balls, put a fuzzy toilet seat on and have them all pee sitting down"). An exchange between Leykis and one equally hysterical caller illustrates some of the recurrent themes of the broadcast:

LEYKIS: We're talking about this report called *Gender in Televised Sports*, by a Professor Michael Messner from the University of Southern California, [who] is the author of this ridiculous, preposterous survey that says women deserve more coverage during sportscasts on TV. And I say, BULL! I have more to say than that, but what're you gonna do? I have Brad on a cell phone. You're on the *Tom Leykis Show*.

BRAD: HELLOOOOOOO, TOM!

LEYKIS: Hello, Brad!

BRAD: How's it hangin'?

LEYKIS: Hangin' right, Brad.

BRAD: Good man. Hey listen: About 90 to 95 percent of the sports that are being performed by athletes, whether it be professional or collegiate, are performed BY MEN! NOT WOMEN!

LEYKIS: Well, about 95 percent of the coverage—er, 95 percent of the attendance—is in men's events, put it that way. College football, college basketball, pro football, pro basketball. C'MON!

BRAD: The only pro events that women have are golf and, basically, basketball. But you know what? There's no woman basketball player like a Shaquille O'Neal to even be worth reporting.

LEYKIS: No.

BRAD: And there's no Tiger Woods in the women's golf league.

LEYKIS: And what are we supposed to be covering? Little Suzie's run at the parallel bars over at the junior high school? I mean what exactly are we supposed to be putting on TV?

BRAD: NOTHING! NOTHING WITH WOMEN, BECAUSE THERE'S NOTHING WORTH WATCHING!

LEYKIS: Right.

BRAD: There's really nothing! I mean, I don't sit at home and watch figure skating. I don't watch some gymnastics—

LEYKIS: [interrupting] Figure skating is a pussy-assed sport anyway. Figure skating is not even a sport. If figure skating is a sport, then so is ballet [with Brad laughing approvingly in the background]. C'mon, I've said this on the air before: they take points off for having bad make-up or the wrong length of hair or a bad costume. That's not a sport!

BRAD: The only thing that I was actually impressed with was with this college girl who pitched a perfect softball game. But what really surprised me was that she struck out all twenty-seven batters! THAT'S worth reporting, because that's something, that's, you know, news!

LEYKIS: What was her life partner's name?

BRAD: I don't know, probably Butch.

Leykis and Brad both laughed heartily, and the show soon cut to an advertisement for *NFL Insider Magazine*.

In this exchange, Leykis and Brad defended the contested boundaries of men's sports. Sports are something that *men* do. Women do not do sports. And when it turns out that some women *do* do sports, well, then they are not real women. In short, either women athletes are too soft and feminine to be worth considering as serious athletes ("pussy-assed figure skaters"), or they are butch lesbians who are worthy only of derision. Brad's contention that 95 percent of all the sports being played out there are by men and that the only pro events that women have are golf and basketball spoke volumes concerning the ways that major sports media largely ignore existing women's sports while lavishly promoting and aggressively building audiences for men's college and professional sports.[25] Further, Brad's claim that there is no female equivalent to Shaquille O'Neal or Tiger Woods is most telling. On the one hand, one might have to concede his point about O'Neal: The last time I checked, WNBA centers were hitting well better than 50 percent of their free throws. But with respect to Tiger Woods, there actually are two rough equivalents in Karrie Webb and Annika Sörenstam, who in recent years have dominated the LPGA and broken records in much the same way as Woods has dominated the PGA. In 1999, Webb recorded one of the most impressive seasons in LPGA history,[26] winning six tournaments and recording twenty-two top-ten finishes. In 2000, she won seven tournaments and had seventeen top-ten finishes. When Webb won the LPGA Championship in June 2001, she became at age twenty-six the youngest woman in history to win the career Grand Slam.[27] In 2000–2001, Annika Sörenstam emerged as a major challenger to Webb's domination of LPGA competition. In March 2001, Sörenstam's tournament score of fifty-nine became the lowest score ever on the LPGA tour, and she became the highest career money winner on the tour. However, while Tiger Woods is a household name, far fewer people know the names Karrie Webb or Annika Sörenstam. And the reason for this is simple: the major sports media and commercial sponsors constantly serve up images and commentary on Woods while either ignoring Webb and Sörenstam or relegating images, commentary, and advertisements featuring them to marginal media and smaller commercial markets. In short, the comments by Brad on the *Tom Leykis Show*—that there is "no female equivalent to Tiger Woods out there"—illustrate my main point: If sports consumers like Brad focus on the cultural center, 95 percent of what they see is big men playing big men's sports and promoting big products. Put another way, if *SportsCenter*, the major TV networks, and *Sports Illustrated* don't show us Karrie Webb or Annika Sörenstam, then as important cultural symbols, they do not exist.

Selective Incorporation of Standout Women Athletes

Sports media and commercial interests that promote sports do sometimes seize on the image of a woman athlete and pull her to the center of cultural discourse, at least temporarily. They seem most likely to do so when there is a high profit potential (and this usually means that the individual woman can be neatly packaged as heterosexually attractive) and when nationalism can be invoked.[28] A recent example of this is the way the mass media and commercial sponsors positioned U.S. track star Marion Jones well in advance of the 2000 Olympics as "our" hope and as "our" representative and champion versus the rest of the world. African American male athletes have been positioned this way in the past: Jesse Owens versus Hitler, Joe Louis versus Max Schmeling; and a few, such as Tommie Smith and John Carlos at the 1968 Mexico City Olympic Games, resisted being used this way.

In addition to inviting a global analysis, the cases of Smith and Carlos, Louis, Owens, and more recently Jones invite a complex analysis of the intersections of race and gender. Utilizing such an analysis, cultural studies scholar Sarah Banet-Weiser argues that the media, commercial sponsors, and the WNBA itself launched the new women's professional basketball league by foregrounding images of the athletes as mothers and attractive models.[29] The WNBA women, the promotional hype promised, offer fans a "return to the purity of the game," and this return to purity was positioned against the backdrop of the image of the rich, spoiled, violent, highly sexualized, and very black bad boys of the NBA.[30] In short, the athletes of the WNBA are coded as women; the athletes of the NBA are coded as black.

Similarly, Marion Jones was positioned by mass media and corporate sponsors such as Nike as the pure, smiling, girl next door who just happened to be really fast. She was coded largely in gender terms, as an icon of the arrival of women athletes in the 2000 games. However, during the games, when the story broke that her husband, shot putter

Figure 7. The Nike swoosh and the American flag signal track and field star Marion Jones's arrival as a central icon of the sport-media-commercial complex. A woman athlete like Jones is pulled to the center of sport symbolism under particular conditions: if she is viewed as conventionally attractive and athletically talented, and when she can invoke patriotism as "our hope for a gold medal" in international events. Photograph courtesy of Allsport Photography USA, Inc.; reprinted with permission.

C. J. Hunter, had tested positive for an illegal anabolic steroid, cameras could not stop focusing on this huge African American man, and commentators salivated over the question of whether this man's misbehaviors would rub off on and possibly even bring down Marion Jones. The media's focus on this story, I believe, suddenly made race salient. Marion Jones, "our girl," through her association with her huge, black, supposedly bad-boy drug-taking husband, suddenly became black, other, and a tarnished suspect.

Cultural studies scholar Craig Watkins has argued that the popular idea that some successful African American athletes such as Michael Jordan have "transcended" race and become honorary whites "is both reductive and racist."[31] Indeed, this belief should have been put into the cultural trash bin by now, especially since we witnessed how O. J. Simpson, once seen by many as a superstar who had achieved "racial transcendence," was so thoroughly racially coded once he was accused of murder (even to the point where a national news magazine artificially darkened his face on its mug shot-like cover photo).[32] In the context of U.S. culture, race and gender are never transcended; they are always already there. The point I want to make, rather, is that when we look at the cultural imagery of athletes such as Marion Jones and try to make sense of the confluence of race and gender, it behooves us to consider how and why, in certain contexts and under certain conditions, race or gender becomes more salient as a meaning-making theme. As I argued in chapter 2, this point has been hammered home by sport studies scholars who have shown how male athletes' sexual transgressions and violence against women have been projected largely onto African American male athletes. The institutional center of sport clearly generates its own problems, and part of the way these problems are managed is through a racialization of deviance.

Reading the Center

A recent national survey found eight- to seventeen-year-old children to be avid consumers of sports media, with television most often named as the preferred medium.[33] Girls watch sports in great numbers, but boys are markedly more likely to be regular consumers of televised sports. The most popular televised sports with boys, in descending order, are pro football, men's pro basketball, pro baseball, pro wrestling, men's college basketball, college football, and extreme sports.[34] What are kids seeing and hearing when they watch these programs? In particular, what kinds of values concerning gender, race, aggression, violence, and consumerism are boys exposed to when they watch their favorite televised sports programs, with their accompanying commercials? Children Now, a children's advocacy organization, asked my colleagues Darnell Hunt and Michele Dunbar and me to shed light on these questions by analyzing these televised sports and their accompanying commercials.[35] Our analysis revealed that sports programming presents boys with narrow and stereotypical messages about race, gender, and violence. We identified ten distinct themes that, together, make up what we call the televised sports manhood formula:

White males are the voices of authority. The play-by-play and ongoing "color commentary" in National Football League (NFL), professional wrestling, National Basketball Association (NBA), extreme sports, and major league baseball (MLB) broadcasts that we examined was conducted exclusively by white male play-by-play commentators. With the exception of ESPN's *SportsCenter*, women and African American men never appeared as the main voices of authority, "in the booth," conducting play-by-play or ongoing color commentary. The NFL broadcasts occasionally cut to field-level color commentary by a white woman, but her commentary was a very brief interlude. Similarly, the NBA broadcasts used African American men and white or African American women for occasional on-court, pregame, and halftime analysis but not for play-by-play commentary. Although viewers commonly see African American male athletes, especially on televised NBA games, they rarely hear or see African American men (or any women) as voices of authority in the broadcast booth.[36] In fact, the only African American commentators that appeared on the NBA shows that we examined were former star basketball players (Cheryl Miller, Doc Rivers, and Isiah Thomas). An African American male briefly appeared to welcome the audience to open one of the extreme sports shows, but he did no play-by-play; in fact, he was used only to open the show with a cool, street, hip-hop style for what turned out to be an almost totally white show.[37]

Sport is a man's world. Images and discussion of women athletes are almost entirely absent in the sports programs that boys watch most. The baseball, basketball, wrestling, and football programs we watched were men's contests so perhaps could not have been expected to cover or mention women athletes. However, extreme sports are commonly viewed as alternative or emerging sports in which women are challenging masculine hegemony.[38] Despite this, the extreme sports shows we watched devoted only a single fifty-second interview segment to a woman athlete. This segment constituted about 1 percent of the total extreme sports programming and, significantly, did not show this woman athlete in action.

Perhaps this limited coverage of women athletes on the extreme sports shows we examined is evidence of what sociologist Robert Rinehart calls a "pecking order" in alternative sports, which develops when new sports are appropriated and commodified by the media. When ESPN first produced the eXtreme games, Rinehart observes, they were sponsored by Miller Lite Ice, Taco Bell, Mountain Dew, Nike's ACG brand, AT&T, and General Motors. This "coopting by corporations," Rinehart argues, is paradoxical: though now sanctioned by a governing body and by some of the largest U.S. corporations, the appeal of extreme sports to many consumers appears to be their "outlaw" nature. To be commercially successful then, extreme sports televised productions and their accompanying commercial advertisements have creatively played with this paradox, highlighting moments of symbolic (masculine) "outlaw" rebellion while constructing an audience of conformist consumers.[39]

Men are foregrounded in commercials. The gender composition and imagery in commercials reinforce the idea that sport is a man's world. Women almost never appear in commercials unless they are in the company of men. Of the 722 commercials we examined, 279 portrayed only men, and only 28 showed only women. That 38.6 percent of all commercials portrayed only men actually understates the extent to which men dominated these commercials, for two reasons. First, nearly every one of the 91 commercials containing no visual portrayals of people included a male voice-over. When we include the "voice-over" group, the proportions shift to over 50 percent of commercials portraying "men only" images and/or voice-overs, and only 3.9 percent portraying only women. Moreover, when we combine the "men only" and "women and men" categories, we see that men were actually visible in 83.5 percent and present (at least in voice) in 96.1 percent of all commercials. Second, in the commercials that portrayed both women and men, women were often (though not exclusively) portrayed in stereotypical and very minor "background" roles.

Women are sexy props or prizes for men's successful sports performances or consumption choices. Though women are mostly absent from sports commentary, when they do appear, it is most often in stereotypical roles as sexy, masculinity-validating props, often cheering the men on. For instance, X-sports on Fox Sports West used a bikini-clad blond woman as a "hostess" to welcome viewers back after each commercial break while the camera moved provocatively over her body. Though she mentioned the show's sponsors, she did not narrate the actual sporting event. The wrestling shows generously utilized scantily clad women (e.g., in pink miniskirts or tight Spandex and high heels), who overtly displayed the dominant cultural signs of heterosexy attractiveness,[40] to escort the male wrestlers to the ring, often with announcers discussing the women's provocative physical appearances. Women also appeared in the wrestling shows as sexually provocative dancers (e.g., the Gorgeous Nitro Girls on TNT).

In sports-related commercials, women are numerically more evident and generally depicted in more varied roles than in the sports programming. Still, women are underrepresented and rarely appear in commercials unless they are in the company of men. A common theme in commercials aimed at boys and men is to depict women as capable either of humiliating men or of affirming men's masculine desirability. And women's supposed masculinity-validating power is clearly linked to men's consumption choices: women will ignore or humiliate the man who is incapable of buying the right product or unwilling to, but women become sexy and accessible "prizes" for men who are wise enough to make the right consumption choices. Both of these themes were rawly depicted in a commercial for Keystone Light Beer that ran on *Sports-Center*. Two white guys are attending a major league baseball game, when one of them unexpectedly appears on the stadium big screen. His buddy says, "Dude, look, you're on! *Do* something!" All the guy can think to do with his sudden ten seconds of fame is to take a drink of his beer. Immediately, the taste of this bitter beer twists and distorts his face. The stadium announcer reacts in shock to his ugliness ("Ay caramba!"), and the camera cuts to two conventionally attractive young women in the crowd, who are totally grossed out ("Eeeew!") by having to look at this man's contorted face. But then the voice-over reassuringly instructs the viewer, "Don't be a victim of bitter beer. Drink Keystone Light, America's never bitter beer, so there's always a great taste and never a bitter face." When the commercial ends, the formerly contorted and humiliated man has returned to normal, and we see him again on the big screen, now holding a Keystone Light and looking healthy, attractive, and confident with the same two young fashion-model-like women standing on either side of him, now adoring him. He says, "I hope my wife's not watching!" as the two women happily wave to the audience.

This madonna-whore juxtaposition of women—wives and girlfriends and other castrating bitches are to be avoided, but sexy dancers or models are desirable objects of consumption—is also evident in a series of 2000–2001 full-page magazine ads for Jim Beam whiskey that, under the umbrella theme of "Real friends. Real bourbon," pitched male bonding through alcohol consumption to a college-aged (or young college-educated) crowd of men. Against a striking red background, black-and-white photos of clean-cut, mostly white young men in bars drinking, laughing, and happily partying together were accompanied by these captions: "Unlike your girlfriend, they never ask where this relationship is going," and "You can count on them never to ask you to get in touch with your feminine side."

Women, the ads imply, demand levels of emotional commitment

Figure 8. (a) Drink the wrong beer, and you'll look ugly and be publicly humiliated. (b) Women, especially, will be disgusted by you. (c) But drink the right beer, and beautiful women will admire you and throw themselves at you.

and expression that men are not ready or willing to submit to. Women are a pain in the ass. Life with the guys (and the booze) is comfortable, comforting, and safe. It's also exciting. The one ad in the series that included an image of a woman showed only part of her body (*Sports Illustrated* ran this one in its 2000 swimwear issue, in 3-D if you were willing to put on the glasses). The guys are drinking again together at a bar. In the foreground, we see the high-heeled legs of what appears to be a dancing female stripper. The guys drink, laugh, and seem very amused with each other. "Your lives would make a great sitcom," the caption reads. "Of course, it would have to run on cable." That the guys mostly seem to be ignoring the woman dancer affirms the strength and primacy of their bond with each other; they don't need her or any other women, it seems to say. On the other hand, her powerfully sexual presence appears to affirm that the bond between the men is safely within the bounds of heterosexuality.[41]

Whites are foregrounded in commercials. The racial composition of the commercials is, if anything, narrower and more limited than the gender composition. African American, Latino, or Asian American people almost never appear in commercials unless the commercial also has white people in it. And when we examined the quality of the portrayals of African Americans, Latinos, and Asian Americans in the "multiracial" commercials, we found that people of color are far more often than not relegated to minor roles, literally "in the background" of scenes that feature whites, and/or they are relegated to stereotypical or negative roles. For instance, a Wendy's commercial that appeared on several of the sports programs in our sample showed white customers enjoying a sandwich with the white owner while a barely perceptible African American male walked by in the background.

Aggressive players get the prize; nice guys finish last. Viewers of televised sports are continually immersed in images and commentary about the positive rewards that come to the most "aggressive" competitors and of the negative consequences of playing "soft" and lacking aggression. Commentators consistently laud athletes who most successfully employ "physical" and "aggressive" play and "toughness." For instance, after

Figure 9. This bourbon advertisement is part of a series that affirmed the strength and primacy of young men's bonds with each other. The ad suggests that these guys don't need the exotic dancer who is working to entertain them—or any other women, for that matter.

having his toughness called into question, NBA player Brian Grant was awarded "redemption" by *SportsCenter* because he showed that he's "not afraid to take it to Karl Malone." *SportsCenter* also informed viewers that "the aggressor usually gets the calls [from the officials], and the Spurs were the ones getting them." In pro wrestling commentary, this is a constant theme. WWF announcers praised the "raw power" of wrestler Shamrock and approvingly dubbed Hardcore Holly as "the world's most dangerous man." NBA commentators suggested that it's okay to be a good guy off the court, but one must be tough and aggressive on the court: Brian Grant and Jeff Hornacek are "true gentlemen of the NBA . . . as long as you don't have to play against them. You know they're great off the court; on the court, every single guy out there *should* be a killer."

When players are not doing well, they are often described as hesitant and lacking aggression, emotion, and desire (e.g., desire for a loose ball or a rebound). For instance, commentators lamented that "the Jazz aren't going to the hoop; they're being pushed and shoved around," that Utah was responding to the Blazers' aggression "passively, in a reactive mode," and that "Utah's got to get Karl Malone toughened up." *Sports-Center* echoed this theme, opening one show with a depiction of Horace Grant elbowing Karl Malone and asking of Malone, "Is he feeble?" Similarly, NFL broadcasters waxed on about the virtues of aggression and domination. Big "hits," ball carriers who got "buried," "stuffed" or "walloped" by the defense, and players who got "cleaned out" or "wiped out" by a blocker were often shown on replays, with announcers enthusiastically describing the plays. By contrast, announcers declared that it's a very bad thing to be "passive" and to let yourself get "pushed around" and "dominated" at the line of scrimmage. Announcers also approvingly noted that "going after" an opposing player's injured body part is just smart football; in one NFL game, the Miami strategy to blitz the opposing quarterback was lauded as brilliant: "When you know your opposing quarterback is a bit nicked and something is wrong, Boomer, you got to come after him."

This injunction for boys and men to be aggressive, not passive, is reinforced in commercials, where a common formula is to play on the insecurities of young males (e.g., that they are not strong enough, tough enough, smart enough, rich enough, attractive enough, decisive enough, etc.) and then attempt to convince them to avoid, overcome, or mask their fears, embarrassments, and apparent shortcomings by buying a particular product. These commercials often portray men as potential or actual geeks, nerds, or passive schmucks who can overcome their geeki-ness (or avoid being a geek like the guy in the commercial) by becom-ing decisive and purchasing a particular product. This is also a common theme on commercials that run on the *Tom Leykis Show*, as discussed above.

Boys will be (violent) boys. Announcers often take a humorous "boys will be boys" attitude in discussing fights or near fights during contests, and they also commonly use a recent fight, altercation, or disagreement between two players as a "teaser" to build audience excitement. Fights, near fights, threats of fights, or other violent actions are overemphasized in sports coverage and often verbally framed in sarcastic language that suggests that this kind of action, though reprehensible, is to be expected. For instance, when *SportsCenter* showed NBA centers Robinson and O'Neal exchanging forearm shoves, the commentators said, simply, "much love." Similarly, in an NFL game, a brief scuffle between players was met with a sarcastic comment by the broadcaster that the players were simply "making their acquaintance." This is, of course, a constant theme in pro wrestling. My colleagues and I found it noteworthy that the supposedly spontaneous fights outside the wrestling ring (what we call unofficial fights) were given more coverage time and focus than the supposedly official fights inside the ring. We speculate that wrestling producers know that viewers already watch fights inside the ring with some skepticism as to their authenticity, so they stage the unofficial fights outside the ring to bring a feeling of spontaneity and authenticity to the show and to build excitement and a sense of anticipation for the fight that will later occur inside the ring.

Give up your body for the team. Athletes who are "playing with pain," "giving up their body for the team," or engaging in obviously highly dangerous plays or maneuvers are consistently portrayed as heroes; conversely, those who remove themselves from games because of injuries raise questions about their character, their manhood. This theme cuts across all sports programming. For instance, *SportsCenter* asked, "Could the Dominator be soft?" when an NHL star goalie decided to sit out a game because of a groin injury. Heroically taking risks while already hurt was a constant theme in extreme sports commentary. For instance, one bike competitor was lauded for "overcoming his fear" and competing "with a busted up ankle," and another was applauded when he "popped his collarbone out in the street finals in Louisville" but came back to "his bike here in Richmond, just two weeks later!" Athletes appear especially heroic when they go against doctors' wishes not to compete. For instance, an X Games interviewer adoringly told a competitor, "Doctors said don't ride, but you went ahead and did it anyway, and escaped serious injury." Similarly, NBA player Isaiah Rider was lauded for having "heart" for "playing with that knee injury." Injury discussions in NFL games often include speculation about whether the player will be able to return to this or future games. A focus on a star player in a pregame or halftime show, such as the feature on 49er Garrison Hearst, often contains commentary about a heroic overcoming of serious injuries (in this case, a knee blowout, reconstructive surgery, and rehabilitation). When one game began, commentators noted that thirty-seven-year-old "Steve Young has remained a rock. . . . Not bad for a guy who a lotta people figured was—what?—one big hit from ending his career." It's especially impressive when an injured player is able and willing to continue to play with aggressiveness and reckless abandon: "Kurt Scrafford at right guard—bad neck and all—is just out there wiping out guys. . . ." And announcers love the team leader who plays hurt: "Drew Bledsoe gamely tried to play in loss to Rams yesterday; really admirable to try to play with that pin that was surgically implanted in his finger during the week; I don't know how a QB could do that. You know, he broke his finger the time we had him on Monday night, and he led his team to two come-from-behind victories, really gutted it out, and I think he took that team on his shoulders and showed he could play and really elevated himself in my eyes, he really did."

Sports are war. Commentators in our study consistently (an average of nearly five times during each hour of sports commentary) used martial metaphors and language of war and weaponry to describe sports action (e.g., *battle, kill, ammunition, weapons, professional sniper, depth charges, taking aim, fighting, shot in his arsenal, reloading, detonate, squeezes the trigger, attack mode, firing blanks, blast, explosion, blitz, point of attack, a lance through the heart*, etc.). Some shows went beyond commentators' use of war terminology and actually framed the contests *as* wars. For instance, one of the wrestling shows offered a continuous flow of images and commentary that reminded the viewers that "RAW is WAR!" Similarly, NFL *Monday Night Football* broadcasts were introduced with explosive graphics and an opening song that included these lyrics: "Like a rocket burning through time and space, the NFL's best will rock this place . . . the battle lines are drawn. . . ." This sort of use of sports-war metaphors has been a common practice in televised sports commentary for many years, serving to fuse (and confuse) the distinctions between values of nationalism with team identity and athletic aggression with military destruction.[42] War themes were also reinforced in many commercials, including commercials for movies, other sports programs, and the occasional commercial for the U.S. Military.

Show some guts! Commentators continually depict and replay big hits, violent crashes, and incidents of athletes engaging in reckless acts of speed or showing guts in the face of danger. This theme was evident across all of the sports programs in our study but was especially predominant in extreme sports, which continually depicted crashing vehicles or bikers in an exciting manner. For instance, when one race ended with a crash, it was showed again in slow-motion replay, with commentators approvingly dubbing it "unbelievable" and "original." Extreme sports commentators commonly raised excitement levels by saying "he's on fire!" or "he's going huge!" when a competitor was obviously taking greater risks. An athlete's ability to deal with the fear of a possible crash, in fact, is the mark of an "outstanding run": "Watch out, Richmond," an X Games announcer shouted to the crowd, "he's gonna wreck this place!" A winning competitor laughingly said, "I do what I can to smash into [my opponents] as much as I can." Another competitor said, "If I crash, no big deal; I'm just gonna go for it." NFL commentators introduced the games with images of reckless collisions, and during the game, a "fearless" player was likely to be applauded: "There's no chance that Barry Sanders won't take when he's running the football." In another game, the announcer noted that receiver "Tony Simmons plays big. And for those of you not in the NFL, playing big means you're not afraid to go across the middle and catch the ball and make a play out of it after you catch the ball." Men showing guts in the face of speed and danger was also a major theme in forty of the commercials that we analyzed.

The Televised Sports Manhood Formula

Tens of millions of people, many of them children, watch televised sports programs with their accompanying commercial advertisements. Though there are certainly differences across different kinds of sports as well as across different commercials, when my colleagues and I looked at all of the programming together, we identified ten recurrent themes, outlined above. Taken together, these themes codify a consistent and (mostly) coherent message about what it means to be a man. We call this message the televised sports manhood formula:

> *What is a real man? A real man is strong, tough, aggressive, and above all, a winner in what is still a man's world. To be a winner he has to do what needs to be done. He must be willing to compromise his own long-term health by showing guts in the face of danger, by fighting other men when necessary, and by giving up his body for the team when he's injured. He must avoid being soft; he must be the aggressor, both on the "battlefields" of sports and in his consumption choices. Whether he is playing sports or making choices about which snack food or auto products to purchase, his aggressiveness will net him the ultimate prize: the adoring attention of conventionally beautiful women. He will know if and when he has arrived as a real man when the voices of authority—white males—say he is a real man. But even when he has finally managed to win the big one, has the good car and the right beer, and is surrounded by beautiful women, he will be reminded by*

these very same voices of authority just how fragile this real manhood is: After all, he has to come out and prove himself all over again tomorrow. You're only as good as your last game (or your last purchase).

There is an ideological center to sports culture, and this is it. The major elements of the televised sports manhood formula are evident, in varying degrees, in the football, basketball, baseball, extreme sports, and *SportsCenter* programs and in their accompanying commercials. But it is in the dramatic spectacle of professional wrestling that the televised sports manhood formula is most clearly codified and presented to audiences as an almost seamless package. Boys and young men are drawn to televised professional wrestling in great numbers. Consistently each week, from four to six pro wrestling shows rank among the top ten rated shows on cable television. Professional wrestling is not a "real sport" in the way that baseball, basketball, football, or even extreme sports are. It is a highly stylized and choreographed "sport as theater" form of entertainment. Its producers have *condensed*, and then *amplified*, all of the themes that make up the televised sports manhood formula. Where violence represents a thread in the football or basketball commentary, it makes up the entire fabric of the theatrical narrative of televised pro wrestling. In short, professional wrestling presents viewers with a steady stream of images and commentary that represent a constant fusion of all of the themes that make up the televised sports manhood formula: this is a choreographed sport where all men (except losers) are real men, where women are present as sexy support objects for the men's violent, monumental "wars" against each other. Winners bravely display muscular strength, speed, power, and guts. Bodily harm is (supposedly) intentionally inflicted on opponents. The most ruthlessly aggressive men win, while the passive or weaker men lose, often shamefully. Heroically wrestling while injured, rehabilitating oneself from injuries, and inflicting pain and injury on one's opponent are constant and central themes in the narrative.

In 2001, the head of the World Wrestling Federation Vince McMahon and NBC sports' Dick Ebersol (who two years ago had lost the rights to televise the NFL) each put up a hundred million dollars to launch a new pro football league, the XFL. With its amped-up sex and violence, the XFL was clearly positioning itself to capture the valuable age eighteen to thirty-five male demographic that the NFL had been losing and to which pro wrestling so obviously appealed. And the televised sports manhood formula was its ideological vehicle. NFL players had gotten "soft," it seems, because of rules that protected these spoiled, overpaid players from injury. The XFL would raise the violence level and ensure more exciting collisions by tweaking the rules: there are no fair catches on punts and no quarterback-in-the-grasp stoppages. In the first televised game, Minnesota governor Jesse "the Body" Ventura served as NBC's color commentator and continually (and loudly) bemoaned what he saw as players' lack of toughness. When a quarterback left the game, apparently woozy and beaten up, Ventura criticized him for quitting: "He hasn't even taken a shot to the head yet!"

Cheerleaders were a major part of the XFL marketing strategy and were overtly promoted as sexual partners to the players. Vince McMahon agreed that the cheerleaders are central: "The audience is going to get to know the girls on a first-name basis. Then when the quarterback fumbles or the [receiver] drops the ball—and we know who he's dating— I want our reporters right back in her face on the sidelines demanding to know whether the two of them did the wild thing last night."[43] Commercials promoting the XFL played up this angle: One showed apparently naked cheerleaders getting out of the showers. Another that ran during the first game profiled a player with a cheerleader adoringly draped over his torso. When asked what his "favorite play" was, he responded with a knowing smirk, "I guess right now it'd have to be the bump and run." The creation of the XFL was an overt attempt to use the most obvious elements of the televised sports manhood formula to deliver a young male demographic to sponsors like Anheuser-Busch, AT&T, Burger King, and the U.S. Army. Ratings for the first XFL broadcast in February 2001 were twice as high as had been expected and higher than they had been for game four of the American League Baseball championship series. However, in the ensuing weeks, the television ratings plummeted, and by the spring the league had already declared itself out of business.

Examining the ways that the televised sports manhood formula cuts across sports programming and the accompanying commercials provides important clues to the ways that ideologies of hegemonic masculinity are both promoted by, and in turn serve to support and stabilize, the collection of interrelated institutions that make up the sport-media-commercial complex. The televised sports manhood formula is a master narrative that is produced at the nexus of the institutions of sport, mass media, and corporations that hope to sell products and services to boys and men. As such, this formula appears well suited to discipline boys' and men's bodies, minds, and consumption choices within an ideological field that is conducive to the reproduction of the entrenched interests that profit from the sport-media-commercial complex. The perpetuation of these commercial interests appears to be predicated on boys and men accepting—indeed, glorifying and celebrating—a set of bodily and relational practices that resist and oppose a view of women as fully human and place boys' and men's long-term health prospects in jeopardy.

At a historical moment when hegemonic masculinity has been destabilized by socioeconomic change and by women's and gay liberation movements, the televised sports manhood formula provides a remarkably stable and concrete view of masculinity as grounded in bravery, risk taking, violence, bodily strength, and heterosexuality. And this view of masculinity is given coherence against views of women as sexual support objects or as invisible and thus irrelevant to men's public struggles for glory. Yet, perhaps to be successful in selling products, the commercials sometimes provide a less than seamless view of masculinity. The insecurities of a masculinity in crisis are often tweaked in the commercials when we see weak men, dumb men, and indecisive men being eclipsed by strong, smart, and decisive men and sometimes being humiliated by smarter and more decisive women. In short, this commercialized version of hegemonic masculinity is constructed partly in relation to images of men who *don't* measure up.

The themes that are codified in the televised sports manhood formula both reflect and serve as an ideological support for the interactional tendencies at the center of men's sports culture, as I described them in chapter 2. The dominant images and commentary emitted by the sport-media-commercial complex tweak boys' and men's insecurities and need for connection and respect while proposing that the means to gain such connection and respect are through the paths of violence and risk taking; drinking with the guys; denigrating women and non-aggressive boys; using women as prizes for successful competition with other men and as objectified vessels through which to bond erotically with other men; and suppressing empathy for weakness or vulnerability (in oneself and in others).

The alcohol industry plays a key role in the sport-media-commercial complex. As I discussed in chapter 3, for many years, alcohol (especially beer) advertisements have asserted a strong presence in radio and television sports broadcasts and magazines and at live sports venues. A decade ago, media scholar Lance Strate argued that beer commercials offer male television viewers a sort of "manual on masculinity."[44] Beer is a working man's reward for a job well done, the commercials seem to say, and it is best consumed in some public place, among other men. The consumption of beer confirms one's individual sense of masculinity, solidifies one's membership in a community of men, and positions men as consumers of sexy women. And this is a lesson that alcohol commercials teach to boys and young men far before they have reached legal drinking age.[45] The alcohol industry's central role in sports advertising and promotion is of special importance when we consider the key role of alcohol (as I discussed in chapter 2) in male athletic peer groups' internal bonding and violence against others. In short, alcohol appears to be a key linking factor among men's peer group interactions, sport institutions, and mass media imagery of athletic masculinity.

Drawing these kinds of analytic connections, however tentative, between the dominant ideologies in sports media and the dominant practices at the center of male athletes' worlds moves us toward answers to commonly asked questions. For instance, why do so many boys and men continue to take seemingly irrational risks, submit to pain and injury, and risk long-term debility or even death by playing while injured? The televised sports manhood formula suggests why: the "costs of masculinity" (pain, injury, risk of premature death), according to this formula, appear to be well worth the price. The boys and men who are willing to pay the price always seem to get the glory, respect, and adulation of others, the championships, the big money, the best consumer products, and the beautiful women. Those who don't or can't pay the price are humiliated or ignored by women and are left in the dust by other men. In short, the televised sports manhood formula is a pedagogy through which boys are taught that "paying the price," be it one's bodily health or one's money, gives one access to the privileges that have been historically linked to masculinity: money, power, glory, and women. And the barrage of images of femininity as modellike beauty displayed for and in the service of successful men suggests that heterosexuality is a major lynchpin of the televised sports manhood formula and, on a larger scale, serves as one of the major linking factors in the conservative gender regime of the sport-media-commercial complex.

Problems at the Center

Thus far I have described a fairly consistent package of ideological images that emanate from the cultural center of the sport-media-commercial complex. However, anyone who reads the daily sports pages knows that a large array of problems and scandals are constantly being generated at the center of the institution of sport: Title IX legal suits filed against high schools and colleges; cheating scandals, leading to NCAA sanctions against big-time college athletic programs; illegal activities by athletes and coaches; violence off the field, including rape and wife or girlfriend abuse by athletes and coaches.[46] How do the mass media deal with these problems at the center of American sport? In particular, how has the media handled the now all-too-common spate of stories about male athletes' violence against women?

A decade ago, my colleague Bill Solomon and I analyzed the press coverage of the news story that boxer Sugar Ray Leonard had admitted to having physically abused his wife, including hitting her with his fists, and to using cocaine and alcohol.[47] As we followed the trajectory of this story in major newspapers, we observed that the press very quickly dismissed and ignored the part of the story that dealt with Leonard's violence against his wife and chose instead to discuss the story as a drug abuse story. In other words, the press decided that wife abuse was "outside the frame" of the story; instead, they employed a familiar "jocks on drugs" narrative of sin and redemption. Leonard took drugs; he apologized and said he wouldn't do it again; he was forgiven for his "mistakes"; he was rapidly repositioned as a hero who could resume his "just say no" campaign among children. We argued at the time that the wife abuse story so quickly disappeared from view because the press essentially accepted Leonard's contention that his violence against his wife was a personal matter. In contrast, it was by then well established that an athlete's drug or alcohol abuse is a *public* matter and thus fair game for media scrutiny.

By the end of the 1990s, the idea that news media should simply ignore male athletes' violence against women as private matters had disappeared. There were simply too many incidents (often high profile) of male athletes accused (and sometimes convicted) of beating up and/or raping their wives, girlfriends, or other women. These included the high-profile cases of boxer Mike Tyson, baseball players Jose Canseco and Darryl Strawberry, golfer John Daly, football players Lawrence Phillips, Christian Peter, O. J. Simpson, Mark Chmura, Jake Plummer, and Cornelius Benett, and basketball players Robert Parrish and Jason Kidd. In the 1990s, these stories pushed their way into the frame of media focus, so the question became not *whether* to cover these stories but, rather, *how* to cover them. In an insightful 1999 study, sport studies scholar Mary McDonald compared press coverage of two stories of domestic violence by high-profile sports men—college football coach Dan McCarney, a white man, and major league baseball player Wilfredo Cordero, a Latino man.[48] White men such as McCarney who are violent to women, McDonald suggests, are viewed by the sports media as individually pathological aberrations in an otherwise good system and thus as potential sources of confession and redemption narratives. As such, they become valuable public relations symbols for teams and leagues. Conversely, violence by athletes of color like Cordero tends to be viewed as a logical result of cultural deficiency or a natural racial proclivity to be violent or misogynist. This racialized media frame tends quickly to redeem white males while projecting violence and misogyny onto men of color. In either case, the role of the broader culture of sport in encouraging and rewarding misogyny and violence is not questioned, and sports reporters thus avoid disrupting the smooth and lucrative relationship that they enjoy as promoters of the sport-media-commercial complex.

The 1990s also saw the introduction of HIV-AIDS stories in sport. Big-time men's sports have tended to affirm and celebrate an imagery of masculinity as necessarily fused with a virile heterosexuality. Since HIV-AIDS has been so thoroughly culturally coded as a "gay disease," its appearance in big-time men's sports may have been particularly shocking and potentially disruptive. Shortly after basketball star Ervin "Magic" Johnson announced his HIV-positive status, he vehemently denied rumors that had circulated for years that he was bisexual, a denial that the mainstream media quickly and fully accepted. As sociologist Jim McKay pointed out, the media also placed any "blame" for Johnson's having contracted the virus firmly on the shoulders of women. Johnson was a "marked man," whose only crime had been his nice-guy tendency to do his best to "accommodate" the hordes of aggressive, "wanton women" who had targeted him.[49] Sociologists Shari Dworkin and Faye Linda Wachs examined media coverage of Johnson and two other high-profile athletes who announced that they were HIV-positive—diver Greg Louganis and boxer Tommy Morrison. Dworkin and Wachs observed, as McKay had, that Johnson, "a self-identified heterosexual man, was not stigmatized" by the media when he announced his HIV-positive status. Instead, "he was framed by the mainstream American print media unequivocally as a hero and was lauded for courageously battling a socially stigmatized disease." When white boxer Tommy Morrison contracted the disease, the media did not laud him as a hero as they had Johnson. Morrison's working-class background was noted as a source of his having made "irrational, immature decisions" to allow himself to be targeted by women as "the world's biggest bimbo magnet."[50] What linked coverage of Johnson's and Morrison's HIV-positive announcements was the press's tendency to emphasize the question of how the virus could have been contracted by a heterosexual and then supply the answer: they were just being normal men, unable to resist when scores of sexy women aggressively pursued them.

When gay diver Greg Louganis announced that he had contracted HIV, the press reacted very differently. Despite the fact that Louganis for years had been in an apparently monogamous relationship with one man (and therefore had far fewer sexual partners than Johnson or Morrison had), there still appeared to be no need to question how he contracted the virus: the fact that he was gay seemed answer enough to this question. It was simply assumed that a gay man is likely to contract HIV-AIDS. Dworkin and Wachs concluded that in the sports media, "gay men and 'promiscuous' women are viewed as the virulent agents or problematic vehicle for transmission, while hegemonic masculinity, and the norm of virile male heterosexuality is protected and reaffirmed."[51] Thus, just as the sports media tend to suggest that men of color are primarily to blame for violence against women while deflecting blame either from white men or from the institution of sport, so too do the media project blame onto either heterosexual women or gay men for male athletes' sexual promiscuity and any subsequent contraction of HIV. These tendencies tend to deflect potential critical questions about the routine practices and cultural imagery of heterosexual masculinity that are at once a main source and outcome of the sport-media-commercial complex.

Sports Audiences

In this chapter, I have outlined how the sports media have responded to challenges they faced in the explosion of women's sports by silencing, marginalizing, trivializing, or selectively incorporating imagery of women athletes. I have also outlined the major themes and tendencies at the center of the sports media, codified in the televised sports manhood formula. However, we must be cautious in coming to definitive conclusions as to how the media's current treatment of women athletes as well as its promotion of the values embedded in the televised sports manhood formula might fit into the worlds of sports spectators and fans. It is not possible, merely on the basis of my (or anyone else's) textual analysis of sports programs, to explicate precisely what kind of impact broadcast sports, sports in magazines, and their accompanying commercials have on audiences. Do boys and men swallow the televised sports manhood formula whole? What is the appeal of watching violent sports?[52] Does watching violent sports tend to make some boys and men accept violence, celebrate violence, and act more violently in their daily lives?[53] Do certain groups of boys and men (by age, race-ethnicity, social class, sexual orientation, etc.) derive or construct different meanings from televised sports and their ads? How do the readers of *Sports Illustrated* (most of whom are male) interpret and make meaning of the annual swimwear issue or the similarly coded photo spread of Anna Kournikova? Do *SI* readers view the highly paradoxical photo of Jenny Thompson as consistent with conventional media sexual objectification of women, or does this image break the normal media coding of female athletes, thus jarring and challenging audiences to think of women's bodies in new ways? What meanings do girls and women derive from watching central men's sports? How do girls and young women respond to the overtly liberal feminist messages in ads by Nike and other commercial promoters of sports? Even when women athletes are trivialized or devalued in media portrayals, do some audiences nevertheless create more positive interpretations and meanings?[54] Are boys' and men's conceptions of gender challenged or changed when strong and successful women athletes (like the U.S. champion soccer team) are pulled to the center of cultural discourse? Are girls and women empowered by the proliferation of images of strong women, even if those images are relegated mostly to marginal media? Will young girls who are exposed to more images of powerful, successful, and athletic women choose in the future to rally around these images rather than the image of Barbie? These kinds of questions are best approached through direct research with audiences, very little of which has thus far been conducted in sport studies. However, audience research in general tells us that audiences interpret, use, and draw meanings from media variously, on the basis of factors such as social class, race-ethnicity, and gender.[55]

It is also important to go beyond my emphasis in this chapter on the ways that the dominant themes at the center of the sports media reinforce the hegemony of current race, gender, and commercial relations. In addition to these continuities, there are some identifiable discontinuities within and among the various sports programs and within and among the accompanying commercials. For instance, television commercials are far more varied in the ways that they present gender imagery than sports programs themselves are. Though the dominant tendency in commercials accompanying sports programs is either to erase women or to present them as stereotypical support- or sex-objects, a significant minority of commercials present themes that set up boys and men as insecure and/or obnoxious schmucks and women as secure, knowledgeable, and authoritative. In addition, a few athletes such as Dennis Rodman offer up images that are profoundly mixed and paradoxical in their gender, sexual, and racial meanings.[56] Audience research with people of all ages and backgrounds would shed fascinating light on how people variously decode and interpret these more complex, mixed, and paradoxical gender images against the dominant, hegemonic image of the televised sports manhood formula.

I end this chapter where it began: at the Rose Bowl, with over ninety thousand spectators and a television audience of millions cheering a women's soccer match. Women athletes and women's sports are clearly here to stay. No longer simply symbolically annihilated, they are nevertheless still largely marginalized by the central sports media. However, the continued rise in the popularity of women's sports and the proliferation of problems generated at the center of men's sports are two major destabilizing forces that will continue to fundamentally challenge the dominant values, symbology, and interests of the sport-media-commercial complex.

CHAPTER 5

Contesting the Center:
Just Do What?

In the early 1970s, Virginia Slims became one of the first major corporations to sponsor professional women's sports with its support of women's professional tennis. The tobacco company pitched its anorexically skinny cigarette to women with a slogan appropriated from the second wave of feminism: You've come a long way, baby![1] Since then, girls' and women's athletic participation has soared. And during that same stretch of time, women also narrowed the smoking and lung cancer gaps between themselves and men.[2]

In the 1990s, Nike implored and encouraged girls and women to "Just Do It" in sports, just like the men. A series of Nike television commercials featuring strong, athletic women inspired a whole generation of girls and young women.[3] And indeed, research began to illustrate the positive benefits of athletic participation for girls and women. In this same decade, however, the women's equivalent of men's "pain principle" in sports blossomed, because female athletes learned that they too were expected to risk their long-term health for short-term athletic gains. Knee injuries among women basketball and soccer players skyrocketed.[4] And young girls in elite-level gymnastics and figure skating often face regimes of emotional and sexual abuse from coaches, encouragement to train and compete while in pain, and severe dieting that results in serious injuries, eating disorders, depression, and even suicide attempts.[5]

At the end of the 1990s, the WNBA was born with great fanfare, complete with television contracts and the institutional backing of the NBA. The initial television ads for the new women's league borrowed a common line from playgrounds in cities throughout the United States: "We Got Next!" Ten years ago, the women basketball players (most of them African American) who were students in my university classes used to tell me, proudly, that they had it better than the men players. "The men," they'd tell me, "are so focused on the false dream of playing in the NBA, they ignore their schooling. We *know* that our athletic scholarships are a ticket to a college degree, and we focus on that."[6] Today, equity advocates celebrate the fact that girls and young women too can dream of pro basketball careers. But is this development entirely beneficial? It sure hasn't been such a productive dream for most young *male* athletes. Thirty-two percent of male high school basketball and football players (and 43 percent of African American male athletes) think they will make it to the pros. In fact, their chances of going pro are about 1 in 2,340.[7] And now, sociologist Sohaila Shakib finds evidence in her research with Los Angeles area high school girls' basketball teams that poor African American girls are increasingly likely to view their basketball skills as a ticket to the WNBA big time.[8]

Women athletes *have* come a long way. Girls and women in sports *are* "just doing it." They are no longer waiting to be invited. They have asserted that, like it or not, they "got next." At this exciting moment in history, though, it behooves us to ask whether coming a long way and just doing it represent a tidal wave of fun and healthful opportunities for the masses of girls and women or simply a trickle of high-profile career opportunities for a few and serious injury and eating disorders for the many. Does "we got next" mean that girls and women will someday enjoy the status, prestige, and power that have been associated with sports, or does it mean that poor, especially African American, girls will now be given the dubious opportunity to focus their aspirations on the distant mirage of athletic fame and fortune while overlooking the very real opportunities that high school and college education might actually afford them? In other words, as girls and women assert themselves and are pulled, however tenuously, closer to the center of sport, will athletic participation be a healthy and empowering experience for them, or will they simply be subject to all of the "costs of masculinity" (health, relational, financial) that male athletes have paid out for so many years? These questions point to the key paradoxes and tensions in today's shifting gender regime of sport.

Athletic progress for girls and women in the post–Title IX era has not been without its costs, questions, and dilemmas. But make no mistake about it: the mass movement of girls and women into sports has empowered women in ways that have challenged and destabilized the masculinist center of American sport.[9] In this book, I have pointed mainly to how this contested center has reasserted itself, by continuing (1) to sex segregate children, coaches, and sports media; (2) to structure athletic programs inequitably; (3) to promote, justify, and glorify men's violence; (4) to allow, perhaps even encourage, group-based dynamics of misogyny and homophobia and suppression of empathy to operate as the core values system of men's sports; and (5) to render women athletes invisible in sports media or to promote imagery that ghettoizes or belittles them. These reactionary responses powerfully reassert a masculinist, corporate center to sport. But they also give us hints at the very real vulnerabilities of this center.

This book has not been a story of a fundamental transformation of sport. Clearly, there are entrenched interests (commercial, masculine, white, and heterosexual) that have responded to challenges in ways that have largely held sport's institutional and cultural center intact. However, neither has this simply been a story of social reproduction or the recuperative powers of sport to remain unchanged. Rather, it is a dynamic story of power at play—of challenges to the center, operating at the level of everyday group practice, of institutions, and of cultural symbol—that are variously resisted, crushed out, ghettoized, and partly incorporated by the center. The results are partial changes in institutions, a shifting terrain of cultural imagery, and a new set of relational contexts that create the possibility for new kinds of experiences and, thus, new kinds of challenges. Girls' and women's quest for equity and fairness will continue to be fundamental to these challenges. The ways that the gender regime of sport (and, indeed, that of the entire sport-media-commercial complex) responds to these challenges will have a profound ripple effect on the larger gender order. Currently, I see three trends that are pulling the gender regime of sport simultaneously (albeit quite unevenly) in different directions: the ghettoization model, the just do it model, and the social justice model.[10]

The Ghettoization Model

Women's movement into sports is dramatic and, I believe, irreversible. But current struggles for equity and fairness might result in women's sports being remarginalized and reghettoized. A similar thing happened once before. Sport historians describe how the twentieth century opened with a dramatic "wave of athletic feminism" that accompanied the first wave of feminism.[11] Women athletes were in the forefront of challenging Victorian limits on women's use of public space and constraining notions about natural female frailty. By the late 1920s, though, women's burgeoning athleticism began to meet a virulent backlash (from educators, medical doctors, and religious leaders) that expressed a fear of a growing "mannishness" among physically active women. By the 1930s, the explosion of female athleticism was largely contained. Men's sports were reestablished as the unquestioned center of athletics, and an easily ignored sphere of limited female exercise continued on the margins.

To the extent that competitive women's sports persisted throughout the middle decades of the twentieth century, they survived in two highly marginalized athletic ghettos: women's schools and universities, and popular public sports organizations (both amateur, such as the Amateur Athletic Union, and professional, such as the All American Girls Baseball League in the 1940s). Women physical educators in schools and universities warded off fears of mannishness by carefully developing and promoting what sociologist Nancy Theberge has called an "adapted model" of sports—playing games that had very different rules from the games that the men played.[12] Adapted-model sports ensured that women engaged in less strenuous activity that required less movement, less bodily contact, and very little, if any, bodily aggression. "The moderate, wholesome athlete idealized by physical educators," writes historian Susan Cahn, "fused appropriate female athleticism with a middle-class concept of womanhood characterized by refinement, dignity, and self-control."[13] The more market-driven promoters of women's popular sports, by contrast, countered fears of mannishness in a different way: by promoting women athletes' sex appeal. To these promoters, "sport would enhance the sexual appeal of young women, at the same time heightening the viewing pleasure of audiences entranced by attractive female competitors."[14] Cahn describes both of these tendencies as facilitating a shift, but also a new form of containment, in the dominant conception of femininity:

> To alter public impressions of the masculine female athlete, physical educators and promoters of popular sport formulated competing concepts of athletic womanhood: the healthy, wholesome athlete of moderate ability and limited activity; and the exuberant, sexy, competitive athlete. Both ideals incorporated athletic enjoyment and competence into notions of femininity. Yet neither fundamentally challenged the commonsense belief that rugged sport and athletic ability were masculine in character.... The model of the athlete as beauty queen appeared to admit energy, vigor and muscle tone into the concept of femininity. However, these were usually presented as benefits accrued toward marriage and motherhood.... The athletic beauty-queen model depended on cultural images and practices *outside* of sport—beauty contests, pageantry, sexual appeals—for legitimacy. In the end women athletes found acceptance not simply for their skill but for their usefulness and attractiveness to men. The unmodified "athlete" remained a male figure.[15]

Aspects of these two mid-twentieth-century forms of ghettoization (adapted-model women's sports and the portrayal of women athletes as sexualized beauty queens) are echoed in tendencies in women's sports today. Cahn's summary statement—that "the unmodified 'athlete' remained a male figure"—captures the essence of women's athletic ghettoization today. As I noted in my discussion of backlash in chapter 4, opponents of equality for women athletes, such as radio talk show host Tom Leykis and many of his listeners, appear to be threatened precisely by the idea that women are claiming the image, rights, and privileges of the role of "athlete." As long as women quietly play adapted forms of sports in their separate and unequal ghettos or allow themselves to be marketed as media sex goddesses, the unmodified cultural definition of "athlete" remains securely male.

There is plenty of evidence that women's sports continue to be institutionally marginalized, as my discussion in chapter 3 of smaller budgets, limited facilities, and lower salaries in girls' and women's sports illustrated. There is also evidence that some of this marginalization is taking the form of adapted-model sports: women's basketball, for instance, is now much closer to the men's game than it was forty years ago but is still played with some different rules and with a smaller ball; girls are channeled very early into softball (an adapted form of baseball), while boys play the higher-status baseball.[16] And media coverage of women's sports is largely ghettoized, as I discussed in chapter 4. Positive, respectful coverage of women's sports is mostly relegated to marginal niche markets, while the televised sports manhood formula continues to be projected, largely uncontested, into tens of millions of American homes every day.

There are some limited benefits to ghettoization. Just as it did nearly a century ago, ghettoization helps women's sports sidestep the vicious counterpunch of patriarchal backlash. Today, some older women who worked as physical educators and coaches in the pre–Title IX era will tell you that they have very mixed feelings about the "progress" that has been made in the last thirty years. Women's sports in that earlier era were underfunded and devalued, they agree, but they also provided relatively autonomous safe havens, where girls and women could participate in healthy exercise, experience some limited forms of bodily empowerment, learn leadership skills, and develop beneficial health practices. So too today: as long as they stay safely and quietly on the margins, women's sports can continue, even thrive, with some relative autonomy.

Few advocates of women's sports, though, would favor a return to the extreme levels of ghettoization that characterized these sports in the pre–Title IX era. Those inside the walls of a ghetto may feel some protection, safety, and autonomy, but these very same walls are holding them inside, containing and limiting their choices. Today's girls and young women assume that they have the right to unfettered opportunities to play sports; they do not want to cower within the safe but constraining walls of a new female protectionism. Further, ghettoization ensures the containment of any challenge that girls' and women's sports might pose to the day-to-day culture of masculinity, to the inequitable distribution of institutional resources, status, and prestige afforded men and women athletes in schools, universities, and professional athletics, and to the dominant masculinist symbolism of the sports media.

The Just Do It Model

Girls' and women's agency, especially their assertive quest for equal athletic opportunities and resources in schools and public spaces, resists the imposition of a purely marginalized status. In this book, I have emphasized the continued problems and sex inequities in sport, but a glance at the past thirty years or so reveals tremendous change. Clearly, with respect to numerical participation, struggles for equitable opportunities for girls and women in communities, schools, and colleges and increased media attention to women's sports, significant progress has been made. The glass is half full. Girls' and women's sports are gradually nudging closer to the institutional and cultural center, and this movement is due to a combination of forces, all of which spring from the successes of second-wave feminism. These forces include (1) assertive and effective deployment of equal opportunity laws that have pressed schools, colleges, and communities to commit more resources to girls' and women's sports; (2) a general shift in cultural values toward viewing vigorous exercise and competitive sports as healthy and positive for girls and women; and (3) selective promotion of women's sports and imagery of female athleticism by market forces emanating from the sport-media-commercial complex.[17]

In some ways, pressing for equal opportunities for girls and women help to alter the masculinist center of sport. One of the most impressive aspects of this change is the extent to which many fathers of girl athletes have begun to coach and teach their daughters to play sports (as most fathers previously did only with sons). And some of these fathers (few of whom would have defined themselves as feminists) have become equity activists when unfair school- or community-based sports programs have blocked their daughters. We have also seen, though, how a quest for simple equal opportunities for girls and women in sports can invoke a vitriolic backlash. This backlash may be grounded in some men's fears that including women in "their" sports will destroy the homosocial bond that has become so foundational to their sense of self. Others may resist women's inclusion in sports because they know (or sense) that the equation of athleticism with men and masculinity has served as an important ideological underpinning of men's social power and privilege.

Sex Segregation versus Integration: What's at Stake?

True equal opportunity—allowing girls and women the right to play with boys and men in integrated sports—may most directly threaten these privileges. For instance, in 2000, Heather Sue Mercer won a lawsuit against Duke University, which she claimed had unfairly denied her the opportunity to compete as a placekicker on its Division I football team.[18] After Mercer made the game-winning twenty-eight-yard field goal in a season-ending intrasquad scrimmage, Duke head coach Fred Goldsmith told reporters that she had made the team. However, when practice started for the next season, Goldsmith cut Mercer from the team, and she says that the coach suggested to her that she should try out for beauty pageants instead of the football team. Situations like the Mercer case are becoming increasingly common. Given the rapidly closing skill and muscle gap between women and men athletes, and given the reality that certain sports are not available to girls and women, more of them are claiming the right to compete in boys' and men's high school and college football, wrestling, and ice hockey programs.

What's at stake in giving girls and women equal opportunities in sports? And why do some men resist these efforts? We should not underestimate the possibility that some men, especially those who have their hands on athletic department budgets, are simply defending men's historical "rights" to control these resources. But I think the threat of women's playing with men, especially in the most masculine sports such as football, wrestling, and ice hockey, runs far deeper than mere budgets. A major ideological outcome of the high visibility of these sports has been their ability to provide ideological "proof" of the natural physical superiority of all men over all women. This belief is dealt a severe blow when a woman football player takes the field and catches a pass or kicks a field goal; when a high school girl wrestler pins a boy; when a girl absorbs an aggressive body check from a boy ice hockey player and simply gets up and keeps playing. But people rarely have the opportunity to witness such an occurrence, because sport has been organized as segregated and unequal, thus reinforcing what sport studies scholar Mary Jo Kane calls an "oppositional binary," a belief that men and women are categorically different (and thus unequal).[19] But when we grant girls and women equal opportunities to play sports alongside boys and men, a different truth is revealed: males and females are not categorically different. We all exist on a "continuum of difference," where some women are taller, stronger, faster, and better athletes than some men, and vice versa. Increasingly, advocates of women's sports are deploying this idea in their strategies to secure equal opportunities for girls and women.[20]

As I discussed in chapter 1, the main tendency in North American children's sports is to enforce early sex segregation, which delivers a powerful message to children that boys and girls are as naturally and categorically different as Barbie Girls are from Sea Monsters. Equal opportunity for girl athletes promises to expose the falsehood of this oppositional gender binary by empirically demonstrating the continuum of difference. The potential power of this lesson was brought home to me dramatically a few years ago, when my older son played his first-ever T-ball game as a six-year-old. The teams were integrated, though each team had only one or two girls. The first time a girl on the opposing team stood up to the tee to hit, she swung mightily, missed, and nearly fell down. The boys on my son's team laughed so wildly at her, some of them tumbled to the ground. On her second swing, she connected and drove a screaming line drive right up the center of the diamond. Again, my son's teammates fell down, but this time to get out of the way of the ball while the girl circled the bases with a home run. This incident passed without much comment by anybody, but it struck me as a powerful learning experience—for the girl, that she could withstand ridicule, rise to the occasion, and beat the boys; for the boys, that girls can be as good as, sometimes even better than, boys at physical competition. Segregated sports deny children this kind of early demonstration of the reality of the continuum of difference.

But does this mean that we should simply and immediately sex integrate all sports? I sometimes ask my students this question: Imagine a whole generation of young adults who have been raised in a society of absolute equal opportunity in sports—equal numbers of teams and facilities, equal status from peers, equal encouragement from parents and coaches, equal attention in the mass media. Would we then see equal numbers of women playing at the highest levels alongside men on pro ice hockey, baseball, basketball, or football teams? My students puzzle and argue over this hypothetical question. Some stubbornly insist that, indeed, women have been held back by lack of opportunities and that, under conditions of equal opportunity, women's natural equality with men would be revealed, and professional teams would eventually become fully sex integrated. Others express the less politically popular (in my classes, at least) view that men are still going to be stronger and faster, with more power and body mass, and that even conditions of equal opportunity won't change that fact enough to make women capable of playing in the NFL, NBA, or NHL.

This question and the responses to it expose the limits of the liberal just do it model of equal opportunity in sports. Even if we can imagine a world where girls and boys are given absolute equal opportunities in sports (i.e., a world in which children are not constrained by sex inequalities), we must also confront two related facts that the just do it model of equal opportunity too often ignores: first, women's and men's bodies exist on a continuum of difference, yes, but there are still average differences between them; and second, the most popular and valued sports (football, basketball, ice hockey) are historically organized around the most extreme possibilities of *men's* bodies.

Take, for instance, the relationship between body height and the game of basketball. If we line up all of the students in a high school or a university according to height, tremendous overlap between the sexes will be revealed (some women are taller than some men). However, two other realities will also be revealed: first, men's average height will likely be about five inches more than women's average height; and second, at the tallest end of the line, all or nearly all of the people will be men. Now, if we overlay these collective height differences between the sexes onto basketball, a game that by its rules, strategies, and goals tends to favor and reward taller players over shorter ones, we can see that, at least at its highest levels (big time college and professional basketball), very few women will be big enough to compete equally with men. Under conditions of absolute equal opportunity, I believe some women would be big, strong, and good enough athletes to play with the men in big time college and pro basketball, baseball, football, and ice hockey. But it seems to me that these sports would still remain disproportionately dominated by men. Before concluding, though, that men are (even if simply "on average") naturally better athletes than women, we need to recognize that there are other aspects of bodies that tend to favor and reward more extreme possibilities of *women's* bodies. For instance, most likely very few, if any, men could compete at the top levels of women's gymnastics on a balance beam, and women's higher average body fat ratios give them an advantage in long-distance cold-water swimming.

The question then becomes not whether women's or men's bodies are "superior" but, instead, what are our cultural values? What kinds of physical activities do we support, valorize, and celebrate as "sport"? A quick look at the last century shows that we tend culturally to elevate sports that entail explosive physical power and domination expressed through aggressive bodily contact and collision. In other words, we most highly value and reward those sports that express the most extreme possibilities of male bodies. As I discussed in chapter 3, these sports—football, ice hockey, basketball, baseball—developed historically as masculine-gendered institutions. The values upon which they are based (today summarized in the televised sports manhood formula) are sold by the sport-media-commercial complex as *the* sport values. As long as the dominant institutional forms of sport are gendered in this way, women athletes will be operating at a decided disadvantage to men, even under conditions of equal opportunity.

For these reasons and others, integration of women and men in sports is unlikely to develop too rapidly. True, there are some notable instances of coed sports among children, among adults in community leagues, and even at the professional level (e.g., mixed doubles in tennis).[21] But most sports are, and will continue to be for the foreseeable future, sex segregated. This means that nearly all cases for equal opportunity for girls and women are going to originate from separate teams and leagues, operating from sport's institutional margins, and will be aimed at gaining access to resources and opportunities currently being monopolized by those at the center. Can separate ever be fully equal? Can an acknowledgement of "difference" coexist with institutional equity?[22] Can girls' and women's sports ever be fully incorporated into the center? Should they always want to be?

Just Do . . . Corporate Individualism?

The just do it model has been partly successful, largely because it operates within the parameters of liberal traditions of individual equal opportunity. Advocates of women's sports have deployed existing laws—and forged new ones, when necessary—to press for increasing resources for girls and women. They have also been adept at taking up long-standing cultural values of equal opportunity for all and strategically turning them toward arguments for fairness for girls and women in sports, arguments that make any opposition appear to be outright antidemocratic and un-American. The Women's Sports Foundation, a high-profile advocacy organization begun by Billie Jean King in 1974, effectively fuses strategies of advocating numerical equity, research, and educational work that promote positive images of the healthy benefits of sports for girls and women with corporate promotion of women's sports.[23] Feminist scholars have argued that the WSF epitomizes both the contributions and the limitations of the liberal feminist ideals of equal opportunity in sports for girls and women.[24]

There are two general limitations of the just do it model, both of which are grounded in its mostly unexamined individualism: (1) its lack of a critical institutional analysis, and (2) its increasing reliance on large corporations to provide the financial support and cultural imagery that define and promote a certain kind of equity for girls and women in sports. Are there arguments against strategizing to get major corporations involved in promoting and funding girls' and women's sports? Advocates of this strategy—especially in the United States, where the government takes an extremely laissez-faire approach to sport[25]—might reply, why not? After all, corporate sponsorship and promotion are some of the most important driving forces behind the success of *men's* sports. If women have hopes of being able to "do it" like the men, they need the same kinds of financial support and promotion. And despite corporate America's role as the driving force behind the cultural hegemony of the televised sports manhood formula, there really is no corporate conspiracy to freeze out women's sports. Corporations are gendered organizations, yes, but they also kneel before the bottom line: if they believe they can make a buck off women's sports, they will promote women's sports. Indeed, marketing data show that women purchase a disproportionate amount of the sports and fitness equipment and 86 percent of the sports apparel in the United States.[26] Drawing from this data, the Women's Sports Foundation has convinced several major corporations to support their research, scholarships, and other advocacy work for women's sports.[27] Clearly, the WSF's relationship with these corporations has helped to fund some important advances in girls' and women's sports. What's in it for the sponsors? Some corporations see an untapped market and want to capture it: the Gatorade folks know that women consume sports drinks, too; Reebok and Nike want to sell shoes and clothing to women; Mervins wants to pitch its sports bras and other fitness apparel to women; General Motors and Chrysler know that women buy cars; Miller wants women to drink its beer; Phillip Morris would love to see young women light up. It is in these corporations' interests to support and promote women's sports. And so, what's the problem with this?

The just do it model approaches sex equity as though the institutional center is the place to be, and women deserve the right to be there with the men. This belief, of course, is based on simple notions of fairness: the center is where the power, status, excitement, and resources are; a few shouldn't be allowed to monopolize it just because they happen to have been born male. But the just do it model operates from a naively optimistic liberalism that assumes that if we simply open doors, women will be able to march "from the margins to the center," and everything will be okay. As I discussed in chapter 3, when we look at what has happened to other "marginal sports" that promoters have pulled toward the center (such as certain extreme sports like snowboarding and skateboarding), we can see the mixed results.[28] These sports were created in the first place by people who were disenchanted with the rigid rules, hierarchical control, star system, and win-at-all-costs values that characterize institutional sport. The cultural margins appeared to them be a place of relative autonomy, community, creativity, and individuality that were relatively unfettered by the rigidity of institutional sport. Once pulled to the center by television and corporate sports promoters, though, these sports increasingly have taken on the trappings of other sports: rationalized systems of rules, hierarchical and individualistic star systems, the creation of "rebel" athletes who look like walking corporate billboards, and the elevation of win-at-all-costs values.

Drawing a distinction between individuality and individualism is a key to understanding what happens as social forms are pulled closer to the institutional center. *Individuality* might be thought of as the uniqueness of every person, based on one's personal style, creative abilities, and actions. *Individualism* might be seen as the social ideology that is expressed as an aggressive desire to be on top of or to be seen as better than others. Seen this way, the former concept is creative and conducive to community; the latter is hierarchical and destructive of community.

Institutional life (as most children and adults experience it in schools, families, media, sports, churches, and workplaces) tends to crush individuality and replace it with a distorted quest for individualism. Consumer capitalism then thrives on tapping the insecurities inherent in people's quest for individualism: The most hip ads hail the consumer to "buy this and be a rebel" (just like the hundreds of millions of other rebels out there). As millions of consumers express their rebellious individualism by conforming to the latest corporate fashions, marketing experts comb the margins of culture, seeking new expressions of creative style and individuality, and then they pull these expressions into the center by mass producing and marketing them. Style becomes fashion, as moments of creative individuality are converted through corporate marketing into opportunities for the masses to pursue individualism through consumption.[29] The just do it model of advocacy for women's sports equity has bought into both the promise and the limitations of this corporate individualism.

To the extent that equity activists are successful in pressing the liberal feminist or third-wave feminist-inspired just do it model closer to the center, sport culture and institutions will change in some significant ways.[30] In a more equitable system, girls and women will enjoy a greater share of opportunities and resources; salaries and corporate endorsement contracts of high-profile women athletes and coaches will be closer to those of their male counterparts; a more diverse imagery of women athletes will be available in popular culture. These would all be changes to applaud. But the just do it model's uncritical, even celebratory, joining of forces with corporate individualism is also fully compatible with a reproduction of many of the most unhealthy aspects of sport. Under such a model, resources will be mobilized with the goal of producing a few high-profile women stars who can deliver audiences of willing consumers to large corporations. Meanwhile, the masses of young female athletes will be taught and encouraged (just like the boys) to take unhealthy bodily risks and to suppress their empathy for others while they engage in dog-eat-dog competition to reach the largely mythical "top."

And here is where a distinction might very well be drawn between *playing sports* and being a highly committed *athlete*. A recent survey commissioned by the Women's Sports Foundation hints at this distinction.[31] The researchers found differences between teens who played some sports and those who were "highly involved" in sports (those which I am calling athletes). Teenaged boys and girls appear to derive some health benefits from playing sports: they are statistically less likely than nonathletes to use illicit drugs, drink alcohol, smoke cigarettes, or attempt suicide. In addition, girls who play sports have been found to have more positive body images than girls who do not play sports and are more likely to use seatbelts when riding in cars. On the other hand, "highly involved athletes" have been found to be *more* involved in dangerous risk taking and unhealthy practices: they are more likely to use anabolic steroids, more likely to binge drink, and twice as likely to be suicidal. Highly involved girl athletes are also more likely than nonathletes to use dieting and exercise to control their weight and to use extreme forms of weight control like vomiting and/or laxatives.

Just as we have seen that health and other dangers (especially the triad of men's violence) are associated with highly involved male athletes, we see growing evidence of an emerging set of problems particular to girls as more of them are pulled to the center of athletic institutions and culture. And this dynamic is played out differently for different groups of boys and girls. When I wrote *Power at Play*, I noted that the white, middle-class men I interviewed generally found that having played sports had aided them, both in the transition to a career outside sports and in their future careers in education, medicine, and other professions. By contrast, the poor, working-class, and mostly African American men I interviewed tended to face more difficult transitions to postsports life and found that having been a highly involved athlete did not benefit them much, if at all, in postsports jobs or careers. Race and class-based structures of opportunity similarly constrain and enable girls' choices. So, we should expect that as girls' overall sports participation continues to boom (bringing benefits to many participants), a disproportionate number of those who come to define themselves centrally as athletes will come from poor, working-class, and ethnic minority backgrounds. The implications of these findings are, I think, that we should encourage the most widespread and equitable system of opportunities in schools, sports organizations, and city parks and recreation centers for all children to enjoy the benefits of playing sports. But we simultaneously should question and resist the ways that the hierarchical, elite star system shaped by the interests of the sport-media-commercial complex is constantly filtering down and shaping school and community sports. Parents, teachers, coaches, media, and sports organizations should carefully consider the extent to which, for girls *and* for boys, playing sports can be a very good thing; becoming a highly involved athlete may not be a very good thing.[32] And if, as a society, we truly care about eliminating poverty and racism, we would do better to invest massively in better schools, housing, health care, and decent-paying jobs than to encourage impoverished youth to use sports as a way up and out of poverty.[33]

Considering these distinctions—between playing sports and being an athlete, between individualism and individuality—raises the more general question of why we should assume that the centripetal force, which pulls everything toward the center, is necessarily always a good thing. The center, after all, is a place of athletes and individualism; the margins are where people play sports and where there may be more space for individuality to thrive. And perhaps the concept of margins and center is an inadequate analogy to describe the processes at work here, because the idea of the center seems always to be defined as the ideal place to be. Instead, as sociologist Kum-Kum Bhavnani has suggested, perhaps it is a mistake to try to make social change by advocating a movement of less powerful people from the margins to center.[34] When some previously marginalized people succeed in moving to the center, she implies, they succeed only in becoming a part of the system that oppresses whatever groups still remain at the margins. Rather than fighting to become the latest perpetrators of the problem, like the pigs in Orwell's famous fable *Animal Farm*, Bhavnani advocates embracing positions of marginality as ideal locations from which groups can wage a "permanent revolution" against the distorted human relations at the center.

This debate concerning the relationship of the margins to the center summarizes the paradoxical space between the just do it model and the ghettoization model in women's quest for equality in sport and other institutions. To the extent that some women manage to "just do it" in ways that enable them to share men's institutional power and privileges, they may simply become more effective agents in re-creating similarly oppressive social relations, perhaps in racial-ethnic or class relations. To the extent that women refuse to move to and operate within this impure and corrupt center, they may retain their ability to shape and promote different, less oppressive, even oppositional notions of sport and physical activity. These ideas from the margins hold the potential to demonstrate alternatives to the sport-media-commercial complex's dominant structures, practices, and symbols of gender, race, sexuality, and commercialization. But they may also simultaneously doom themselves to all the limitations of marginal status: fewer resources and opportunities, less power, continued vulnerability to second-class status. If women's sports remain on the margins, any new ideas or practices generated there would be unlikely to challenge the center of sport; as such, women's sports would become a comfortable ghetto that relieves pressure from, rather than challenging and changing, the center.

The Social Justice Model

The ghettoization model and the just do it model are the major social tendencies at work today. These twin trends are also two aspects of the same social process. Neither will fundamentally alter the values or power relations at the center. Ghettoization is a result of the center's interactional, institutional, and symbolic power to push girls' and women's sports away from where the most highly valued action is. Like a swirling whirlpool in a surging river, the center exerts a powerful centrifugal force that pushes girls' and women's sports away from the center into quiet eddies and pools near the shores of the river. But the agency of girls and women, with the support of women's sports advocates, has presented us with an alternative model, based on the liberal ideal of equal opportunity. Girls and women have resisted ghettoization and have assertively pushed themselves toward the center, demanding equity and fairness.

Working in concert with this agency, the powerful, swirling whirlpool of the center exerts a magnetic centripetal force that sucks in anything that gets too close, subjecting it to the center's own powerful current and motion. The market today provides the main impetus in the centripetal force at sport's center. As some women's sports and some women athletes are pulled into the swirling waters of the sport-media-commercial complex, they will surely be dazzled by the dizzying power of it all. But ultimately, they will be sucked down and into the same forms and forces that have made commercialized men's sports such an attractive nuisance in American life.

To avoid the twin pitfalls of either being pushed into the quiet marginal eddies of irrelevance or being sucked into the belly of the beast, a third model needs to be counterposed to the ghettoization model and the just do it model. The social justice model fights against the oppressive and unjust aspects of ghettoization at the same time as it recognizes that fundamental social critique and oppositional strategies can be forged from the margins. It also acknowledges the paradoxes of the corporate individualist just do it model of equal opportunity and attempts to work with it creatively rather than ignore it. Moving toward social justice, at this historical juncture, involves adopting a simultaneous quest for simple fairness and equal opportunities for girls and women *along with* critical actions aimed at fundamentally transforming the center of men's sports. The social justice model recognizes that men, especially poor men and racial-ethnic and/or sexual minority men, are dehumanized, exploited, and hurt by the sport-media-commercial complex. Why should women want to be incorporated equally into this? Instead of simply joining in the corporate chorus that tells girls to just do it, the social justice model asks the crucial question: Just do *what*?

It is the asking of this fundamental question—Just do *what*?—that makes the social justice model distinct from the liberal just do it model. To be sure, the real world is complicated; nothing falls neatly into any one of the three models that I have described in this chapter. Instead, when we look at concrete sport formations, we see complex interweavings of aspects of these three models. For instance, I have discussed the

Women's Sports Foundation as the epitome of the liberal-corporate just do it model. But there are aspects of WSF activism that shade into the social justice model. For instance, their research and activism around sexual harassment in sport challenge some of the fundamental gender relations of sport's center. And while earlier critics were probably correct that WSF was slow to deal with lesbian issues and homophobia in sport, in recent years WSF has directly taken on these issues. Liberal and more radical versions of feminism exist in a creative tension within organizations like the WSF.[35]

The rise of sports in gay communities, including the now successfully institutionalized Gay Games, is similarly paradoxical. The very existence of muscular and athletic gay men disrupts the dominant ideological equation that athleticism equals heterosexual masculinity. However, the dominant forms of gay men's sports are developing within a just do it model. As sport philosopher Brian Pronger has argued, gay athletic organizations have largely replicated and celebrated, rather than challenged or changed, the distorted and unhealthy hypermasculinity so central to men's sports.[36]

To give another example of this lived complexity, aspects of the ghettoization model, the just do it model, and the social justice model can be seen in the current formation of the WNBA. Women's professional basketball is a ghettoized sport: the game is played according to adapted rules (smaller ball, etc.), the league name is gender marked (*Women's* National Basketball Association), the players get far less pay than their NBA counterparts,[37] and they get far less and poorer quality media exposure. But the WNBA can also be seen as representing the current apex of the ideology and practice of the corporate just do it model of women's sports. Additionally, the WNBA's practices sometimes shade toward a social justice model of feminism. For instance, a WNBA game that I attended a year ago featured "breast cancer awareness night" along with several invited community women's organizations, including the group I was with, the California Women's Law Center. It struck me that the community relations and marketing strategies of the WNBA are clearly different from those of the NBA: I'd not go to a Lakers game and expect to see invited groups of progressive activists joining in a celebration of "testicular cancer awareness night." The WNBA promotion can be seen, on the one hand, as clever marketing that promotes a second-wave feminist issue, women's health, and uses it to link up with progressive women's communities with the goal of pulling them in as customers. But it is also a sign of the way that the rise of women's sports is organically connected to the feminist movement, at least to liberal feminist sensibilities that have seeped into the culture at so many levels.

Similarly, before the beginning of the 2001 season, the WNBA Los Angeles Sparks decided openly to pitch their product to the local lesbian community. This was a major departure in marketing strategy. In 1998, Sparks president Johnny Buss had cautiously distanced the team from the lesbian market, saying, "I know the lesbian community is showing up, so I leave them alone. I'd rather focus on pulling in more males. Would it hurt if most of our spectators were lesbian? That's hard to say." Perhaps responding to the slight drop-off in attendance in the 2000 season, the Sparks decided to shift partly away from their previous marketing strategy of targeting heterosexual families with children. When they announced their upcoming pep rally at Girl Bar Los Angeles, a lesbian dance club, Sparks marketing officials said, "We want to market this basketball team to fans whoever they might be, be they an inner-city youth basketball team or someone of an alternative lifestyle." This overt shift to marketing to Los Angeles lesbians was treated cooly by WNBA officials, who called it a "local promotion; a team matter."[38]

These examples of WNBA marketing illustrate the complex paradoxes at work today in commercialized women's sports: the specific form of today's emergent women's pro basketball simultaneously plays a progressive destabilizing role in current gender and sexual relations, even as it is being shaped by many of the same conservative market forces that control men's sports. Ultimately, though, the WNBA does not epitomize the social justice model as I am outlining it, because it fails to ask the critical question Just do *what*? If it is commercially successful, the WNBA will in most ways replicate, rather than challenge or alter, the dominant social relations in sport and in the larger society. On the other hand, the WNBA's commercial success may ultimately be predicated on its ability to broaden the institutional and cultural center of sport, making it more inclusive of "others" (lesbians, African American women), and this would in some ways further destabilize the white, heterosexual, masculine-dominated center.

Taking on the Center

What makes activism for social justice different from the liberal just do it model? First, activist groups that have formed around specific issues are beginning to identify the ways that problems like sexual violence, structural inequities in sport, and corporate-media domination are inter-related threads that make up the same institutional and cultural fabric. As such, they are forming organizations and coalitions that connect these various issues. One group that does this well is an educators' organization, the Association for Gender Equity Leadership (AGELE), which fights simultaneously for sex equity for girls in sport, antiviolence programs to protect girls *and* boys from sexual and homophobic violence and bullying, and programs that celebrate and enhance cultural and racial-ethnic diversity and equality.[39] Second, activist groups are beginning to work together to confront the ways that various institutions, such as sport, the media, schools, and corporations, intertwine to promote, perpetuate, and often profit from inequitable and violent sports. And third, social justice activists are recognizing that social change happens at various levels, so activism needs to take place simultaneously at the local interactional level, where people "do" gender and race and class relations, as well as at the levels of social institutions and cultural production and consumption. To be sure, this kind of radical activism is not happening on a widespread basis. However, I will discuss below some promising examples of social justice activism and change in and around sport.

Sport does not exist in a vacuum; it is organically intertwined with various other institutions, many of which (such as schools, universities, the mass media, medicine, and the law) have been far more successfully contested by women's quest for equality than sport has. As such, men's sports are increasingly under fire from schools, universities, legal advocacy agencies, and sometimes even the media to "clean up their act," especially with respect to athletes' violence against women. This pressure from outside sport—in particular, the efforts by public school, college, and university administrations to ensure that campuses are safe places for girls and women—has created an opening for antirape activists and professionals to intervene directly into the inner circles of men's sport cultures. Several such intervention programs (e.g., the University of Massachusetts Mentors in Violence Program and Athletes for Sexual Responsibility at the University of Maine) that link resources from campus counseling centers, women's issues centers, and athletic departments have sprung up in recent years.[40] Many of the individuals who are organizing these interventions are health professionals who have been involved in sex education and antirape organizing that is organically linked to feminist organizing for social justice.

The mere existence of antirape intervention programs is a sign of a crisis at the heart of men's sports. But to what extent do these programs really work? Antirape programs in sport have yet to be systematically examined to assess their effect (if any) on the sexist and homophobic attitudes and dynamics of male athletic peer groups that enable the assaultive behaviors of some.[41] I suspect that these programs will have little effect, especially when they are one-shot interventions that are not organically linked to longer-term institutional attempts to address men's violence at its psychological, peer group, and organizational roots. At their best, such programs may provide a context in which some individual boys and men will be empowered to remove themselves from the role of passively complicit (but not fully comfortable) participants in the daily practices that feed an athletic rape culture. Some of these boys' and young men's suppressed empathy for girls and women might be reawakened and validated, especially if they can be encouraged to understand the links between their own marginalization within the male peer group and that group's denigration and victimization of women. These young men might then take the risk to break the silence and speak out against the dominant discourse and practices of the group. The result of this might be that a few girls and women, and indeed some boys and men, will be safer than they might otherwise have been. This outcome alone, even if only occasional, would make these programs worth developing and institutionalizing in a widespread manner.

But ultimately, if intervention programs focus their attentions only at the level of men's group-based interactions, while leaving the larger institutional and cultural contexts untouched, they are unlikely to alter fundamentally the annual reproduction of sport as a pedagogical site for boys' and men's learning of the triad of violence. In fact, at their worst, rape awareness sessions for athletes may serve as a school's or university's public relations window dressing while allowing the athletic department and its teams to continue with business as usual. A commitment to address the root causes of men's violence against women will ultimately run up against the need to fundamentally rethink both the dominant conceptions of gender in the society and the specific ways that gender difference and hierarchy continue to be constructed in sport.

This larger confrontation with sport will more often than not mean taking on the entrenched institutional power of football teams and coaches in schools and universities. From their positions of privilege at the center of the gender regimes of schools and universities, football programs are often the major impediments to sex equity. Football programs like to position themselves as the goose that laid the golden egg, but as I have shown, most football programs drain campus budgets while claiming a disproportionate number of scholarships and other resources for men athletes. Meanwhile, football programs are consistently among the most powerful enforcers of the homophobia, misogyny, and suppression of empathy that underlie the triad of men's violence on campuses.

Corporate domination of city governments also plays an increasingly important and conservative role in defining and shaping sport priorities. In cities and their surrounding communities, debates have recently emerged about the mostly hidden environmental and social costs involved when huge amounts of public resources are committed to building stadia and other athletic facilities that will be used primarily by elite professional or Olympic athletes. In 1989, when Toronto opened its new stadium with great fanfare, progressive sport scholar and activist Bruce Kidd scathingly dubbed it "the Men's Cultural Centre."

> [The Men's Cultural Centre] constitutes a massive subsidization and celebration of men's interests.... It was initiated by male politicians well known for their hostility to feminist causes. At a time when women's crisis centers go underfunded, the developers obtained 25 acres of prime downtown public land and $85 million in public funds for the stadium ... which will stage male team games for predominantly male audiences.[42]

Kidd's analytic connection between the corporate-patriarchal commitment of public funds to men's sports and the lack of public response to men's violence against women is among precisely the kind of institutional connections that activists increasingly began to make in the 1990s. As Helen Lenskyj's research has shown, local community opposition to staging the Olympics was organized in Sydney, Atlanta, and other cities by coalitions of low-income-housing activists, tenant unions, anti-poverty activists, racial-ethnic minority and aboriginal groups, and environmentalists.[43] These groups challenge the feel-good, trickle-down corporate logic and propaganda used to promote cities' Olympic bids. Instead, they argue for broader and deeper community commitment to growth and development that is premised on social justice and community participation rather than on the staging of a brief, high-profile, expensive, elite sporting event that succeeds in lining the pockets of a few local businessmen and large corporate and media promoters.

Taking on masculinist sport and the violence and inequities associated with it also means engaging in a critical confrontation with the sport-media-commercial complex's dominant imagery of the televised sports manhood formula. One strategy along these lines is pedagogical: we need to take advantage of young people's incipient skills at reading media critically. Sociologist Jim McKay has outlined a creative classroom pedagogy that engages students in critical readings of race, gender, violence, and commercial themes in sports media texts.[44] Along these same lines, when I show my students Jackson Katz's *Tough Guise*, a documentary film that vividly analyzes the conventional ways that men are portrayed in media (including sports media and advertisements), they are not only adept at understanding Katz's critique of narrowly destructive conventions of masculinity; they are often able to go beyond the film, carrying the critique into discussions of other media and of their daily lives.

Though some young people have the ability to interpret sports media critically, they certainly are not abandoning sports media in droves. They are, however, increasingly diverse in their tastes, and this may make people in broadcast media a bit nervous. For instance, the NFL—until very recently, the undisputed king of televised sports—appears to be experiencing erosion of its fan base in the crucial age eighteen to thirty-four male demographic. The controversial emergence and rapid demise of the XFL, as discussed in chapters 3 and 4, are indicators of both the volatility of this fan base and the willingness of the sport-media-commercial complex to amp up the televised sports manhood formula in an attempt to capture today's younger male viewers. The hand-wringing of mainstream sports media people concerning the XFL's assault on the "purity" of sport is further evidence of crisis tendencies at the center of the sport-media-commercial complex. Yet it is also evidence of the continued profitability of televised sports violence. To confront this reality, sport scholar Lawrence Wenner has proposed that antiviolence activists develop an annual "sports violence profile," which would be distributed to media, accompanied by an annual "Bad Sport Award" and a "Good Sport Award" given out to deserving individuals and organizations.[45] The goal of this kind of media activism would be to chronicle, analyze, and publicly expose the media's promotion of violence in sports and to point to and applaud positive alternatives.

Taking on men's violence in sports also means confronting the central role of alcohol consumption and the alcohol industry in sport. In chapter 2, I discussed how alcohol consumption is often a key aspect of the more dangerous and violent dynamics at the center of male sport cultures. Though it does not "cause" men's violence against women or against other men, it seems to be one of the factors that facilitates that violence.[46] As I pointed out in chapter 3, institutionally, alcohol (especially the beer industry) plays a key economic role on college campuses and in professional sports. And, as I noted in chapter 4, the imagery of masculinity promoted in sports broadcasts and magazines is heavily influenced by liquor-industry advertisements. Alcohol facilitates and perpetuates masculinist interactions, structures, and cultural symbolism in sport. It is, in the words of sport studies scholar Lawrence Wenner, a key part of "a high holy trinity of alcohol, sports, and hegemonic masculinity."[47] Thus, activism around alcohol and sport, such as the antibinge drinking program launched at the University of Iowa in 1996, promises to confront a key linking factor within the sport-media-commercial complex.[48]

As an entity that clearly profits from the distorted social relations at the center of men's sports, the alcohol industry is an obvious target for today's social activists. But what about those corporations that have recently been in the forefront of promoting women's sports? I believe that radical analysis and activism around gender and sport must also engage and creatively expose the institutional relations and advertising imagery of seemingly "women friendly" corporations. For instance, as I described in chapter 3, Nike arrived at the promotion of women's sports later than some of its competitors, such as Reebok, but through its powerfully successful advertising campaigns, managed eventually to position itself as what cultural studies scholars C. L. Cole and Amy Hribar call a "celebrity feminist."[49] Many female consumers have identified with Nike's slogans and imagery as powerfully affirming signs of their arrival as women athletes who will no longer be held back. Meanwhile though, the production policies of Nike (and indeed, those of many other similar corporations) have been premised on the exploitation of extremely low-paid (mostly female) workers in other parts of the world.[50] Current activists have exposed this in several ways. For instance, the Canadian-based organization Adbusters has distributed "counteradvertisements" that appropriate the imagery and slogans of Nike and other corporations in ways that creatively expose the institutional oppression and exploitation that lie beneath the corporate individualist messages and signs of liberation.[51]

Figure 10. Employing a strategy of "culture jamming," Adbusters distributes "counteradvertisements" that appropriate the imagery and slogans of corporations to expose the institutional oppression and exploitation that lie beneath the corporations' messages.

Similarly, when Nike offered its web site customers the option to use their own creativity to "build your own" sneaker, complete with a word of your choice or "iD" printed on the side, MIT graduate student Jonah Peretti asked Nike to print the word *sweatshop* on his shoe.[52] When Nike refused to do so, Peretti protested in what eventually became a very public back-and-forth exchange between him and the corporation. Peretti wrote to Nike:

> Your Web site advertises that the NIKE iD program is "about freedom to choose and freedom to express who you are." I share Nike's love of freedom and personal statement. The site also says that "If you want it done right ... build it yourself." I was thrilled to be able to build my own shoes, and my personal iD was offered as a small token of appreciation for the sweatshop workers poised to help me realize my vision. I hope that you will value my freedom of statement and reconsider your decision to reject my order.

When Nike again refused to print *sweatshop* on Peretti's shoes, he jammed them one more time with this reply:

> Dear NIKE iD, Thank you for the time and energy you have spent on my request. I have decided to order the shoes with a different iD, but I would like to make one small request. Could you please send me a color snapshot of the 10-year-old Vietnamese girl who makes my shoes? Thanks, Jonah Peretti

Peretti's and Adbusters' creatively humorous "culture jamming" exposes the exploitation that underlies the celebration of Nike's (and others') corporate individualism and celebrity feminism. This kind of activism also highlights how important it is for today's increasingly fashionable cultural studies analysis of signs and symbols to be joined with critical institutional analysis of sport and its related institutions. Indeed, antisweatshop activism—such as the Workers Rights Consortium, a coalition of activists on sixty college campuses—has recently exposed the links between university athletic programs and large shoe and apparel manufacturers that routinely exploit workers in poor nations as well as vulnerable immigrant workers in the United States.[53] These burgeoning movements are very promising, especially because they are beginning to make the important connections among global corporate circuits of production, U.S. consumption of symbols (including those of sports teams), and local (gender, race, and class) relations on campuses and in communities.[54]

Activists' attempts to link efforts to confront male athletes' violence against women and sex equity struggles in sport and communities and efforts to expose the institutional underpinnings of the sport-media-commercial complex are important, not only because sport is today a key site of gender contest, but also because of sport's economic and symbolic ties to other institutions. The opening of the twenty-first century has seen an impressive display of forces at play: as women continue to press for equity, the center of sport reasserts itself as a key institutional site for the construction of hegemonic masculinity. The institution of sport tends not only to reflect but also to amplify and reassert those aspects of masculinity that have been successfully contested in many other parts of the larger gender order. The center of sport daily reproduces and valorizes dominant values of male heroism based on competition and winning, playing hurt, handing out pain to opponents, group-based bonding through homophobia and misogyny, and the legitimation of interpersonal violence as a means of success. Thus, directly intervening in men's athletic programs or developing pedagogical methods of criticizing dominant sports media not only might help make the world safer for some women and men; a fundamental confrontation with the root causes of athletic men's violence against women is also likely to have a positive ripple effect throughout the larger gender order.

I introduced this book with the image of Los Angeles Lakers center Shaquille O'Neal. When I wrote the first chapter, O'Neal was the league's most valuable player on the defending NBA championship team.

He had the Superman *S* logo tattooed on his huge, muscular shoulder, and it seemed to fit. He appeared to be invincible. However, as the 2000–2001 season progressed, it became apparent that opposing teams had a strategy. Rather than cowering in fear, they decided that in the closing minutes of a tight game, they would intentionally foul O'Neal. In essence, they were giving him uncontested free throws from fifteen feet away. If he were to make most of them, the Lakers would win. But for the first half of the season, O'Neal barely managed to hit 40 percent; the free throw line, it seemed, was Shaq's kryptonite. Moreover, by mid-season, it became apparent that Superman had sore feet. Strained and aching arches hampered O'Neal's play. When he sat out several games, including the midseason All Star game, to rest his feet, his team floundered. In short, opposing teams found and exploited the one weak spot in the game of this talented and seemingly invincible center, and he was hampered by his own vulnerable and, it turns out, very human body. Eventually though, O'Neal returned to the lineup with rested feet and discovered a free throw stroke that was good enough to raise his season average to over 50 percent. By the end of the regular season, he and his teammates had recovered their winning ways and successfully defended their championship. O'Neal and the Lakers once again appeared invincible, but the championship came only weeks after midseason grumbling about the team's "bad chemistry" and about O'Neal's personal shortcomings and vulnerabilities.

Like Shaquille O'Neal, the institutional center of sport at times seems invincible, able to repel most challenges and absorb others in ways that allow ultimately for a neat reproduction of business as usual. A close look, though, reveals instability at the center due to (1) problems—particularly off-field violence—generated by men's athletic culture; (2) the destabilizing influence of institutions such as schools, universities, and the law, which often have very different goals and core value systems from those at the center of sport; and (3) the continued challenges from the margins of sport by girls and women pressing for equity and fairness. These challenges and instabilities suggest that further shifts are inevitable—indeed, that the center of sport is vulnerable to conscious interventions that aim to bring about progressive changes in it and in the wider societal field of gender, race, sexual, and class relations.

We should not underestimate the extent to which everyday practices of men's sports and the dominant cultural imagery of sport still tend to support and legitimize men's power and privileges over those of women.[55] However, it is also crucial to recognize that there is a soft underbelly to sport's masculinist center. As I pointed out in chapter 2, there is often a disjuncture between what boys and men want and what they get from sports. Routinely, boys and men have their very human need for closeness, intimacy, and respect thwarted by cutthroat competition, homophobia, and misogyny, which leave them cut off from and fearful of becoming vulnerable with others. Instead, their need for connection is converted into a narrow form of group-oriented bonding based on competitive one-upmanship, self-destructive behaviors, and sexually aggressive denigration of others. To the extent that boys do not get to experience institutional contexts that allow them the opportunity for healthy, respectful connection with others, they will probably continue to find experiences in sports and the dominant cultural imagery of men's sports to be comforting havens in which to construct identities and relationships. On the other hand, to the extent that adults can create institutional and symbolic contexts, both inside and outside sport, that allow boys to experience a full range of emotional expression and connection with others (including respectful, egalitarian relations with girls), fewer boys and young men will find affinity with the homophobia, misogyny, and violence that characterize the current masculinist center of sport culture. So prepared, more boys and men might join with girls and women in the feminist project of leveling the playing field and simultaneously changing the rules of the game to make the world more just, equitable, and healthy for all.

Notes

Introduction

1. Women's Sports Foundation, *The Wilson Report*.

2. National Federation of State High School Associations, "2000–2001 Athletics Participation Summary."

3. Sport scholars R. Vivien Acosta and Linda Jean Carpenter have been compiling longitudinal data on college women's sports participation rates, coaching, and administration since 1978. See Acosta and Carpenter, *Women in Intercollegiate Sport*.

4. Acosta and Carpenter, *Women in Intercollegiate Sport*, report that soccer has had the greatest growth rate of any college sport in the past twenty-three years. In 1978, it was available on only 2.8 percent of college campuses. By 2000, soccer was available on 84 percent of college campuses and had overtaken softball as the most popular college women's sport.

5. See, for instance, a journalist's account of a girls' high school basketball team: Blais, *In These Girls, Hope Is a Muscle*. High-profile women professional athletes, too, have begun recently to write autobiographies that at times suggest that a veritable revolution has recently taken place in women's sports. See, for instance, Holdsclaw with Frey, *Chamique*.

6. Sport scholars have argued that windsurfing and other sports that exist outside what I am calling the center of sport culture can serve as an alternative—perhaps even a challenge—to the routine reconstruction of gender hierarchy. See Wheaton and Tomlinson, "The Changing Gender Order in Sport?" For a discussion of the significance of the growth of extreme sports, see Rinehart,

"Inside of the Outside." For a discussion of scholarly examinations of sport "subcultures," see Crosset and Beal, "The Use of 'Subculture' and 'Subworld' in Ethnographic Works on Sport."

7. For general discussions of the expansion and significance of sports media, see Jhally, "The Spectacle of Accumulation"; Wenner, ed., *MediaSport*; Rowe, *Sport, Culture and the Media*.

8. C. L. Cole has argued that the concept of sport studies is a limited way to conceptualize the object of study. Instead, she proposes a "feminist cultural studies" that "requires rethinking the categories of and relations among sport, gender, sexuality, nature, the body, race, class, difference, science, power, representation, subjectivity, and opposition." Cole, "Resisting the Canon," 23. See also Rail, "Seismography of the Postmodern Condition." Though I draw from some of the same cultural studies theories that inform Cole's and Rail's works, I argue in this book that there still is an institutional center to what we define as sport.

9. Nearly all of this gap can be explained by the existence of boys' football, a sport for which there is no girls' counterpart. In 2000–2001, high school football accounted for by far the largest number of boy participants (1,012,420), followed by basketball, track and field, and baseball, each with roughly half a million participants. The largest number of participants in girls sports were in basketball (452,728), track and field (415,666) and volleyball (390,814). National Federation of State High School Associations, "2000–2001 Athletics Participation Summary."

10. Suggs, "Uneven Progress for Women's Sport." Acosta and Carpenter also document this uneven progress from the mid-1970s to the present, including data that illustrate the ways that leadership of college women's sports (coaches, athletic directors) has fallen disproportionately into men's hands since the passage of Title IX. Acosta and Carpenter, *Women in Intercollegiate Sport*.

11. Patricia Adler and Peter Adler observed in their study of peer cultures in grade school, "The major factor affecting boys' popularity was athletic ability. . . . In several schools we observed, the best athlete was also the most popular boy in the grade." Adler and Adler, *Peer Power*, 39. Sohaila Shakib has pointed out the various peer, family, and cultural factors that lead many preadolescent and adolescent girls to drop out of sports, despite the obvious benefits they receive from playing sports. Shakib, "Male and Female High School Basketball Players' Perceptions of Gender and Athleticism."

12. Not surprisingly, the study also found that boys tend to consume sports media at higher rates than girls do. Amateur Athletic Foundation of Los Angeles, *Children and Sports Media*.

13. Connell, *Gender and Power*, defines the gender order in dynamic, societywide scale, as the "current state of play in this macro-politics" of institutional gender relations. Distinct from, but linked to, more face-to-face "sexual politics," the concept of the gender order captures "the conflict of interest on this society-wide scale, the formation and dissolution of general categories and the ordering of relationships between institutions, [which] together amount to a macro-politics of gender" (139).

14. My favorite example of this is of the man whom I interviewed for a previous book, *Power at Play*, who, after telling me that a woman had recently been promoted to be his boss, added, "A woman can do a job as well as I can do— maybe even be my boss. But I'll be *damned* if she can go out on the [football] field and take a hit from Ronnie Lott!" Messner, *Power at Play*, 168.

15. In sport studies, the most systematic application of Connell's theories of gender is Jim McKay's comparative study of gender and affirmative action in sport in Australia, Canada, and New Zealand. McKay, *Managing Gender*.

16. Sut Jhally introduced the concept of the "sport-media complex" to describe the interlocking institutional interests and practices of big-time sports and mass media. Jhally, "The Spectacle of Accumulation." A recent study of televised sports that boys watch most, which included an examination of commercials, led my colleagues and me to expand this concept to the sport-media-commercial complex to capture the interests of commercial promoters and sponsors of sports. See Messner, Dunbar, Hunt, "The Televised Sports Manhood Formula." Varda Burstyn introduced a similar concept, which she called the "the sport nexus," to describe an institutional "entity consisting of sport in its associations with the mass media, corporate sponsors, governments, medicine, and biotechnology." Burstyn, *The Rites of Men*, 17.

17. For instance, college women's sports are much more tightly controlled by men and much less autonomous since they were brought under the auspices of the NCAA and since most women's athletic departments were folded into men's athletic departments. As many scholars of women's sports have pointed out, the "success" of college women's sports has not been without its paradoxical outcomes: moving from far out in the margins, closer to the center, has entailed costs. See Cahn, *Coming on Strong*. Similarly, as I will discuss in the

final chapter, some alternative, or extreme, sports, such as skateboarding, are currently being pulled closer to the center of the sport-media-commercial complex.

18. Feminist women of color have led the way in arguing for the importance of studying the simultaneity of race, class, gender, and sexual orientation as interlocking group-based systems of inequality. See, for instance, Baca Zinn, Weber Cannon, Higgenbotham, and Thornton Dill, "The Costs of Exclusionary Practices in Women's Studies"; Baca Zinn and Thornton Dill, "Theorizing Difference from Multiracial Feminism"; and Collins, *Fighting Words*. The idea that one cannot look simply at gender without considering its interplay in a matrix of domination has been well integrated into sport studies over the past fifteen years. A most recent exemplary work that deals with gender and (racial-ethnic, class, sexual, national, and religious) difference is Hargreaves, *Heroines of Sport*.

19. I draw distinctions between interaction, structure, and culture with the full knowledge that these levels of analysis are always mutually intertwined. The things that people do—our interactions and performances—are never free-floating, are always variously constrained and enabled by structural and cultural contexts. The distinction between "structure" and "culture" has been a subject of debate among theorists for many years. I use the term *structure* to refer to institutionalized systems of social relations (the kinds of rules, divisions of labor, and hierarchies one finds in sport or school organizations, for instance) and *culture* to refer to systems of meaning (the symbology of sports media, for instance). As my discussion of the "sport-media-commercial complex" will illustrate, institutional hierarchies and systems of meaning are parts of the same social processes; for instance, sports media can be analyzed as part of an institutional matrix (structure) and as a source of dominant sport symbology (culture). Theorist Sharon Hays has argued that rather than being something entirely distinct, "culture must be understood as a social structure.... Culture is both constraining and enabling. Culture is a social structure with an underlying logic of its own. In conceiving of culture in this way, I argue that social structure consists of *two* central, interconnected elements: systems of social relations and systems of meaning." Hays, "Structure and Agency and the Sticky Problem of Culture." Questions relating to the relationship between structure and culture have been taken up in sport studies as well. See Hargreaves, *Sport, Power and Culture*.

1. Center Snap

1. Empirical evidence has pointed for years to the conclusion that there is more difference *within* the categories "women" and "men" than there is

between them. For the classic and the most recent statements of this position, see Maccoby and Jacklin, *The Psychology of Sex Differences*; and Fausto-Sterling, *Sexing the Body*. In terms of physical abilities, there are some identifiable *average* differences between women and men, but these differences are never categorical. And it is social practices—especially as constructed and promoted through institutions like sport, whose major concern is the development and display of bodies— that produce ideologies of categorical difference between the sexes. For the development of this idea in sport scholarship, see Kane, "Resistance/Transformation of the Oppositional Binary"; Messner, "Sports and Male Domination"; Willis, "Women in Sport in Ideology"; Young, "Throwing Like a Girl."

2. MacInnes argues that modernity undermined patriarchy, so gender was created as a fiction to deal with built-in contradictions of inequality in modern societies that had been constructed on the idea of equality. MacInnes, *The End of Masculinity*. Sport is a quintessentially modern institution in this regard, because it helps to construct (even as other institutions are more and more contested) this fiction of gender as natural, binary sex difference. For historical accounts of the role of sport in modern gender relations, see Burstyn, *The Rites of Men*; Cahn *Coming on Strong*; Crosset, "Masculinity, Sexuality and the Development of Early Modern Sport"; Kimmel, "Baseball and the Reconstitution of American Masculinity."

3. Unlike the long-term, systematic ethnographic studies of children conducted by Barrie Thorne or the Adlers, this chapter takes one moment as its point of departure. See Thorne, *Gender Play*; and Adler and Adler, *Peer Power*. I do not present this moment as somehow "representative" of what happened throughout the season; instead, I examine this as an example of what Arlie Hochschild calls "magnified moments," which are "episodes of heightened importance, either epiphanies, moments of intense glee or unusual insight, or moments in which things go intensely but meaningfully wrong. In either case, the moment stands out; it is metaphorically rich, unusually elaborate and often echoes [later]." See Hochschild, "The Commercial Spirit of Intimate Life and the Abduction of Feminism," 4. A magnified moment in daily life offers a window into the social construction of reality. It presents researchers with an opportunity to excavate gendered meanings and processes through an analysis of institutional and cultural contexts. The magnified moment analyzed in this chapter took place over the course of a morning. Immediately after the event, I recorded my observations with detailed notes. I later slightly revised the notes after developing the photographs that I took at the event.

4. Much of this chapter is adapted from Messner, "Barbie Girls vs. Sea Monsters."

5. Butler, *Gender Trouble*.

6. Walters, "Sex, Text, and Context," 250.

7. Kessler and McKenna, *Gender*.

8. West and Zimmerman, "Doing Gender."

9. See, for instance, Lorber, *Paradoxes of Gender*; and Risman, *Gender Vertigo*.

10. Or, conversely, theories of performativity can easily fall into a celebration of apparently free-floating "transgressions" of gender norms and boundaries. In ignoring the constraining nature of social contexts, theories of performativity can fall into a simplistic voluntarism.

11. Lorber, *Paradoxes of Gender*, 37.

12. Acker, "Hierarchies, Jobs, Bodies."

13. Connell, *Gender and Power*.

14. Most of the structural inventory presented here is from a content analysis of the 1998–1999 Regional AYSO yearbook, which features photos and names of all of the teams, coaches, and managers. I counted the number of adult men and women occupying various positions. In the three cases where the sex category of a name was not immediately obvious (e.g., Rene or Terry) and in the five cases where simply a last name was listed, I did not count it. I also used the AYSO Yearbook for my analysis of the children's team names. To check for reliability, another sociologist independently read and coded the list of team names. There was disagreement on how to categorize only 2 of the 156 team names.

15. The existence of some women coaches and some men team managers in these AYSO leagues' organization manifests a *less* extreme sexual division of labor than that of the same community's Little League Baseball organization, in which there are proportionally fewer (by about half) women coaches. Similarly, Chafetz and Kotarba's study of parental labor in support of Little League baseball in a middle-class Houston community revealed an apparently absolute sexual division of labor, where nearly all of the supportive "activities off the field were conducted by the women in the total absence of men, while activities on the field were conducted by men and boys in the absence of women." Chafetz and Kotarba, "Little League Mothers and the Reproduction of Gender," 52. Perhaps youth soccer, because of its more recent (mostly post–Title IX) history in the

United States, is a more contested gender regime than the more patriarchally entrenched youth sports like Little League Baseball or youth football.

16. For examinations of the ways that (mostly invisible and undervalued) women's labor supports and enables boys' and men's sports and leisure, see Maree Boyle and Jim McKay, "'You Leave Your Troubles at the Gate'"; and Thompson, *Mother's Taxi*.

17. The term *homosocial* refers to contexts that are either all-male or all-female. The four-to-five-year-old kids' games and practices were absolutely homosocial in terms of the kids because of the formal structural sex segregation. However, eight of the twelve girls' teams at this age level had male coaches, and two of the fourteen boys' teams had female coaches.

18. Butterfield and Loovis, "Influence of Age, Sex, Balance, and Sport Participation in Development of Kicking by Children in Grades K–8."

19. See, for instance, Attfield, "Barbie and Action Man"; Chin, *Purchasing Power*; Kinder, ed., *Kids' Media Culture*; Seiter, *Sold Separately*.

20. Walters, "Sex, Text and Context," 246.

21. Rogers, *Barbie Culture*.

22. By 1994, over 800 million Barbies had been sold, worldwide. Over $1 billion was spent on Barbies and accessories in 1992 alone. Two Barbie dolls were purchased every second in 1994, with half of the sales taking place in the United States. DuCille, "Dyes and Dolls," 49. The first quotation comes from Rand, "Older Heads on Younger Bodies," 383. The second quotation comes from DuCille, "Dyes and Dolls," 50.

23. Rand, "Older Heads on Younger Bodies," 386.

24. Ibid.

25. Ibid., 391.

26. Spigel, "Barbies without Ken," 316.

27. Ibid., 328.

28. Ibid.

29. If we extrapolate Barbie's bodily proportions to a "real woman," she would be "33–18–31.5 and stand five feet nine inches tall, with fully half of her height accounted for by her 'shapely legs.'" Rogers, *Barbie Culture*, 23.

30. Spigel, "Barbies without Ken," 345.

31. Connell defines emphasized femininity as the form of femininity that "is defined around compliance ... [with] the global subordination of women ...

and is oriented to accommodating the interests and desires of men." Connell, *Gender and Power*, 183.

32. Rogers, *Barbie Culture*, 14.

33. Baumgardner and Richards, *Manifesta*; Heywood and Drake, eds., *Third Wave Agenda*.

34. Klein, "Duality and Redefinition."

35. Campenni, "Gender Stereotyping of Children's Toys."

36. Bradbard, "Sex Differences in Adults' Gifts and Children's Toy Requests"; Robinson and Morris, "The Gender-Stereotyped Nature of Christmas Toys Received by 36-, 48-, and 60-month-old Children."

37. Etaugh and Liss, "Home, School, and Playroom."

38. Raag and Rackliff, "Preschoolers' Awareness of Social Expectations of Gender."

39. Rogers, *Barbie Culture*, 30.

40. Unlike Barbie, whose bodily dimensions have remained identical over the years, the G.I. Joe action toy has pumped up to greater and more cartoonish levels of extreme muscularity over the past fifteen years or so. Pope, Olivarda, Gruber, and Borowiecki, "Evolving Ideals of Male Body Image as Seen through Action Toys."

41. Jordan and Cowan, "Warrior Narratives in the Kindergarten Classroom," 728.

42. Connell, "Cool Guys, Swots and Wimps," 291.

43. Messner, *Power at Play*.

44. This is not to suggest that gender is not there or not important in boys' and men's homosocial groups. Indeed, gender's unspoken nature, its *invisibility* in boys' and men's homosocial institutions, is a major way that privilege operates. Just as race finally becomes marked and overtly salient in a previously all-white organization such as the U.S. Congress or in a class-privileged all-white residential neighborhood only after a few people of color break the color bar, so too gender in men's privileged homosocial realms is often unmarked unless and until girls and women challenge the homosocial boundaries. (Thanks to Shari Dworkin for reminding me of this crucial point.)

45. See Hasbrook, "Young Children's Social Constructions of Physicality and Gender." Colette Dowling has summarized much of the research on the social processes that—despite girls'and women's dramatic movement into sports— continue to push girls away from physically empowering athletic experiences. Dowling, *The Frailty Myth*. Sohaila Shakib's doctoral dissertation on girls and

high school basketball illustrates how peer group, family, and school influences on girls are such that postadolescent girls who decide to *stay* in sports must make some decisions and adjustments in their lives that run against the grain of gender arrangements and expectations in their social contexts. Shakib, "Male and Female High School Basketball Players' Perceptions of Gender and Athleticism."

46. This trilevel analysis of structure, interaction, and culture may not be fully adequate to plumb the *emotional* depths of the magnified Barbie Girls vs. Sea Monsters moment. Though it is beyond the purview of this chapter, an adequate rendering of the depths of pleasure and revulsion, attachment and separation, and commitment to ideologies of categorical sex difference may involve the integration of a fourth level of analysis: gender at the level of personality. See Chodorow, *The Power of Feelings*. Object relations theory has fallen out of vogue in feminist sociology in recent years, but as Christine Williams has argued, it might be most useful in revealing the mostly hidden social power of gender to shape people's unconscious predispositions to various structural contexts, cultural symbols, and interactional moments. See Williams, "Psychoanalytic Theory and the Sociology of Gender."

47. Dworkin and Messner, "Just Do . . . What?"

2. Playing Center

1. "Six Football Players Arrested for Hazing."

2. See Benedict, *Athletes and Acquaintance Rape*; and Totten, *Guys, Gangs, and Girlfriend Abuse*. Journalist Laura Robinson offers an especially chilling description of violence and sexual assaults by Canadian hockey players. See Robinson, *Crossing the Line*.

3. "Six Football Players Arrested for Hazing."

4. Jeffrey Benedict and Alan Klein compared national crime data with arrest and conviction rates of male collegiate and professional athletes accused of felony sexual assault; they concluded that when athletes are accused of sexual assault, they are more likely than nonathletes to be arrested or indicted but significantly less likely to be convicted. Benedict and Klein, "Arrest and Conviction Rates for Athletes Accused of Sexual Assault."

5. Boeringer, "Influences of Fraternity Membership, Athletics and Male Living Arrangements on Sexual Aggression"; Fritner and Rubinson, "Acquaintance Rape"; Koss and Gaines, "The Prediction of Sexual Aggression by Alcohol Use, Athletic Participation and Fraternity Affiliation."

6. Crosset and his colleagues also surveyed reports to campus police

departments, and although they found that male athletes were more likely to be reported for sexual assault than male nonathletes, the difference was not statistically significant. In their analysis of the two sets of data—Judicial Affairs offices and campus police offices—they argued that there are good reasons to expect that college women are more likely to report assaults to Judicial Affairs than to campus police, and so the (statistically significant) data from the former are a better reflection of reality than the data from the latter. Crosset, Benedict, and McDonald, "Male Student Athletes Reported for Sexual Assault."

7. Crosset, "Athletic Affiliation and Violence against Women."

8. Crosset et al., "Male Student Athletes and Violence against Women."

9. McPherson, "Sport, Youth, Violence and the Media."

10. Clarke, "Fear of a Black Planet."

11. Davis, *Woman, Race and Class*; Staples, *Black Masculinity*.

12. For a thoughtful discussion of this dilemma, see Berry and Smith, "Race, Sport, and Crime."

13. Robinson, *Crossing the Line.*

14. Kaufman, "The Construction of Masculinity and the Triad of Men's Violence." Joseph A. Kuypers explores another dimension of the issue of men's violence: he argues that men derive benefits through the threat and use of violence, and thus have a collective self-interest in maintaining it. Kuypers, *Man's Will to Hurt.*

15. This section of the chapter is a substantially revised version of Messner and Stevens, "Scoring without Consent."

16. Lefkowitz, *Our Guys*, 23–24.

17. Ibid., 25.

18. Lefkowitz's descriptions of the assault are retrospective constructions, based in part on the victim's descriptions and on subsequent bits of information that came out in the trials. The precise numbers on just how many boys in the basement participated physically in the assault and how many acted as a supportive audience are thus somewhat speculative.

19. Fine, *With the Boys.*

20. Julian Wood argues that this sort of competitive sexual talk among boys is a sort of group pedagogy through which boys are "groping toward sexism" in their attitudes and practices toward girls and women. Wood, "Groping toward Sexism."

21. See Kupers, "Rape and the Prison Code."

22. Hasbrook and Harris, "Wrestling with Gender," 27.

23. Adler and Adler, *Peer Power*, 65.

24. Eveslage and Delaney, "Trash Talkin' at Hardwick High."

25. Curry, "Fraternal Bonding in the Locker Room."

26. Sabo, "The Myth of the Sexual Athlete."

27. Indeed, Hasbrook and Harris, "Wrestling with Gender," 20, report this sort of verbal and physical aggression by higher-status boys toward lower-status boys taking place in their study of first graders.

28. Messner, *Power at Play*, 99.

29. In their study of peer cliques in grade schools, Adler and Adler describe the status hierarchy in this way: "At the high end was the popular clique, comprising the exclusive crowd. Below them were the wannabes, the group of people who hung around the popular clique hoping for inclusion. Next was the middle group, composed of smaller, independent friendship circles. At the bottom were the social isolates, who found playmates only occasionally, spending most of their time by themselves." Adler and Adler, *Peer Power*, 75. Rather than describing the dynamics between differently situated cliques, I am mostly describing here the internal dynamics of an "exclusive crowd" of male athletes.

30. Adler and Adler, *Peer Power*, 67–68.

31. Farr, "Dominance Bonding through the Good Old Boys' Sociability Group."

32. Lyman, "The Fraternal Bond as a Joking Relationship."

33. I develop this argument in Messner, "Studying Up on Sex."

34. Lefkowitz, *Our Guys*, 183–84.

35. Curry, "Booze and Bar Fights," 171–72.

36. Messner, "Riding with the Spur Posse."

37. As a result, the high school removed eight players from the nationally ranked lacrosse team and cancelled the rest of the season. See Anderson and Satterfield, "St. Paul's Cancels Varsity Lacrosse Season."

38. Sanday, *Fraternity Gang Rape*.

39. Messner, *Power at Play*, 94–95.

40. I originally wrote of this incident as part of an autobiographical short story. Messner, "Indignities."

41. James Messerschmidt argues that when boys are teased or ridiculed in schools for not being enough of a man, they experience this as a "masculinity challenge." Some boys respond to this subordination among other boys by using

sexual violence against women as a "hegemonic masculine project." Messer-schmidt, "Becoming 'Real Men'"; Messerschmidt, *Nine Lives.*

42. Benedict, *Athletes and Acquaintance Rape*, 2.

43. Ibid., 1–2.

44. An implicit assumption in this goal orientation to sex with women is the notion that "normal sex" goes through predictable scripted stages, from "foreplay" to the ultimate goal and destination of sexual intercourse.

45. Indeed, in Tim Beneke's work with convicted rapists, he notes that many of these men say they were motivated by a desire for revenge against women for the humiliation they have felt as a result of the sexual power that they perceive women to have over them. Beneke, *Men on Rape.*

46. Beneke notes that men often learn to project this subjectivity onto women through their use of pornography, which offers images of women not as simply passive objects but as active subjects whose desire is for the consumer. Beneke, *Proving Manhood.*

47. McKabe, "Jocks and Puck Bunnies."

48. Spain, "The Spatial Foundations of Men's Friendships and Men's Power"; Sanday, *Female Power and Male Dominance.*

49. Lefkowitz, *Our Guys*, 280.

50. "They Said It: Kobe Bryant."

51. Silver, "Dirty Dogs."

52. Glauber, "We're Paid to Be Violent."

53. "Quotebook," *Los Angeles Times.*

54. Segrave, Moreau, and Hastad, "An Investigation into the Relationship between Ice Hockey Participation and Delinquency."

55. Nixon, "Gender, Sport, and Aggressive Behavior outside Sport."

56. Messner, *Power at Play*, 65–66.

57. Canada, *Fist Stick Knife Gun.*

58. I develop this line of argument in much more depth in *Power at Play*, where I argue that the specific kind of connection that boys and men experience in sports is a distant and thus "emotionally safe" form of connection. This has (mostly negative) ramifications for the development of friendships, for intimate relations with women, and for athletes' retirement and disengagement from sports. Psychologist William Pollack reaches a similar conclusion, arguing that boys often find sports to be one place where they find emotional connection. Pollack concedes that "the positive benefits to boys dim when sports cease to be played"; still, he

tends to overstate the benefits of sports and ignores the range of social-scientific studies of sport that point to negative outcomes. Pollack, *Real Boys*, 273.

59. Ferguson illustrates how dynamics of gender and race in public schools serve as self-fulfilling prophecies, tracking African American boys into failure in the classroom, into the school's "punishment room," and ultimately (and inevitably, according to some of the teachers) into the criminal justice system. Ferguson, *Bad Boys*.

60. MacIntosh, "White Privilege."

61. Philosopher Brian Pronger has argued that an oppressive territorialization of the male body, which closes off intimate and erotic connection with other bodies and channels desire into violent directions, is the key outcome of modern sport, which he sees as a major expression of fascism. Pronger, "Outta My Endzone"; Pronger, "Homosexuality and Sport."

62. Curry, "Booze and Bar Fights," 168, 169–70.

63. Ibid., 170.

64. Several studies have shown that college male athletes and fraternity members tend to have higher rates of alcohol consumption than other college students, including more drinks per week and higher rates of binge drinking. Boswell and Spade, "Fraternities and Collegiate Gang Rape"; Leichliter et al., "Alcohol Use and Related Consequences among Students with Varying Levels of Involvement in College Athletics." A study of teen athletes found that male and female teen athletes are no more likely to drink than nonathletes, but "highly involved athletes" are more likely to binge drink than nonathletes. Miller et al., *The Women's Sports Foundation Report*.

65. Curry, "Booze and Bar Fights," 169.

66. Adams and Russakoff, "At Columbine High, a Darker Picture Emerges."

67. Indeed, Messerschmidt points out that although many boys are challenged by bullying, not all respond with violence. Boys' responses to bullying vary, and this variance can be explained by boys' being differently situated in family, school, and peer contexts. Messerschmidt, *Nine Lives*.

68. As Rocco L. Capraro puts it, ". . . college men's drinking appears to be profoundly paradoxical. . . . [They drink] not only to enact male privilege but also to help them negotiate the emotional hazards of being a man in contemporary American college." Capraro, "Why College Men Drink," 307.

69. Young, "Young at Heart," 61.

70. The extent of brain damage to boxers has been well documented for many years. Stories of champions and top contenders suffering from dementia pugilistica (a medical term that describes a malady that used to be called punch-drunk) and other forms of boxing-induced brain damage, such as Floyd Patterson, Muhammad Ali, Jerry Quarry, Sugar Ray Robinson, and Wilfredo Benitez are only the most recent high-profile examples of the logical outcome of boxing. These and other cases led to the American Medical Association in 1986 calling for a ban on boxing. More recent research has increased awareness of the danger and extent of head injuries in other sports, especially football and soccer. Crosset sites recent studies that note a connection between men's head injuries and their violence against women: "... batterers are more likely to have sustained moderate or severe head injuries than nonbatterers.... A history of significant head injury increased the chances of marital violence sixfold.... Like alcohol consumption, head injury is not the direct cause of violence against women but clearly one that may play a role in some athlete violence against women." Crosset, "Athletic Affiliation and Violence against Women," 160.

71. These statistics, of course, do not include the much larger number of routine, smaller injuries that do not result in a player sitting out a game. Gutierrez and Mitchell, "Pain Game."

72. Young and White, "Researching Sports Injury."

73. Dwyer Brust, Roberts, and Leonard, "Gladiators on Ice."

74. As reported in Gold and Weber, "Youth Sports Grind Is Tough on Body, Spirit."

75. Dwyer Brust, Roberts, and Leonard, "Gladiators on Ice," 27.

76. Messner, *Power at Play*, 122–23.

77. Brian Pronger has written about sport as a disciplinary practice particular to modernity, through which men learn to close off their bodies to connection with others. Instead, the body is experienced as a means of overcoming others. Pronger, "Outta My Endzone."

78. Pollack, *Real Boys*.

79. Sabo, "Pigskin, Patriarchy and Pain." The pain principle in sport can also be seen as paradigmatic of (and indeed, a pedagogy for) a more general cultural view of men's instrumental orientations to their own bodies. A few scholars have recently pointed to gender-related health patterns among men that help to explain the fact that, on average, men die seven years earlier than women do and have higher death rates from suicide, heart disease, accidents, and other major

killers. Research points to the conclusion that these health risks among men are closely correlated with boys' and men's conformity to narrow conceptions of masculinity that include risk taking, violence, and instrumental orientations to the body. For excellent general overviews, see Sabo and Gordon, eds., *Men's Health and Illness*; and Courtenay, "Constructions of Masculinity and Their Influence on Men's Well-Being." Taking this observation to a different level, scholars have pointed out how different groups of men—broken down by social class, race-ethnicity, sexual orientation, age, and so forth—have very different levels of vulnerability to certain diseases and dangers. See, for instance, Staples, "Health among African American Males."

80. Messner, *Power at Play*, 72.

81. White, Young, and McTeer, "Sport, Masculinity, and the Injured Body," 171.

82. Green, *The Dark Side of the Game*, 215, 125.

83. Courtenay, "Constructions of Masculinity and Their Influence on Men's Well-Being," 1385.

84. The "no más" reference is to the famous 1980 welterweight championship fight between Roberto Duran and Sugar Ray Leonard. Feeling that he was losing the fight, Duran refused to return to the ring for a new round, saying, "No más." He was roundly criticized for quitting instead of continuing the fight until he was knocked out. I critically examined this idea that boxers must fight until the very end in Messner, "Why Rocky III?"

3. Center of the Diamond

1. "Joanie Smith" is a pseudonym.

2. This story is distilled from Eric Anderson's description of these incidents in chapter 7 of his book. See Anderson, *Trailblazing*.

3. Economist Andrew Zimbalist observes that Raveling's total compensation package was actually worth over four hundred thousand dollars a year. Stanley was asking for parity only with Raveling's base salary. Zimbalist, *Unpaid Professionals*, 76.

4. Ibid., 78.

5. Ibid., 77.

6. Stanley went on to co-coach the Stanford basketball team, then spent two years at the helm of the UC Berkeley team, and in 2000 signed on as a coach of the WNBA Los Angeles Sparks basketball team.

7. "Court Rejects Stanley's Suit."

8. The California Women's Law Center argued that the City of Los Angeles Department of Recreation and Parks' discrimination against the West Valley Girls Softball League "came against a background of severely limited opportunities for girls to participate in city recreational programs. Girls comprise less than 20% of participants in its team sports programs, and this is deficient. Based on Department of Recreation and Park statistics, of the 58,000 city-wide youth participants in team sports, girls comprise a mere 18% of those playing team sports. Almost 17,000 boys play basketball at park leagues throughout the city, but only 5000 girls play. 4800 boys play soccer, but only 950 girls play soccer citywide. 20,500 boys play baseball, but only 2200 girls play baseball. Citywide, only 2000 girls play softball. Girls comprise barely 17% of those playing softball and baseball combined." California Women's Law Center, "1999 President's Pro Bono Service Award for District 7."

9. Acker, "Gendered Institutions," 567. For key works on the gendered organization, see Acker, "Hierarchies, Jobs, Bodies"; and Brittan, "The Epistemology of the Gendered Organization."

10. In the United States, the modern institution of sport was constructed primarily by and for white, middle-class, heterosexual men, partly in response to a "crisis of masculinity" brought on by modernization of work and families and by the women's movement. Eventually, men of color and working-class men fought for and largely won the right to involvement in sports, thus shifting the forms, meanings, and styles of masculinization that took place in sports. For the foundations of this historical argument, see Crosset, "Masculinity, Sexuality and the Development of Early Modern Sport"; and Kimmel, "Baseball and the Reconstitution of American Masculinity: 1880-1920." In *Power at Play*, I argue that throughout the twentieth century, there was an elective affinity between boys' and men's developing masculine identities and the gendered institution of sport.

11. Sociologist Jim McKay has developed perhaps the most sophisticated analysis of divisions of labor and power in the gendered institution of sport. McKay, *Managing Gender*.

12. A 1997 NCAA study found that the average base salary of Division I-A head coaches in men's basketball was $99,283, compared with $60,603 for head coaches of women's teams. Zimbalist, *Unpaid Professionals*, 80.

13. Nor has the institution of sport ever been static. There is a rich history

of girls and women contesting the masculinist gender regime of sport. Historian Susan Cahn describes U.S. sport throughout the twentieth century as a site of contest for gender, sexual, racial, and class relations. Cahn, *Coming on Strong*.

14. Anderson, *Trailblazing*, 172, 174.

15. For a discussion of Title IX and sex equality in schools, analyzed from the point of view of feminist legal theory, see Brake, "The Struggle for Sex Equality in Sport and the Theory behind Title IX." Toby Miller, Jim McKay, G. Lawrence, and David Rowe argue that initiatives like Title IX are unlikely to lead to fundamental changes in the gender order. Title IX discourse is "underpinned by orthodox liberal-feminist definitions of fairness, which assume that equality can be achieved by getting more women to the same starting point as men. But increasing the numbers of women in sporting organizations will not necessarily change masculine cultures, or the stresses that women experience in combining work and family responsibilities. Therefore, if an organization attempts to recruit more women, but retains policies that are based on sameness rather than difference, it is unlikely there will be any impact on . . . the white male heterosexual and largely ablebodied ruling monoculture." T. Miller et al., *Globalization and Sport*, 114. Miller and his colleagues' emphasis on the need for more radical institutional change is important. But there is also evidence to suggest that liberal initiatives such as Title IX, rather than simply contributing to a restabilized corporate-managerial business-as-usual, tends to destabilize local gender regimes in ways that open space for further contest and (potentially more radical) change. This question, of course, reiterates an age-old debate concerning the extent to which liberal reform merely stabilizes oppressive systems or creates possibilities for truly fundamental progressive insititutional change.

16. The California Women's Law Center is a nonprofit policy and advocacy center established in 1989 to advance, secure, and protect the civil rights of women and girls. In 1998, the CWLC, along with the ACLU of Southern California, sued the city of Los Angeles in the case, *Baca et al. v. City of Los Angeles, Department of Recreation and Parks et al.* The case was settled out of court on February 26, 1999, when the city of Los Angeles, through the City Council and the Board of Commissioners of the Department of Recreation and Parks, agreed to adopt a citywide gender equity program (called Raise the Bar Program) designed to correct past deficiencies and to develop interest and encourage participation in girls' athletic activities. The city also agreed to provide a permanent home to the West Valley Girls' Softball League. An analysis of data provided by

the city's Department of Recreation and Parks was conducted by UCLA law students Syd Whalley and Brady M. Bustany. They reported that by 2000, boy participants in city youth sports programs still outnumbered girls by a three-to-one ratio. However, there was evidence that Raise the Bar was bringing about some change. In 1998, girls constituted only 18.7 percent of participants. This proportion of girl participants rose to 21.6 percent in 1999 and to 25.6 percent in 2000, an increase that exceeded the goals set by the legal settlement. Whalley and Bustany, "Gender Equity in Youth Team Sports by the Department of Recreation and Parks in the City of Los Angeles."

17. A foundational work in sport studies that illustrates the social class dynamics of structural constraint and human agency is Gruneau, *Class, Sports, and Social Development*. When Don Sabo and I wrote the introduction to our first edited collection on men, gender, and sport, we attempted to look at agency and constraint in terms of gender, race, and class. See Messner and Sabo, "Toward a Critical Feminist Reappraisal of Sport, Men, and the Gender Order." One thing that was mostly missing from our model, though (and this is a common blind spot in progressive sociology), was the fact that it is not only oppressed and marginalized groups who are historical agents. Privileged groups of people also exercise agency. This book focuses largely on the agency exercised by those at the institutional and cultural center of sport, an agency that is enabled by positions of authority and privilege but is also shaped in response to the agency of those at the margins.

18. Title IX is patterned after the language of Title VII of the Civil Rights Act of 1964, which prohibited discrimination of students on the basis of race, color, or national origin. Title IX reads, "No person in the United States shall, on the basis of sex, be excluded from participation in, be denied the benefits of, or be subjected to discrimination under any educational program or activity receiving federal financial assistance." Much of my description of the dynamics of Title IX struggles over the years is drawn from Linda Jean Carpenter's beautiful narrative of her life with Title IX. See Carpenter, "Letters Home." See also Harris, "The Reform of Women's Intercollegiate Athletics."

19. In 1979, NCAA lawyers who were frustrated by the U.S. Department of Health, Education, and Welfare's provisions for enforcement of Title IX, stated: "This whole Title IX effort can ... be viewed as an attempt by the Federal government to take over control of higher education in America" and that the proposed 1979 Athletics Policy Interpretation of Title IX was a result of "the

entrenched thinking of HEW's cadre of young, female lawyers." As quoted in Carpenter, *Letters Home*, 139.

20. According to the National Women's Law Center, although we do know that girls' participation in sports has continued to grow, national data on sex equity in sports at the elementary, middle school, and high school levels do not exist. However, the law center points out that anecdotal evidence suggests persistent vast inequities: "We receive many calls from disgruntled parents, athletes, and coaches complaining of gender inequality in their school athletics program. Some of the more common problems raised are the failure to offer enough girls' sports; the scheduling of girls' sports in the 'off-season,' causing the girls to miss out on scholarship and recruiting opportunities; the authorization of paid coaching positions for boys' teams and volunteer coaching positions for girls' teams; and the provision of generally inferior equipment and facilities." National Women's Law Center, "The Battle for Gender Equity in Athletics in Elementary and Secondary Schools."

21. In 1998, in what some commentators called "the most important litigation to date on sex discrimination in intercollegiate athletics," a federal judge ruled against Brown University in clarifying the legal definition of "substantial proportionality." The ruling states that the proportion of female athletes at an institution should be within 3.5 percentage points of the proportion of female undergraduates. Naughton, "Judge Approves Settlement of Brown U.'s Title IX Case." In 2000, the U.S. Department of Education's Office of Civil Rights announced what would become known as the One Percent Rule—a policy that is hailed as a tremendously important clarification of Title IX. In 1997, the National Women's Law Center filed a Title IX complaint with the Office of Civil Rights, claiming that twenty-five universities failed to give female athletes their share of scholarship money. The outcome, the One Percent Rule, stipulates that a gap no wider than 1 percentage point should exist between the percentage of scholarship athletes of one sex and the percentage of total scholarship aid awarded to that sex. The National Women's Law Center hailed this new ruling as a great victory for sex equity in sports. "Education Dept. Resolves Last of 25 Bias Complaints Filed by Women's Group."

22. For instance, a survey in 2000 found that 79 percent of adults approved of Title IX, and 76 percent even approved of cutting back on men's sports if that were necessary to improve access for girls and women. Suggs, "Poll Finds Strong Public Backing for Gender Equity in College Athletics."

23. Acosta and Carpenter, *Women in Intercollegiate Sport.*

24. A similar dynamic occurred, but in the opposite direction, when the previously male (and higher-status) occupation of clerical work was rapidly deskilled and "feminized" during a period of rapid industrialization and bureaucratization in the early twentieth century. See Reskin and Roos, *Job Queues, Gender Queues.*

25. This fact is well documented by sport economists and sociologists. See Sperber, *Beer and Circus;* and Zimbalist, *Unpaid Professionals.*

26. The researchers assigned "grades" to individual schools and averaged the grades by divisions, with full gender equity being awarded a 4.0 grade. Division I-A schools, defined as schools that sponsor major football and basketball programs, averaged a 2.48 grade. Division I-AA schools that usually sponsor major basketball and smaller football programs got a 2.51. Division I-AAA programs that sponsor major basketball programs but no football received a 2.86. Division II programs that limit athletic scholarship and other expenses to provide competitive but financially less costly athletic programs received a 2.5. And Division III schools that do not award athletic scholarships received a 2.77. Sabo, *The Women's Sports Foundation Gender Equity Report Card.*

27. Eitzen, *Fair and Foul*, 118.

28. The elite college football programs that are members of the BCS are all of the schools from the Atlantic Coast, Big East, Big Ten, Big 12, Pacific Ten, and Southeastern conferences. Suggs, "Female Athletes Thrive, but Budget Pressures Loom," A-46.

29. Suggs, "U. of Kansas to Drop Men's Swimming and Tennis."

30. Suggs, "Supreme Court Won't Hear Title IX Lawsuit."

31. Suggs, "2 Appeals Courts Uphold Right of Universities to Reduce Number of Male Athletes."

32. Jacobson, "Among Big Sports Programs, Gender Equity Is No. 1 Reason for Cutting Men's Teams, Report Says."

33. Jacobson, "Among Big Sports Programs. . . ."

34. National Women's Law Center, "Title IX and Men's Minor Sports."

35. Weistart, "Title IX and Intercollegiate Sports: Equal Opportunity?" 296.

36. Sabo writes that "separatist, elitist, or wounded-giant sexism benefits the elite men who sit atop the administrative hierarchies that were formed in the historical heyday of patriarchal sport." Sabo, "Different Stakes," 207.

37. Of course, this kind of accounting would have to recognize that equipment and uniform costs in some sports are much higher than in others.

38. Concerning college sports, economist Andrew Zimbalist observes: "The NCAA wants it both ways. When confronted by the challenges of Title IX and gender equity, the NCAA and its member schools want to be treated as a business. AD's argue that it is justifiable to put more resources into men's than women's sports, because men's sports generate more revenue. But when the IRS knocks on its door, the NCAA and its member schools want their special tax exemptions as part of the non-profit educational establishment and they claim special amateur status in order to avoid paying their athletes." Zimbalist, *Unpaid Professionals*, 6.

39. For earlier Marxist analyses of sport, see Brohm, *Sport*; and Rigauer, *Sport and Work*. Responding critically to the economistic reductionism of these early works, hegemony theorists insisted on viewing sport as intricately intertwined with the capitalist economy but also as a relatively autonomous cultural realm. See Gruneau, *Class, Sports, and Social Development*; and Hargreaves, *Sport, Power and Culture*. Taking a different theoretical tack, Eric Dunning explores sport and commercialization from a figurational perspective. Dunning, *Sport Matters*.

40. Zimbalist, *Unpaid Professionals*, 127.

41. Sperber, *Beer and Circus*, 216.

42. As of February 2001, there were thirteen major league baseball players who were signed to multiyear contracts, each of which is paying more than $80 million, topped by Texas Rangers shortstop Alex Rodriguez's ten-year, $253 million contract. In March 2001, NFL quarterback Brett Favre signed a ten-year $100 million contract. That same day, less stellar players also signed big contracts: New York Giants cornerback Jason Sehorn ($36 million for six years with a $10 million signing bonus); the Pittsburgh Steelers' Jerome Bettis ($35 million for six years); and Tennessee Titans wide receiver Derrick Mason ($23.45 million for five years). The top-paid NBA player is the Minnesota Timberwolves' Kevin Garnett, who is earning $127 million from 1997 to 2002. In the NHL, the Pittsburgh Penguins' Jaromir Jagr is earning $48 million from 1998 to 2004.

43. Jhally, "The Spectacle of Accumulation"; Gruneau, "Making Spectacle." In the 1990s, scholars began to study concretely how these institutional relations operate. In particular, see Real's discussion of "MediaSport" commodification, Bellamy's analysis of integrated marketing in sport, Whitson's

exploration of sport's global "circuits of promotion," and Rowe, McKay, and Miller's analysis of sport, nationalism, and media. Bellamy, "The Evolving Television Sports Marketplace"; Real, "MediaSport"; Rowe, McKay, and Miller, "Come Together"; Whitson, "Circuits of Promotion"; Miller et al., *Globalization and Sport.*

44. Messner, Dunbar, and Hunt, "The Televised Sports Manhood Formula."

45. With respect to college sports, the dynamics of the sport-media-commercial complex have been critically illuminated by scholars Murray Sperber and Andrew Zimbalist. See Sperber, *Beer and Circus*; and Zimbalist, *Unpaid Professionals.*

46. The "What are *you* doing?" ad appears incoherent until the final frame of the ad. During most of the ad, three white, apparently middle-class (and slightly effeminate—perhaps gay?) guys are in their apartments drinking expensive imported beers and asking each other, in increasingly obnoxious ways, "What are *you* doing?" The ad ends with a view of two African American guys sitting on a couch, looking stunned, apparently having watched these three nutty, dumb white guys acting up with their imported beers. The encoded message, I think, is intended to play on middle-class white guys' fears of being feminine (and appearing gay): Drinking an expensive imported beer becomes a sign *not* of valued higher-class status but of a stigmatized feminine status. The black guys offer a contrast: they are just regular (masculine) guys who *know* what they're doing—in terms of both their beer and their manhood.

47. Sperber, *Beer and Circus*, 49; emphasis in the original.

48. Ibid., 184.

49. Warren Farrell was among the first to analyze the Super Bowl as a corporate-sponsored "machismo ritual." See Farrell, "The Super-Bowl Phenomenon."

50. The largest categories of advertisers for the 2001 Super Bowl were dot.com companies (seventeen total ads) and snack food companies (sixteen total ads, the largest of which was Pepsi, with six ads).

51. The extent of alcohol ads varied across different televised sports: Alcohol ads made up 9.1 percent of baseball ads, 13.3 percent of ESPN *SportsCenter* ads, 3.8 percent of ESPN X Games ads, 6.8 percent of NBA ads, 8.9 percent of NFL ads, 0 percent of professional wrestling ads. Overall, auto-related ads and snack food ads were the two largest categories, followed by ads for other

shows on the same networks, with alcohol ads fourth. See Messner, Hunt, and Dunbar, *Boys to Men*.

52. I will reflect more on the content of beer and other alcohol ads in chapter 4.

53. They also gleefully read and share his recent autobiography. See Hawk, *Hawk*.

54. Humphreys, "'Shredheads Go Mainstream?'"

55. Wheaton and Tomlinson, "The Changing Gender Order in Sport?"

56. Weidman and Beal, "Authenticity in the Skateboarding World."

57. I explore the dynamics of this different race-class contextualization of life choices for boys and young men in *Power at Play*.

58. White men's internalized fears of African American men are often highly sexualized. Paul Hoch suggests that white men tend to project the image of an oversexed "black beast" onto African American males as a means of sublimating white males' own repressed sexual desires. Hoch, *White Hero, Black Beast: Racism, Sexism and the Mask of Masculinity*. And psychologists Chester Pierce and Wesley Profit observed that white males reveal deep fear of African American males by tending not to "reveal weakness, inferiority, uncertainty, or anxiety in front of Black males." Their research also revealed that "white men in the presence of Black men spend many more seconds covering their genitals than when they are by themselves." Pierce and Profit, "Racial Group Dynamics," 169.

59. Kusz, "BMX, Extreme Sports, and the White Male Backlash."

60. This racial dynamic was played out starkly on an extreme sports show my colleagues and I analyzed as part of a study of televised sports. The show was introduced by an African American male, using hip-hop music. Once this cool "black style" was established, the actual bike competition included all-white competitors in front of what appeared to be an all-white crowd. Messner, Dunbar, and Hunt, "The Televised Sports Manhood Formula."

61. Robert Rinehart, in his study of corporate-media commodification of in-line skating, concludes that "skating culture as [the skaters] once knew it is also morphing, changing to fit the demands of a voracious television audience (or at least an audience perceived to be voracious by television bosses and advertisers)." Rinehart, "Dropping into Sight."

62. In addition to an invitation to pay to join Tony Hawk's fan club, the official Tony Hawk web site includes links to Birdhouse skateboards, a full line of Tony Hawk shoes, Arnette sunglasses and goggles, EXPN (ESPN's extreme

sports site), TSG helmets, Techdeck bikes, skateboards, and surfboards, Tony Hawk Proskater 2 and other electronic games, Hawk clothing (shirts, pants, hats, etc.), and Bagel Bites ("the official hot snack sponsor of the ESPN X Games!").

63. Parts of this final section of the chapter were previously published in Dworkin and Messner, "Just Do ... What?" 348–50.

64. Zimbalist, *Unpaid Professionals*, 143.

65. The Nike swoosh logo seems indeed to be everywhere. It is nearly impossible to watch a televised sports game without seeing the swoosh on play-ers' uniforms and on the walls of stadiums or arenas. The athletic gear worn by coaches and athletes and the school clothing sold in the student bookstore at my university (and at many others) all have the swoosh on them. The uniforms that the kids in my son's YMCA basketball league wear are all swooshed. People even choose to buy shirts, hats, and other clothing (besides Nike shoes) with the swoosh on them. Robert Goldman and Stephen Papson call the omnipresence of the Nike sign "overswooshification." Goldman and Papson, *Nike Culture*, 1.

66. Goldman and Papson, *Nike Culture*, 5.

67. As noted in Goldman and Papson, *Nike Culture*, 132.

68. Rather than seeing Nike's relationship to feminism as one of simple appropriation or co-optation, Cole and Hribar argue that Nike is part of a more general "postfeminist" historical moment. "Postfeminism can be characterized as the process through which movement feminism was reterritorialized through the normalizing logic ... governing 1980s America. While movement feminism generated spaces and identities that interrogated distributional and relational inequalities, meanings, differences, and identities, the postfeminist moment in-cludes spaces that work to homogenize, generate conformity, and mark Others, while discouraging questioning. It is, in other words, a normalizing discourse." Cole and Hribar, "Celebrity Feminism," 356. For a discussion of how racism is sometimes tied in to this cultural dynamic, see McKay, "Enlightened Racism and Celebrity Feminism in Contemporary Sports Advertisements."

69. Nike's ads are probably most appealing to younger, post–Title IX female viewers, because they address this generation of girls' and women's common worldviews. As Goldman and Papson observe, Nike ads communicate two general themes. First, they communicate an "irreverent, winking attitude about everything that smacks of commodity culture. Nike adopts a self-reflexive posture" that appeals to younger, media-savvy viewers who are jaded by over-exposure to commercial images and appeals. And second, Nike ads express a

"motivational ethos" (condensed in its Just Do It slogan) that "integrates themes of personal transcendence, achievement, and authenticity." Goldman and Papson, *Nike Culture*, 3. I suspect that, together, these twin themes resonate with younger women who might define themselves as media-savvy, individualist "third-wave feminists." I will address this issue more in the final chapter.

70. Cole and Hribar, "Celebrity Feminism," 365.

71. Don Sabo, who has worked for years with the Women's Sports Foundation, gave me an important insight into this dynamic: "Certain women's movements have always *used* the media, as much as possible. Mass media become vehicles for communication when effectively manipulated. The Women's Sports Foundation has become adept at using print and electronic media. We'd use our research studies and events to garner media attention—get them in the 'same room' via an 'event' or through a celebrity presence and, then, lay a message on them or communicate key information that had implications for fomenting social change and change in public awareness." Don Sabo, personal communication, May 31, 2001.

72. Take Action for Girls, "The Two Faces of Nike," 2.

73. Zimbalist, *Unpaid Professionals*, 141.

74. Current academic debates over how to assess the value of an athletic shoe sometimes pit those employing a more traditional Marxist labor theory of value against more recent cultural studies scholars who argue that the value of current commodities is determined more by the cultural cachet of its commodity sign. So, for instance, the labor theory of value would see a $70 pair of Nike shoes, note that workers who made the shoe were paid about $1.60, and, after subtracting the costs of materials and other incidentals, would call the remaining profit surplus value that has been unfairly extracted from the exploited workers. Goldman and Papson, while not denying that exploitation of workers is an important factor, argue that this labor theory of value approach is "outdated and erroneous." "In today's athletic footwear commodity chain, the symbolic workers (e.g., advertisers, marketers, and designers) contribute the greater share of value to the product." Goldman and Papson, *Nike Culture*, 11. In other words, the Marxist object of study, "the point of production," is not the main point; rather, Nike's focus is on "the point of consumption." Cole and Hribar demonstrate the importance of employing both levels of analysis: "As Nike attempts to mobilize U.S. women around Cheryl Swoops, Third World women will be organizing around the sneaker as they continue in their attempt to

develop international strategies to mobilize against transnationals like Nike." Cole and Hribar, "Celebrity Feminism," 366.

4. Center of Attention

1. The three studies were based on 1989, 1993, and 1999 data and were published in 1990, 1994, and 2000, respectively. See: Amateur Athletic Foundation of Los Angeles, *Gender Stereotyping in Televised Sports*; Amateur Athletic Foundation of Los Angeles, *Gender Stereotyping in Televised Sports: A Followup to the 1989 Study*; Amateur Athletic Foundation of Los Angeles, *Gender in Televised Sports: 1989, 1993, and 1999*.

2. Gerbner, "The Dynamics of Cultural Resistance."

3. It is of course debatable whether new media sources should simply be looked at as "marginal" to the traditional center of sports media or whether perhaps new developments will involve the growth of multiple "centers." This question is perhaps most applicable to the development of what Stephen McDaniel and Christopher Sullivan call "cybersport." See McDaniel and Sullivan, "Extending the Sports Experience."

4. A key part of the symbolic marginalization of women's sports and women athletes is asymmetrical gender marking. Men's events, leagues, and records are symbolically represented as the universal norm (e.g., "the national championship game," "the National Basketball Association," and "the most points ever scored in a game"), while women's events, leagues, and records are always gender marked (e.g., "the women's national championship game," "the Women's National Basketball Association," and "the most points ever scored in a women's game"). This asymmetrical gender marking tends to position women's sports and women athletes symbolically as secondary and derivative to men's sports. My colleages and I have tracked this asymmetrical gender marking in our studies of women's and men's televised sports. See Messner, Duncan, and Jensen, "Separating the Men from the Girls"; Amateur Athletic Foundation of Los Angeles, *Gender in Televised Sports: 1989, 1993, and 1999*.

5. I first made the argument that women athletes represent a "contested ideological terrain" in the late 1980s. With participation rates of girls and women continuing to rise and with the expansion of electronic media and commercialization of women's sports beginning to grow, this ideological contest has continued but shifted. Messner, "Sports and Male Domination." There is also a rich foundation of research on ways that the mass media have covered women

athletes. Key texts and overviews of the research include Duncan and Hasbrook, "Denial of Power in Televised Women's Sports"; Cohen, "Media Portrayals of the Female Athlete"; and Kane, "Media Coverage of the Post–Title IX Female Athlete."

6. Parts of this section of the chapter were previously published in Messner, Duncan, and Cooky, "Silence, Sports Bras, and Wrestling Porn."

7. The finding in our study that *SportsCenter* devoted only 2.2 percent of its airtime to covering women athletes and women's sports was consistent with findings in other recent studies. Eastman and Billings, "Sportscasting and Sports Reporting." Billings also observed that ESPN's highly promoted series of shows on their "top one hundred athletes of the century" included eighty-nine men, eight women, and three horses. As such, the list echoes cultural biases against women athletes in the past and reinforces them today. Billings, "In Search of Women Athletes."

8. Farred, "Cool as the Other Side of the Pillow."

9. Amateur Athletic Foundation of Los Angeles, *Gender in Televised Sports*.

10. As noted in Deford, "Advantage, Kournikova," 97, 100.

11. On the basis of a Lykos.com count of hits on sports celebrities' web sites, Kournikova ranked number one in early 2001. Sable was two, followed by fellow wrestlers Trish Stratus and the Rock. Basketball players Michael Jordan and Vince Carter ranked numbers five and six, respectively, followed by golfer Tiger Woods (seven), basketball player Allen Iverson (eight), tennis player Martina Hingis (nine), and skateboarder Tony Hawk (ten). This sort of list is most likely a good indicator of the celebrity tastes of young sports fans who have internet access. "Now You Know."

12. Deford, "Advantage, Kournikova."

13. As quoted in Amateur Athletic Foundation of Los Angeles, *Sportsletter*, 1.

14. Guttmann, "Nature, Nurture, and the Athletic Body." Guttmann develops these ideas more fully in his book *The Erotic in Sport*.

15. As quoted in Amateur Athletic Foundation of Los Angeles, *Sportsletter*, 1.

16. In 1970, King led a boycott in protest of pay inequities between women and men on the pro tennis tour and within three years launched the separate women's Virginia Slims pro tour.

17. Sport studies scholar Pat Griffin notes that the existence of lesbians in sports has been met with various kinds of homophobic responses that she categorizes as silence, denial, apology, promotion of a heterosexy image, attacks on lesbians, and preference for male coaches. See Griffin, "Changing the Game." See also Griffin, *Strong Women, Deep Closets*; Lenskyj, "Sexuality and Femininity in Sport Contexts"; and Kane and Lenskyj, "Media Treatment of Female Athletes."

18. Creedon, "Women, Sport, and Media Institutions." This trend has been noted by sport scholars in Australia as well. See Lenskyj, "'Inside Sport' or 'On the Margins'?"; and Mikosza and Phillips, "Gender, Sport and the Body Politic."

19. For informative discussions of race and gender in cultural definitions of feminine beauty, see Banet-Weiser, *The Most Beautiful Girl in the World*; Chancer, *Reconcilable Differences*; Collins, *Black Feminist Thought*; and Zones, "Beauty Myths and Realities and Their Impact on Women's Health."

20. Davis, *The Swimsuit Issue and Sport*.

21. Bordo, *The Male Body*.

22. Anderson, "The Other Side of Jenny," 120–21.

23. Heywood, "Bodies, Babes, and the WNBA, or, Where's Tiger Naked in a Cape When You Really Need Him?"

24. Heywood and Drake, eds., *Third Wave Agenda*.

25. In our comparison of televised coverage of the NCAA women's and men's basketball "Final Four" tournament, my colleagues and I argued that audiences were likely to experience the men's Final Four as pleasurable, exciting, and momentous, while experiencing the women's Final Four as less pleasurable, less exciting and momentous, and even a bit disorienting, partly because of the higher production values of the men's tournament, but also because audiences of the men's games were far more likely to be familiar with the players, coaches, teams, and traditions of that tournament than audiences of the women's games would be with theirs. This difference is due in part to a dramatic asymmetry in "audience building" in the two. Throughout the regular season, men's basketball fans are treated to seemingly countless televised games (including a large proportion of the NCAA tournament games preceding the Final Four), as well as mountains of print coverage. By contrast, few women's regular season games are televised, and far less print coverage is given to these games. Thus, by the time the Final Four tournaments appear on television, the audience for the men's

games has been constructed to enjoy the event as the exciting culmination of something they have been a part of. By contrast, the women's event is likely to be experienced as having dropped into one's television from nowhere—the players, teams, and coaches unfamiliar and alien. See Messner, Duncan, and Wachs, "The Gender of Audience-Building."

26. For an excellent analysis of the gender dynamics of the LPGA, see Crosset, *Outsiders in the Clubhouse*.

27. A career Grand Slam is won when a player has won the championship at least once in each of the tour's four major tournaments (now the Nabisco Championship, the U.S. Open, the LPGA Championship, and the Du Maurier). Webb needed to play in only eight major events before winning her four Grand Slam events. By contrast, Tiger Woods played in fifteen majors on the PGA tour before completing the career Grand Slam.

28. For a discussion of the relationship between nationalism and gender in U.S. media coverage of a women's sport, see Chisholm, "Defending the Nation."

29. Banet-Weiser, "We Got Next."

30. C. L. Cole and Samantha King have argued persuasively that the NBA was successfully marketed in the 1980s through a racialized "sport/gang dyad." "Black urban masculinity was visualized (enacted and encoded) through a fundamental distinction between the athlete (primarily figured as in the urban basketball player) and the criminal (typically figured through the gang member): the tension generated between the two categories served as the ground for well-rehearsed and familiar 1980s stories continually circulated and fed by the mass media industry for public consumption and spectatorship." This juxtaposition created the foundation for the emergence of Michael Jordan as American icon and for the successful public reception of the 1994 film *Hoop Dreams*. Cole and King, "Representing Black Masculinity and Urban Possibilities," 52. But this sport-gang dyad juxtaposition only partly and temporarily succeeded in creating a racial symbology that provided fertile grounds for stabile marketing of the NBA and its players. By the mid- to late 1990s, Jordan had retired, and new tensions had arisen, including public disapproval of skyrocketing player salaries as well as various sex, violence, and family scandals concerning individual players. The subsequent souring of public attitudes about the NBA created fertile groundwork for the "return to the purity of the game" WNBA marketing.

31. Watkins, "Bad Boyz."

32. Hunt, *O. J. Simpson Facts and Fictions*.

33. Amateur Athletic Foundation of Los Angeles, *Children and Sports Media*.

34. There are some differences and some similarities in what boys and girls prefer to watch. The top seven televised sports reported by girls are, in order, gymnastics, men's pro basketball, pro football, pro baseball, swimming/diving, men's college basketball, and women's pro or college basketball.

35. In all, we examined about twenty-three hours of sports programming, nearly one-quarter of which was time taken up by commercials. We examined a total of 722 commercials, which spanned a large range of products and services. We collected both quantitative and qualitative data. For a more detailed discussion of this research and its documentation, see Messner, Dunbar, and Hunt, "The Televised Sports Manhood Formula."

36. Sabo and Jansen, "Seen But Not Heard."

37. The racial coding of extreme sports shows is especially intriguing. Though little research has yet been done on this topic, I speculate that many white, middle-class adolescent boys and young men get involved in sports like skateboarding partly as an alternative to the central sports team sports, which are viewed as dominated by African American males. Nevertheless, these alternative extreme sports liberally borrow African American street styles and codes of clothing and music. The emergent TV portrayals of these sports tend to demonstrate this hybrid coding of black cultural style in a predominantly white sport setting.

38. Wheaton and Tomlinson, "The Changing Gender Order in Sport?"

39. Rinehart, "Inside of the Outside."

40. Though images of feminine beauty shift, change, and are contested throughout history, female beauty is presented in sports programming and commercials in narrow ways. "Attractive" women look like fashion models: they are tall, thin, young, usually (though not always) white, with signs of heterosexual femininity encoded and overtly displayed through hair, makeup, sexually provocative facial and bodily gestures, large (often partly exposed) breasts, long (often exposed) legs, and so on. For a critical discussion of this kind of encoding of femininity, see Banet-Weiser, *The Most Beautiful Girl in the World*.

41. This mediated theme of heterosexual male bonding through alcohol reflects common practices in men's use of "sports bars." Lawrence Wenner, in his fascinating study of sports bars, observes, "Not only do public drinking

and participation in sports serve as masculine rites of passage, their spaces and places often serve as refuge from women." Wenner, "In Search of the Sports Bar," 303.

42. Jansen and Sabo, "The Sport/War Metaphor"; Malszecki and Cavar, "Men, Masculinities, War, and Sport"; Trujillo, "Machines, Missiles, and Men."

43. Stewart, "X Marks the Spot."

44. In the 1990s, the male bonding theme became, if anything, even more central in beer commercials. Sometimes it was spoofed, as in the popular mid-1990s beer commercial that featured teary-eyed men saying, "I love you, man!" to each other. Strate, "Beer Commercials."

45. A 1996 survey by the Center on Alcohol Advertising found nearly as many nine- to eleven-year-old children (73 percent) knew that frogs say "Budweiser" as knew that Bugs Bunny said "What's up, Doc?" (80 percent). Another survey found that eight to twelve year olds could name more brands of beer than they could U.S. presidents. Beer companies in recent years have pounced on the rapidly growing extreme sports market, which is primarily a youth market. See Kilbourne, *Can't Buy My Love*, 160–61.

46. Authors Jeff Benedict and Don Yaeger did a statistical survey of NFL players and crime. Not including traffic or other minor offenses and misdemeanors, Benedict and Yaeger found that 109 NFL players (or 21 percent of the players in the league) had a criminal history, with a total of 264 arrests for serious crimes. The largest number of arrests were for domestic violence (15), aggravated assault and battery (42), and other public safety crimes such as illegal possession of a weapon and trespassing (40). There were seven arrests for rape. Benedict and Yaeger, *Pros and Cons*, 6.

47. Messner and Solomon, "Outside the Frame."

48. McDonald, "Unnecessary Roughness."

49. McKay, "'Marked Men' and 'Wanton Women'"; Rowe, "Accommodating Bodies."

50. Dworkin and Wachs, "The Morality/Manhood Paradox," 56.

51. Ibid., 58.

52. Timothy Beneke argues that the appeal of boys' and men's sports spectating, reading the sports pages, and talking sports with other men lies in "BIRGING—Basking In Reflected Glory … gaining esteem through showing off connections with successful others." Beneke, *Proving Manhood*. For scholarly analysis of the appeal of violent entertainment (including sports) to audiences,

see Goldstein, ed., *Why We Watch*; and Briant, Zillmann, and Raney, "Violence and the Enjoyment of Media Sports."

53. This is a huge and complicated question that connects to years of research and debate about violence, media, and audiences. Though it is beyond the purview of my focus here to delve into these debates, I want to note that since the 1980s, it has been part of the "common knowledge" in the United States that rates of violence against women, especially in the home, rise on Super Bowl Sunday. In 1993, journalist Robert Lipsyte dubbed the Super Bowl the "Abuse Bowl." However, as far as I know no actual research has ever documented this relationship between watching the Super Bowl and higher rates of domestic violence. A few years back, a reporter called several women's shelters after the Super Bowl and found that there was no surge in calls from abused women during or immediately following the event. Canadian researchers studied the relationship between televised NHL playoff games and rates of domestic violence, and their findings were inconclusive. Holman, *Sport, Media and Domestic Violence*. Sabo and his colleagues took a different approach to studying this issue. They began with the assumption that any relationship between watching violent sports and acts of spousal violence is, perhaps like spousal rape rates, extremely difficult to measure accurately. So instead of trying to measure or document a statistical correlation, they located and interviewed eighteen women who had been regularly beaten by male partners who were watching (or had just finished watching) televised sports (mostly hockey, football, and basketball). Often, these men battered the women in view of others, as a "display of power and domination" in front of an "audience" that included "children, extended family members, and male friends." The authors concluded that while no simple cause-effect relationship could be drawn between watching sports and wife beating, watching the sporting event was a key part of a violent matrix. Rather than providing a "symbolic refuge" for these male viewers, watching sports on TV "aroused emotional and cultural associations with masculinity that, in turn, seemed to combine with aspects of life history, individual psychology, the use of drugs and alcohol, and gambling to produce violence against women." Sabo, Gray, and Moore, "Domestic Violence and Televised Athletic Events," 145.

54. Toni Bruce's research on fans of women's televised basketball begins to answer this question in the affirmative. Bruce notes that although viewers were often "frustrated" by the ways that women athletes were "devalued, trivialized, and stereotyped" on TV, these viewers "actively challenged television's view and

created their own, more positive, interpretations." Bruce, "Audience Frustration and Pleasure."

55. Darnell Hunt has provided a solid example of how to study audiences' racialized interpretations of a controversial news item. Hunt, *O. J. Simpson Facts and Fictions*. In sport studies, very little audience research has been conducted so far, though some scholars have laid out the fundamental questions that will be of use to future scholars. See Wenner and Gantz, "Watching Sports on Television"; and Whannel, "Reading the Sports Media Audience."

56. Sociologist Michele Dunbar argues that even though he plays with sexual and gender codes, Dennis Rodman's image appears to constitute an individualized rebellion that is mostly reproductive (rather than disruptive or resistant) of dominant gender and race relations. She does note, though, that her critical reading of Rodman would be enhanced by audience studies. Dunbar, "Dennis Rodman—Do You Feel Feminine Yet?"

5. Contesting the Center

1. Nancy Spencer argues that this ad campaign was an early example of "commodity feminism," in which Virginia Slims was one of the first of several marketers that had begun to capitalize on women's changing attitudes by being attentive to what women wanted to hear about themselves. Spencer, "Reading between the Lines."

2. Despite this closing gap, men's tobacco use is still higher than women's, and this accounts for much of men's higher rates of lung cancer and heart disease. See Courtenay, "Behavioral Factors Associated with Disease, Injury, and Death among Men"; and Waldron, "Contributions of Changing Gender Differences in Behavior and Social Roles to Changing Gender Differences in Mortality."

3. Goldman and Papson, *Nike Culture*.

4. Injuries to the knee's anterior cruciate ligament (ACL) occur at a much higher rate among college women basketball and soccer players than among their male counterparts. In basketball, women received 2.89 ACL injuries per 10,000 "exposures," or chances of getting hurt during practices or games, compared with male athletes' rate of 1.01 injuries per 10,000 exposures; in soccer, female players experienced 3.3 injuries per 10,000 exposures compared with only 1.2 injuries for male players. Explanations for these higher rates of injury range from hormonal differences (a woman's menstrual cycle makes for looser

tendons at certain times of the month), anatomical differences (women's lower center of gravity puts more stress on the knee joint), and training differences (women do not do as much hard jumping training, which tends to tighten the knee). Simply discussing this topic tends to make advocates of women's sports uncomfortable, because it raises the possibility of a resurgence of the myth of female frailty and the rise of restrictive protective legislation for girls and women in sports. Jacobson, "Why Do So Many Female Athletes Enter ACL Hell?"

5. Commentators on women's sports often cite today a dangerous medical condition called the female athlete triad, which consists of an interrelated combination of eating disorders, amenorrhea, and low bone density. This triad is a logical outcome of an emotionally and physically abusive training regimen common among young elite female athletes. For a chilling description of this process see Ryan, *Little Girls in Pretty Boxes*. Advocates of women's sports have also pointed to the prevalence of sexual harassment and sexual abuse of girl and women athletes by coaches and others. See Brackenridge, "'He Owned Me Basically ...'"; Brackenridge and Kirby, "Playing It Safe"; Heywood, "Despite the Positive Rhetoric about Women's Sports, Female Athletes Face a Culture of Sexual Harassment"; and Nelson, *The Stronger Women Get, the More Men Love Football*. A comprehensive study of sexual harassment in Norwegian sports found that athletes were no more likely to experience sexual harassment than nonathletes were. However, elite athletes were significantly more likely to experience sexual harassment than less involved or less accomplished athletes were. Fasting, Brackenridge, and Sundgot-Borgen, *Females, Elite Sports and Sexual Harassment*.

6. Indeed, the graduation rate for women college basketball players, at 67 percent, is considerably higher than the graduation rate for men college basketball players (45 percent). Zimbalist, *Unpaid Professionals*, 73.

7. Zimbalist, *Unpaid Professionals*, 31.

8. Shakib, *Male and Female High School Basketball Players' Perceptions of Gender and Athleticism*.

9. Theberge, "Sport and Women's Empowerment."

10. These three trends are admittedly oversimplified ideal types that I have constructed to help make sense of a complicated world. Later in the chapter, I will discuss how concrete organizations such as the WNBA or the Women's Sports Foundation do not fit neatly into any one category.

11. The term *wave of athletic feminism* is from Twin, *Out of the Bleachers*. For other useful histories of women's sports in the United States and Canada,

see Cahn, *Coming on Strong*; Guttmann, *Women's Sports*; and Lenskyj, *Out of Bounds*.

12. Theberge, "Women Athletes and the Myth of Female Frailty."

13. Cahn, *Coming on Strong*, 74.

14. Cahn, *Coming on Strong*, 77. Cahn deftly notes the class and race antagonisms reflected in these two tendencies. While middle-class physical educators saw themselves as guardians of feminine purity against both the sexual exploitation of the market and the presumed mannishness of working-class women, popular promoters appealed to working-class and African American women "[who] lived in a world in which sex, commerce, and sport were frequently integrated [and therefore] saw nothing wrong with using commercial sexual appeals to build the sports they so thoroughly enjoyed" (79).

15. Cahn, *Coming on Strong*, 81–82.

16. The idea of girls and women playing baseball has always seemed controversial. When the All American Girls' Professional Baseball League was formed during World War II, great care was taken to dress the players in "feminine" clothing (such as skirts, ensuring that sliding would be dangerous). They were also subject to severe dress and behavior codes off the field (and were even trained so as not to look too mannish or tomboyish). The league survived for twelve years, into the early 1950s. See Berlage, *Women in Baseball*; and Pratt, "The All-American Girls' Professional Baseball League." In recent years, commercial promoters have developed some limited women's professional baseball. However (at least after the age of seven, when they are allowed to play T-ball and coach-pitch on sex-integrated teams), girls still are mostly channeled into separate softball leagues, while boys play baseball. Without widespread institutionalized opportunities to play baseball in organizations like Little League Baseball and in schools and colleges, it is unlikely that enough women will develop the requisite skills necessary for the formation of a successful professional baseball league. Softball, then, is a good example of the effect of a separate, adapted model of women's sports. As long as girls don't play baseball, "the national pastime" remains a male preserve.

17. Cole argues that "sentimental and impassioned accounts of Title IX obscure the defining power of multinational corporations in American Culture. They erase the increasingly prominent positions of multinational corporations as underwriters of educational institutions via sports programs, their exclusive rights to vending machines, as well as other contractual agreements across

campuses. If not Title IX, who and what are responsible for the growth of girls' and women's sports? Adidas, Fila, Hyundai, Mary Kay, McDonald's, Nike, Reebok, Sears, the NBA, and the list of multinationals goes on." Cole, "The Year That Girls Ruled," 6.

18. Suggs, "Will Female Kicker's Legal Victory Reshape Gender Roles in Athletics?"

19. Kane, "Resistance/Transformation of the Oppositional Binary."

20. For instance, Eleanor M. Smeal, president of the Feminist Majority, has argued that the point of Heather Sue Mercer's case against Duke University is that women who have the ability to participate alongside men ought to be allowed to. Not all women are able to play college football, but neither are all men. "There is really more variance [in physical abilities] among men and among women than between the sexes," says Smeal, a Duke alumna. "A 4-11 man would have a more difficult time competing on a male basketball team than would a 6-5 woman. So, essentially, lumping all women together makes no sense." Suggs, "Will Female Kicker's Legal Victory . . . ?"

21. Scholars have observed that coed sports are often contradictory or paradoxical contexts with respect to gender. An underlying ideal of coed sports is that women and men should have equal opportunities to play together. However, assumptions of natural differences between the sexes and/or acknowledgement of different skill levels resulting from girls' poorer access to sports experiences have led to the development of adapted rules that reflect and reinforce these assumptions. For instance, Korfball is a coed game that was developed in the Netherlands. A close look reveals that although the game was developed on the basis of antisexist values, men still tend to play more controlling roles both in the game and in Korfball organizations. Summerfield and White, "Korfball." Similarly, Faye Linda Wachs's research on adult coed softball leagues in the United States shows how women and men constantly negotiate the gendered rules of the game and do so in ways that variously challenge and reproduce assumptions of men's natural athletic superiority. Faye Linda Wachs, "Leveling the Playing Field"; see also Henry and Comeaux, "Gender Egalitarianism in Coed Sport."

22. Sociologist Nancy Theberge's superb ethnography of elite-level women's ice hockey in Canada offers valuable insights into these questions about equality and difference. In particular, she discusses the ways that women negotiate gender in a sport that values and rewards bodily aggression. The women's version of ice hockey can be defined as partly adapted—that is, the violent body

checking so celebrated in men's hockey has been largely legislated out of the women's game. Has this difference made the women's game less than the men's game? different from it? better than it? "Women's hockey," writes Theberge, "exists in an uneasy tension with the dominant model of men's hockey.... The challenge lies in defining and implementing models that resist the problems of the dominant model while maintaining features that enable pleasure, satisfaction, and a sense of empowerment." Theberge, *Higher Goals*, 133, 137.

23. Within the parameters of liberal ideals of individual equal opportunity, the WSF's promotion of equality has been important and successful. The organization is a major source and clearinghouse of research and promotional information on girls' and women's sports. Women's Sports Foundation web site: http://www.womenssportsfoundation.org/templates/index.html.

24. For instance, M. Ann Hall notes the important contributions of the WSF in advocating for sex equity for women in U.S. sports. But she also charges that the WSF "has always been reluctant to deal openly with lesbianism because in the past corporate sponsors have threatened to withdraw funding." Ann Hall, *Feminism and Sporting Bodies*, 107.

25. By contrast, Canadian feminist activists have found the state to be an arena in which to struggle for women's sport equity. For instance, in 1980, the Canadian federal government's formation of the Women's Program in Fitness and Amateur Sport involved a commitment of resources and personnel to women's sports. And in 1986 the government set equality of opportunity for women at all levels of national sports as its official goal. Hall, *Feminism and Sporting Bodies*, 93. By contrast, the U.S. government takes an almost entirely laissez-faire approach to sport, leaving control of sport policy to private organizations and local or state school systems. Title IX, of course, is a major federal legal statute used by equity activists in school-based sports. But Title IX was not passed to ensure sex equity in sport; rather, the law was intended to apply broadly to everything within schools, including sports. In short, since the state is mostly out of bounds as a legitimate arena in which to fight for sex equity in sport, U.S. activists are more likely to look to corporate America for resources with which to boost girls' and women's sports.

26. See Hums and Snyder, "Growth in the Women's Sports Industry."

27. The WSF has close ties with various corporations. Reebok was an early supporter of the WSF, years before Nike positioned itself as a visible promoter of women's sports. Miller Brewing Company and Wilson Sporting Goods

have funded major WSF studies in the past. The current WSF web site lists the following businesses as its corporate partners: Allsport Photography (USA), Inc., America Online, Chrysler, Du Pont Lycra, Eteamz.com, FogDog, Gatorade, General Motors, Girlzone.com, Improve Network, Lily of France, Merrill Lynch, Pfizer, Inc., Sports Illustrated for Women, Tampax, and iVillage.com.

28. Heino, "New Sports."

29. For an informative summary of current debates concerning the relationship of "the imperatives of consumption" to identity, community, power, and freedom, see Dunn, *Identity Crisis*.

30. Certain expressions of third-wave feminism are fully consistent with corporate individualism. Third-wave feminism is, at least in part, a generational expression of a feminist consciousness that has been successfully individualized by consumer capitalism (the attraction of Nike's "Just Do It" television commercials to some third-wave feminists is a prime example of this). Heywood describes third-wave feminist sensibility as being defined by young women's taken-for-granted assumptions of individual equal opportunity and a strong (if somewhat enigmatic) identification with popular culture and electronic media. This youthful third-wave sensibility positions itself as a "new," even "radical," feminism, counterposed to the perceived cultural (and sexual) stodginess of a falsely universalized and flattened second-wave feminism. I see third-wave feminism as promising and potentially important but not as a major break from second-wave feminism. Rather, I read it as a newer, youthful continuation of individualist, middle-class liberal feminism that has found fertile ground in the political spaces opened by NOW, Title IX, and affirmative action and in the expansive cultural spaces created by the successful corporate-media co-optation of feminist slogans and symbols. It may be that third-wave feminism is "TINA feminism," or "there is no alternative" feminism. (TINA refers to the now pervasive post–Cold War ideology that there is no alternative to global consumer capitalism.) It is a middle-class feminism that has accommodated itself to and identifies with the rebellious fashions of commodified individualism that Nike and others so successfully sell to young consumers these days.

31. Miller et al., *The Women's Sports Foundation Report*.

32. A recent volume probes these paradoxes of how and in what ways sports participation might or might not be good for youth. Gatz, Rokeach, and Messner, eds., *Paradoxes of Youth and Sport*.

33. I am fully aware that a small but very visible number of poor African American boys and girls eventually are talented enough, committed enough, and

lucky enough to parlay their athletic skills into college scholarships that they would not ordinarily have been able to receive. Given the current structure of opportunity, it is not surprising (or in any way reprehensible) for children and young people to see sports as a possible opportunity for educational and occupational upward mobility. My point here, though, concerns public policy and poverty: there is no evidence that sports opportunities have any effect on race and class inequalities. A social commitment to end or ameliorate poverty needs to go to the root causes of these problems: a shortage of good paying jobs, decent housing, health care, child care, and education.

34. Bhavnani, "Response to Stacey & Thorne's 'Is Sociology Still Missing Its Feminist Revolution?'" The theoretical and strategic uses and limits of the concepts of cultural and societal margins and center have been debated within feminism, especially since the publication of bell hooks's influential work in 1984. See hooks, *Feminist Theory*.

35. The implications of this observation are important for progressive activism. It is not a matter of simplistically labeling organizations like the WSF as "liberal feminist" and then deciding on that basis to accept or reject their politics. Rather, such organizations have internal differences that suggest that progressives can (and currently do) work to nudge such organizations toward more fundamental social justice activism.

36. Pronger, "Outta My Endzone"; Pronger, "Homosexuality and Sport."

37. Indeed, WNBA salaries are far lower than NBA ones. In accordance with a 1999 collective bargaining agreement with the league, the top four WNBA draft picks in 2001 started at a salary of fifty-five thousand dollars a year. The next four earned forty-eight thousand, and so on, down to the league minimum of twenty-eight thousand. Salaries are rising at 5 to 10 percent a year, but established players who have done well are still paid according to their original draft position (e.g., all-star Orlando center Taj McWilliams-Franklin made only thirty-seven thousand dollars last year, far less than this year's top rookies). Gustkey, "WNBA's Marquee Brightens."

38. See Gustkey, "Sparks Are Altering Marketing Strategy," for all quotations in this paragraph.

39. For more information, see the AGELE (formerly the National Coalition on Sex Equity in Education) web site: www.ncsee.org.

40. McPherson, "Sport, Youth, Violence and the Media"; Messner and Stevens, "Scoring without Consent."

41. Antirape activist Alan Berkowitz states that preliminary research

indicates that "men's attitudes may not change as a result of educational interventions and that some program formats may actually reinforce attitudes and
beliefs associated with rape proclivity. Athletes and other members of close-knit,
cohesive groups of men may be particularly resistant to such interventions
because of the strength of group norms, interactions, and emotional bonding."
Berkowitz does note, though, that an important factor that makes such programs
more likely to be effective in changing rape-prone attitudes is "the support
and advocacy of individuals who are respected and credible to the participants.
Among athletes, the role of the coach is crucial." Berkowitz, "The Role of
Coaches in Rape Prevention Programs for Athletes."

42. Kidd, "The Men's Cultural Centre," 32.

43. Lenskyj, *Inside the Olympic Industry*.

44. McKay, "Teaching against the Grain." In a more theoretical vein,
David Andrews has taken the corporate imagery of Michael Jordan as a locus for
developing a "critical pedagogy of representation" that might be used to resist
the "seductive and domineering empire of signs" of which sports media are a key
part. Andrews, "Excavating Michael Jordan," 185–86. See also Andrews, *Michael
Jordan, Inc.*

45. Wenner, "The Sports Violence Profile."

46. See Kantor and Strauss, "The 'Drunken Bum' Theory of Wife
Beating."

47. Wenner, "In Search of the Sports Bar," 302.

48. In 1996, the University of Iowa, with support from the Robert Wood
Johnson Foundation and the American Medical Association, launched a serious
program to curtail dangerous binge drinking, which (as at many universities) was
rampant in its Greek system and surrounding its athletic events. This program
included, in 1999, the university's refusal of Miller Brewing Company's offer to
pay for advertising rights to the school's Hawkeye logo and ad space for the football and basketball teams' weekly television shows. The program limited opportunities for students to drink on campus, but it apparently did not significantly
lessen student drinking; rather, more off-campus drinking establishments sprang
up between 1996 and 2000. This outcome illustrates the complexity of the issue.
Sperber, *Beer and Circus*, 185–87.

49. Cole and Hribar, "Celebrity Feminism."

50. Those who own and control the global media conglomerates, as well
as the corporations that promote mediated sports, are overwhelmingly male. See
Miller et al., *Globalization and Sport*; Rowe and McKay, "Fields of Soap."

51. For the Adbusters web site, see http://www.adbusters.org/home. For the Adbusters story and strategy, see Lasn, *Culture Jam*. Another organization, the Nike Watch Campaign, focuses exclusively on monitoring Nike's worldwide production policies. See http://www.caa.org.au/campaigns/nike. See also Sage, "Justice Do It! The Nike Transnational Advocacy Network."

52. "Jockbeat: Making Nike Sweat."

53. Vander Werf, "Anti-Sweatshop Group Finds Abuses at Korean Factory That Produced College Apparel."

54. Opponents of high school, college, and professional sports teams' use of Native American sports mascots and team names have stepped up their activism in the past ten years. Some teams have chosen to change their names (e.g., Stanford University changed from Indians to Cardinal several years ago). Others (e.g., the Cleveland Indians and Atlanta Braves professional baseball teams) have refused to change, despite facing periodic protests and calls for boycotts of their products. Similarly, opposition to the infantilization and second-class status that is built into many college women's teams (e.g., calling a team the Lady Bulldogs rather than the Bulldogs, like the men's team) has similarly led to some changes and to some intransigent refusals to change, often based on appeals to tradition. What these movements against racist team names and sexist team names have in common is their mutual understanding of the importance of language and symbols and the ways that symbolic infantilization of women or ethnic minorities is linked to their continued second-class institutional status. See Davis, "Protest over the Use of Native American Mascots"; King and Springwood, *Beyond the Cheers*; Spindel, *Dancing at Halftime*; and Eitzen and Baca Zinn, "The De-athleticization of Women."

55. Indeed, in his most recent book, R. W. Connell argues that studies of masculinities have recently tended to downplay the extent to which current gender relations support men's material interests. Progressive gender politics among men, he argues, necessarily will divide, rather than unify, men. Connell, *The Men and the Boys*.

References

Acker, Joan. "Hierarchies, Jobs, Bodies: A Theory of Gendered Organizations." *Gender & Society* 4 (1990): 139–58.

———. "Gendered Institutions: From Sex Roles to Gendered Institutions." *Contemporary Sociology* 21 (1992): 565–69.

Acosta, R. Vivien, and Linda Jean Carpenter. *Women in Intercollegiate Sport: A Longitudinal Study—Twenty-three Year Update*. Brooklyn, N.Y.: Brooklyn College, 2000.

Adams, Lorraine, and Dale Russakoff. "At Columbine High, a Darker Picture Emerges. Were Athletes Given Preferential Treatment and Allowed to Misbehave with Impunity?" *Washington Post National Weekly Edition*, June 21, 1999, 29.

Adler, Patricia A., and Peter Adler. *Peer Power: Preadolescent Culture and Identity*. New Brunswick, N.J.: Rutgers University Press, 1998.

Albert, Edward. "Dealing with Danger: The Normalization of Pain and Risk in Cycling." *International Review for the Sociology of Sport* 34 (1999): 157–71.

Amateur Athletic Foundation of Los Angeles. *Gender Stereotyping in Televised Sports*. Los Angeles: AAFLA, 1990.

———. *Gender Stereotyping in Televised Sports: A Followup to the 1989 Study*. Los Angeles: AAFLA, 1994.

———. *Children and Sports Media*. Los Angeles: AAFLA, 1999.

———. *Gender in Televised Sports: 1989, 1993, and 1999*. Los Angeles: AAFLA, 2000.

———. *Sportsletter* 12, nos. 1 & 2, June 30, 2000.

Anderson, Eric. *Trailblazing: The True Story of America's First Openly Gay Track Coach.* Los Angeles: Alyson Books.

Anderson, Kelley. "The Other Side of Jenny." *Sports Illustrated for Women,* November–December 2000.

Anderson, Lynn, and Lem Satterfield. "St. Paul's Cancels Varsity Lacrosse Season." *SunSpot.net: Maryland's Online Community,* April 3, 2001. http://www.sunspot.net/sports/highschool/bal-stpauls03.story?coll=bal%2D.

Andrews, David. "Excavating Michael Jordan: Notes on a Critical Pedagogy of Sporting Representation." In *Sport and Postmodern Times,* ed. Geneviève Rail, 185–219. Albany: State University of New York Press, 1998.

———, ed. *Michael Jordan, Inc.: Corporate Sport, Media Culture, and Late Modern America.* Albany: State University of New York Press, 2001.

Armstrong, Jim. "Money Makes the Sports Go 'Round." In *Sport in Contemporary Society,* ed. D. Stanley Eitzen, 239–47. 6th ed. New York: Worth, 2001.

Attfield, Judy. "Barbie and Action Man: Adult Toys for Girls and Boys, 1959–93." In *The Gendered Object,* ed. Pat Kirkham, 80–89. Manchester, England: Manchester University Press, 1996.

Baca Zinn, Maxine, and Bonnie Thornton Dill. "Theorizing Difference from Multiracial Feminism." *Feminist Studies* 22 (1996): 321–31.

Baca Zinn, Maxine, Lynn Weber Cannon, Elizabeth Higgenbotham, and Bonnie Thornton Dill. "The Costs of Exclusionary Practices in Women's Studies." *Signs: Journal of Women in Culture and Society* 11 (1986): 290–303.

Banet-Weiser, Sarah. *The Most Beautiful Girl in the World: Beauty Pageants and National Identity.* Berkeley: University of California Press, 1999.

———. "We Got Next: Negotiating Race and Gender in Professional Basketball." In *Paradoxes of Youth and Sport,* ed. Margaret Gatz, Sandra Ball Rokeach, and Michael A. Messner, 93–102. Albany: State University of New York Press, 2002.

Baumgardner, Jennifer, and Amy Richards. *Manifesta: Young Women, Feminism, and the Future.* New York: Farrar, Straus and Giroux, 2000.

Bellamy, Robert V., Jr. "The Evolving Television Sports Marketplace." In *MediaSport,* ed. Lawrence A. Wenner, 73–87. London: Routledge, 1998.

Benedict, Jeffrey R. *Athletes and Acquaintance Rape.* Thousand Oaks, Calif.: Sage Publications, 1998.

Benedict, Jeffrey, and Alan Klein. "Arrest and Conviction Rates for Athletes Accused of Sexual Assault." *Sociology of Sport Journal* 14 (1997): 73–85.

Benedict, Jeff, and Don Yaeger. *Pros and Cons: The Criminals Who Play in the NFL.* New York: Warner Books, 1998.

Beneke, Timothy. *Men on Rape.* New York: St. Martin's Press, 1982.

———. *Proving Manhood: Reflections on Men and Sexism.* Berkeley: University of California Press, 1997.

Berkowitz, Alan. "The Role of Coaches in Rape Prevention Programs for Athletes." In *Rape 101: Sexual Assault Prevention for College Athletes*, ed. A. Parrot, N. Cummings, and T. Marchell, 61–64. Holmes Beach, Fla.: Learning Publications, 1994.

Berlage, Gai Ingham. *Women in Baseball: The Forgotten History.* Westport, Conn.: Greenwood, 1994.

Berry, Bonnie, and Earl Smith. "Race, Sport, and Crime: The Misrepresentation of African Americans in Team Sports and Crime." *Sociology of Sport Journal* 17 (2000): 171–97.

Bhavnani, Kum-Kum. "Response to Stacey and Thorne's 'Is Sociology Still Missing Its Feminist Revolution?'" *Perspectives: ASA Theory Section Newsletter* 18 (summer 1996): 1–10.

Billings, Andrew. "In Search of Women Athletes: ESPN's List of the Top 100 Athletes of the Century." *Journal of Sport and Social Issues* 24 (2000): 415–21.

Blais, Madeleine. *In These Girls, Hope Is a Muscle.* New York: Atlantic Monthly Press, 1995.

Boeringer, S. D. "Influences of Fraternity Membership, Athletics and Male Living Arrangements on Sexual Aggression." *Violence against Women* 2 (1996): 134–47.

Bordo, Susan. *The Male Body.* New York: Farrar, Straus and Giroux, 1999.

Boswell, A. Ayres, and Joan Z. Spade. "Fraternities and Collegiate Gang Rape: Why Some Fraternities Are More Dangerous Places for Women." *Gender & Society* 10 (1996): 133–47.

Boyle, Maree, and Jim McKay. "'You Leave Your Troubles at the Gate': A Case Study of the Exploitation of Older Women's Labor and 'Leisure' in Sport." *Gender & Society* 9 (1995): 556–76.

Brackenridge, Celia. "'He Owned Me Basically . . .': Women's Experience of Sexual Abuse in Sport." *International Review for the Sociology of Sport* 32 (1997): 115–30.

Brackenridge, Celia, and Sandrea Kirby. "Playing It Safe: Assessing the Risk of

Sexual Abuse to Elite Child Athletes." *International Review for the Sociology of Sport* 32 (1997): 407–18.

Bradbard, M. "Sex Differences in Adults' Gifts and Children's Toy Requests." *Journal of Genetic Psychology* 145 (1985): 283–84.

Brake, Deborah. "The Struggle for Sex Equality in Sport and the Theory behind Title IX." *University of Michigan Journal of Law Reform* 34 (fall 2000 and winter 2001): 13–149.

Briant, Jennings, Dolf Zillmann, and Arthur A. Raney. "Violence and the Enjoyment of Media Sports." In *MediaSport*, ed. Lawrence A. Wenner, 253–65. London: Routledge, 1998.

Brittan, Dana M. "The Epistemology of the Gendered Organization." *Gender & Society* 14 (2000): 418–34.

Brohm, J. M. *Sport: A Prison of Measured Time*. London: Ink Links, 1978.

Bruce, Toni. "Audience Frustration and Pleasure: Women Viewers Confront Televised Women's Basketball." *Journal of Sport and Social Issues* 22 (1998): 373–97.

Burstyn, Varda. *The Rites of Men: Manhood, Politics and the Culture of Sport*. Toronto: University of Toronto Press, 1999.

Butler, Judith. *Gender Trouble: Feminism and the Subversion of Identity*. New York: Routledge, 1990.

Butterfield, S. A., and E. M. Loovis. "Influence of Age, Sex, Balance, and Sport Participation in Development of Kicking by Children in Grades K–8." *Perceptual and Motor Skills* 79 (1994): 691–97.

Cahn, Susan. *Coming on Strong: Gender and Sexuality in Twentieth-Century Women's Sport*. New York: Free Press, 1994.

California Women's Law Center. "1999 President's Pro Bono Service Award for District 7: Nomination of Kaye, Scholer, Furman, Hays, and Handler, LLP." Unpublished paper. 1999.

Campenni, C. Estelle. "Gender Stereotyping of Children's Toys: A Comparison of Parents and Nonparents." *Sex Roles* 40 (1999): 121–38.

Canada, Geoffrey. *Fist Stick Knife Gun*. Boston: Beacon Press, 1995.

Capraro, Rocco L. "Why College Men Drink: Alcohol, Adventure, and the Paradox of Masculinity." *Journal of American College Health* 48 (2000): 307–15.

Carpenter, Linda Jean. "Letters Home: My Life With Title IX." In *Women in Sport: Issues and Controversies*, ed. Greta Cohen, 133–54. 2d ed. Oxon Hill, Md.: AAHPERD Publications, 2001.

Chafetz, Janet Saltzman, and Joseph A. Kotarba. "Little League Mothers and the Reproduction of Gender." In *Inside Sports*, ed. Jay Coakley and Peter Donnelly, 46–54. London: Routledge, 1999.

Chancer, Lynn S. *Reconcilable Differences: Confronting Beauty, Pornography, and the Future of Feminism*. Berkeley: University of California Press, 1998.

Chin, Elizabeth. *Purchasing Power: Black Kids and American Consumer Culture*. Minneapolis: University of Minnesota Press, 2001.

Chisholm, Ann. "Defending the Nation: National Bodies, U.S. Borders, and the 1996 U.S. Olympic Women's Gymnastics Team." *Journal of Sport and Social Issues* 23 (1999): 126–39.

Chodorow, Nancy J. *The Power of Feelings: Personal Meanings in Psychoanalysis, Gender, and Culture*. New Haven, Conn.: Yale University Press, 1999.

Clarke, Stuart Allan. "Fear of a Black Planet." *Socialist Review* 21 (1991): 37–59.

Cohen, Greta L. "Media Portrayals of the Female Athlete." In *Women In Sport: Issues and Controversies*, ed. Greta L. Cohen, 171–84. 1st ed. Newbury Park, Calif.: Sage Publications, 1993.

Cole, C. L. "Resisting the Canon: Feminist Cultural Studies, Sport, and Technologies of the Body." In *Women, Sport, and Culture*, ed. Susan Birrell and C. L. Cole, 5–29. Champaign, Ill.: Human Kinetics Books, 1994.

———. "The Year That Girls Ruled." *Journal of Sport and Social Issues* 24 (2000): 3–7.

Cole, C. L., and Amy Hribar. "Celebrity Feminism: Nike Style, Post-Fordism, Transcendence, and Consumer Power." *Sociology of Sport Journal* 12 (1995): 347–69.

Cole, C. L., and Samantha King. "Representing Black Masculinity and Urban Possibilities: Racism, Realism, and *Hoop Dreams*." In *Sport and Postmodern Times*, ed. Geneviève Rail, 49–86. Albany: State University of New York Press, 1998.

Collins, Patricia Hill. *Black Feminist Thought: Knowledge, Consciousness, and the Politics of Empowerment*. Boston: Unwin Hyman, 1990.

———. *Fighting Words: Black Women and the Search for Justice*. Minneapolis: University of Minnesota Press, 1998.

Connell, R. W. *Gender and Power*. Stanford, Calif.: Stanford University Press, 1987.

———. "Cool Guys, Swots and Wimps: The Interplay of Masculinity and Education." *Oxford Review of Education* 15 (1989): 291–303.

———. *The Men and the Boys*. Berkeley: University of California Press, 2000.

Courtenay, Will H. "Behavioral Factors Associated with Disease, Injury, and

Death among Men: Evidence and Implications for Prevention." *Journal of Men's Studies* 9 (2000): 81–142.

———. "Constructions of Masculinity and Their Influence on Men's Well-Being: A Theory of Gender and Health." *Social Science and Medicine* 50 (2000): 1385–401.

"Court Rejects Stanley's Suit." CNN/SI.com, June 3, 1999.

Creedon, Pamela J. "Women, Sport, and Media Institutions: Issues in Sports Journalism and Marketing." In *MediaSport*, ed. Lawrence A. Wenner, 88–99. London: Routledge, 1998.

Crosset, Todd. "Masculinity, Sexuality and the Development of Early Modern Sport." In *Sport, Men and the Gender Order: Critical Feminist Perspectives*, ed. Michael A. Messner and Donald F. Sabo, 45–54. Champaign, Ill.: Human Kinetics Books, 1990.

———. *Outsiders in the Clubhouse: The World of Women's Professional Golf*. Albany: State University of New York Press, 1995.

———. "Athletic Affiliation and Violence against Women: Toward a Structural Prevention Project." In *Masculinities, Gender Relations, and Sport*, ed. Jim McKay, Michael A. Messner, and Donald F. Sabo, 147–61. Thousand Oaks, Calif.: Sage Publications, 2000.

Crosset, Todd, and Becky Beal. "The Use of 'Subculture' and 'Subworld' in Ethnographic Works on Sport: A Discussion of Definitional Distinctions." *Sociology of Sport Journal* 14 (1997): 73–85.

Crosset, Todd W., Jeffrey R. Benedict, and Mark McDonald. "Male Student Athletes Reported for Sexual Assault: A Survey of Campus Police Departments and Judicial Affairs Offices." *Journal of Sport and Social Issues* 19 (1995): 126–40.

Crosset, Todd, J. Ptacek, M. MacDonald, and Jeffrey Benedict. "Male Student Athletes and Violence against Women: A Survey of Campus Judicial Affairs Offices." *Violence against Women* 2 (1996): 163–79.

Curry, Timothy. "Fraternal Bonding in the Locker Room: Pro-Feminist Analysis of Talk about Competition and Women." *Sociology of Sport Journal* 8 (1991): 119–35.

———. "Booze and Bar Fights: A Journey to the Dark Side of College Athletics." In *Masculinities, Gender Relations, and Sport*, ed. Jim McKay, Michael A. Messner, and Donald F. Sabo, 162–75. Thousand Oaks, Calif.: Sage Publications, 2000.

Davis, Angela. *Woman, Race and Class*. New York: Vintage Books, 1981.

Davis, Laurel L. "Protest over the Use of Native American Mascots: A Challenge to Traditional American Identity." *Journal of Sport and Social Issues* 17 (1993): 9–22.

———. *The Swimsuit Issue and Sport: Hegemonic Masculinity in* Sports Illustrated. Albany: State University of New York Press, 1997.

Deford, Frank. "Advantage, Kournikova." *Sports Illustrated*, June 5, 2000.

DeGaris, Laurence. "'Be a Buddy to Your Buddy': Male Identity, Aggression, and Intimacy in a Boxing Gym." In *Masculinities, Gender Relations, and Sport*, ed. Jim McKay, Michael A. Messner, and Donald F. Sabo, 87–107. Thousand Oaks, Calif.: Sage Publications, 2000.

Dowling, Colette. *The Frailty Myth: Women Approaching Physical Equality*. New York: Random House, 2000.

DuCille, Anne. "Dyes and Dolls: Multicultural Barbie and the Merchandising of Difference." *Differences: A Journal of Cultural Studies* 6 (1994): 46–68.

Dunbar, Michele D. "Dennis Rodman—Do You Feel Feminine Yet? Black Masculinity, Gender Transgression, and Reproductive Rebellion on MTV." In *Masculinities, Gender Relations, and Sport*, ed. Jim McKay, Michael A. Messner, and Donald F. Sabo, 263–85. Thousand Oaks, Calif.: Sage Publications, 2000.

Duncan, Margaret Carlisle, and Cynthia A. Hasbrook. "Denial of Power in Televised Women's Sports." *Sociology of Sport Journal* 5 (1988): 1–21.

Dunn, Robert G. *Identity Crisis: A Social Critique of Postmodernity*. Minneapolis: University of Minnesota Press, 1998.

Dunning, Eric. *Sport Matters: Sociological Studies of Sport, Violence and Civilization*. London: Routledge, 1999.

Dworkin, Shari L., and Michael A. Messner. "Just Do ... What? Sport, Bodies, Gender." In *Revisioning Gender*, ed. Myra Marx Ferree, Judith Lorber, and Beth B. Hess, 341–61. Thousand Oaks, Calif.: Sage Publications, 1999.

Dworkin, Shari Lee, and Faye Linda Wachs. "The Morality/Manhood Paradox: Masculinity, Sport, and the Media." In *Masculinities, Gender Relations, and Sport*, ed. Jim McKay, Michael A. Messner, and Donald F. Sabo, 47–66. Thousand Oaks, Calif.: Sage Publications, 2000.

Dwyer Brust, Janny, MPH, William O. Roberts, MD, and Barbara J. Leonard, Ph.D. "Gladiators on Ice: An Overview of Ice Hockey Injuries in Youth." *Medical Journal of Allina* 5 (1996): 26–30.

Eastman, Susan Tyler, and Andrew C. Billings. "Sportscasting and Sports Reporting: The Power of Gender Bias." *Journal of Sport and Social Issues* 24 (2000): 192–213.

"Education Department Resolves Last of 25 Bias Complaints Filed by Women's Group." *Chronicle of Higher Education*, January 21, 2000.

Eitzen, D. Stanley. *Fair and Foul: Beyond the Myths and Paradoxes of Sport*. Lanham, Md.: Rowman and Littlefield, 1999.

Eitzen, D. Stanley, and Maxine Baca Zinn. "The De-athleticization of Women: The Naming and Gender Marking of Collegiate Sport Teams." In *Sport in Contemporary Society*, ed. D. Stanley Eitzen, 123–33. 6th ed. New York: Worth, 2001.

Etaugh, C., and M. B. Liss. "Home, School, and Playroom: Training Grounds for Adult Gender Roles." *Sex Roles* 26 (1992): 129–47.

Eveslage, Scott, and Kevin Delaney. "Trash Talkin' at Hardwick High: A Case Study of Insult Talk on a Boys' Basketball Team." *International Review for the Sociology of Sport* 33 (1998): 239–53.

Farr, Katherine A. "Dominance Bonding through the Good Old Boys' Sociability Group," *Sex Roles* 18 (1988): 259–77.

Farred, Grant. "Cool as the Other Side of the Pillow: How ESPN's *SportsCenter* Has Changed Television Sports Talk." *Journal of Sport and Social Issues* 24 (2000): 96–117.

Farrell, Warren. "The Super-Bowl Phenomenon: Machismo as Ritual. " In *Jock: Sports and Male Identity*, ed. Donald F. Sabo and Ross Runfola, 19–30. Englewood Cliffs, N.J.: Prentice-Hall, 1980.

Fasting, Kari, Celia Brackenridge, and Jorunn Sundgot-Borgen. *Females, Elite Sports and Sexual Harassment*. Oslo: Norwegian Women Project, 2000.

Fausto-Sterling, Anne. *Sexing the Body: Gender Politics and the Construction of Sexuality*. New York: Basic Books, 2000.

Ferguson, Ann Arnett. *Bad Boys: Public Schools in the Making of Black Masculinity*. Ann Arbor: University of Michigan Press, 2000.

Fine, Gary Alan. *With the Boys: Little League Baseball and Preadolescent Culture*. Chicago: University of Chicago Press, 1987.

Foley, D. "The Great American Football Ritual: Reproducing Race, Class, and Gender Inequality." *Sociology of Sport Journal* 7 (1990): 111–34.

Fritner, M. P., and L. Rubinson. "Acquaintance Rape: The Influence of Alcohol, Fraternity Membership and Sports Team Membership." *Journal of Sex Education and Therapy* 19 (1993): 272–84.

Gatz, Margaret, Sandra Ball Rokeach, and Michael A. Messner, eds., *Paradoxes of Youth and Sport*. Albany: State University of New York Press, 2002.

Gerbner, George. "The Dynamics of Cultural Resistance." In *Hearth and Home: Images of Women in the Mass Media*, ed. Gaye Tuchman, Arlene Kaplan Daniels, and James Benet, 46–50. New York: Oxford University Press, 1978.

Glauber, Bob. "We're Paid to Be Violent: Cost Was High for Ex-Dallas Star John Niland." *Newsday*, Sunday, January 12, 1997, B8, B25.

Gold, Scott, and Tracy Weber. "Youth Sports Grind Is Tough on Body, Spirit." *Los Angeles Times*, February 28, 2000, A1.

Goldman, Robert, and Stephen Papson. *Nike Culture*. Thousand Oaks, Calif.: Sage Publications, 1998.

Goldstein, Jeffrey H., ed. *Why We Watch: The Attractions of Violent Entertainment*. New York: Oxford Univerisity Press, 1998.

Green, Tim. *The Dark Side of the Game: My Life in the NFL*. New York: Warner Books, 1996.

Griffin, Pat. "Changing the Game. Homophobia, Sexism, and Lesbians in Sport." *Quest* 44 (1992): 251-65.

———. *Strong Women, Deep Closets: Lesbians and Homophobia in Sport*. Champaign, Ill.: Human Kinetics Books, 1998.

Gruneau, Richard. *Class, Sports, and Social Development*. Amherst: University of Massachusetts Press, 1983.

———. "Making Spectacle: A Case Study in Television Sports Production." In *Media, Sports and Society*, ed. Lawrence A. Wenner, 134–54. Newbury Park, Calif.: Sage Publications, 1989.

Gustkey, Earl. "Sparks Are Altering Marketing Strategy." *Los Angeles Times*, May 4, 2001, D-1.

———. "WNBA's Marquee Brightens." *Los Angeles Times*, May 27, 2001, D-12.

Gutierrez, Paul, and Houston Mitchell. "Pain Game." *Los Angeles Times*, January 25, 2000, D1.

Guttmann, Allen. *Women's Sports: A History*. New York: Columbia University Press, 1991.

———. *The Erotic in Sport*. New York: Columbia University Press, 1996.

———. "Nature, Nurture, and the Athletic Body." Paper delivered at the Olympia's Daughters: Gender, Sport, and the New Millennium Conference, University of Texas, Austin, November 4, 2000.

Hall, M. Ann. *Feminism and Sporting Bodies: Essays on Theory and Practice*. Champaign, Ill.: Human Kinetics Books, 1996.

Hargreaves, Jennifer. *Sporting Females: Critical Issues in the History and Sociology of Women's Sports*. London: Routledge, 1994.

———. *Heroines of Sport: The Politics of Difference and Identity*. London: Routledge, 2000.

Hargreaves, John. *Sport, Power and Culture*. Oxford: Polity Press, 1986.

Harris, C. J. "The Reform of Women's Intercollegiate Athletics: Title IX, Equal Protection and Supplemental Methods." *Capital University Law Review* 20 (1992): 691–721.

Hasbrook, Cynthia. "Young Children's Social Constructions of Physicality and Gender." In *Inside Sports*, ed. Jay Coakley and Peter Donnelly, 7–16. London: Routledge, 1999.

Hasbrook, Cynthia A., and Othello Harris. "Wrestling with Gender: Physicality and Masculinities among Inner-City First and Second Graders." In *Masculinities, Gender Relations, and Sport*, ed. Jim McKay, Michael A. Messner, and Donald F. Sabo, 13–30. Thousand Oaks, Calif.: Sage Publications, 2000.

Hawk, Tony. *Hawk: Occupation—Skateboarder*. New York: Regan Books, 2001.

Hays, Sharon. "Structure and Agency and the Sticky Problem of Culture." *Sociological Theory* 12 (1994): 57–72.

Heino, Rebecca. "New Sports: What's So Punk about Snowboarding?" *Sociology of Sport Journal* 17 (2000): 176–91.

Henry, J., and H. Comeaux. "Gender Egalitarianism in Coed Sport: A Case Study of American Soccer." *International Review for the Sociology of Sport* 34 (1999): 277–90.

Heywood, Leslie. "Bodies, Babes, and the WNBA, or, Where's Tiger Naked in a Cape When You Really Need Him?" Paper delivered at the Olympia's Daughters: Gender, Sport, and the New Millennium Conference, University of Texas, Austin, November 4, 2000.

———. "Despite the Positive Rhetoric about Women's Sports, Female Athletes Face a Culture of Sexual Harassment." In *Sport in Contemporary Society*, ed. D. Stanley Eitzen, 150–54. 6th ed. New York: Worth, 2001.

Heywood, Leslie, and Jennifer Drake, eds. *Third Wave Agenda: Being Feminist, Doing Feminism*. Minneapolis: University of Minnesota Press, 1997.

Hilliard, Dan C. "Televised Sport and the (Anti)Sociological Imagination." In *Sport in Contemporary Society*, ed. D. Stanley Eitzen, 96–106. 6th ed. New York: Worth, 2001.

Hoch, Paul. *White Hero, Black Beast: Racism, Sexism and the Mask of Masculinity.* London: Pluto, 1979.

Hochschild, Arlie Russell. "The Commercial Spirit of Intimate Life and the Abduction of Feminism: Signs from Women's Advice Books." *Theory, Culture & Society* 11 (1994): 1–24.

Holdsclaw, Chamique, with Jennifer Frey. *Chamique: On Family, Focus and Basketball.* New York: Scribner's, 2000.

Holman, Margery. *Sport, Media and Domestic Violence.* Windsor, Ontario: University of Windsor, 1999.

hooks, bell. *Feminist Theory: From Margins to Center.* Boston: South End Press, 1984.

Hughson, John. "The Boys Are Back in Town: Soccer Support and the Social Reproduction of Masculinity." *Journal of Sport and Social Issues* 24 (2000). 8–23.

Humphreys, Duncan. "'Shredheads' Go Mainstream? Snowboarding and Alternative Youth." *International Review for the Sociology of Sport* 32 (1997): 147–60.

Hums, Mary, and Marjorie Snyder. "Growth in the Women's Sports Industry: A Study in Opportunity." In *Women in Sport: Issues and Controversies*, ed. Greta Cohen, 375–402. 2d ed. Oxon Hill, Md.: AAHPERD Publications, 2001.

Hunt, Darnell. *O. J. Simpson Facts and Fictions.* Cambridge: Cambridge University Press, 1999.

Jacobson, Jennifer. "Why Do So Many Female Athletes Enter ACL Hell?" *Chronicle of Higher Education*, March 9, 2001.

———. "Among Big Sports Programs, Gender Equity Is No. 1 Reason for Cutting Men's Teams, Report Says." *Chronicle of Higher Education*, March 12, 2001.

Jansen, Sue Curry, and Don Sabo. "The Sport/War Metaphor: Hegemonic Masculinity, the Persian Gulf War, and the New World Order." *Sociology of Sport Journal* 11 (1994): 1–17.

Jhally, Sut. "The Spectacle of Accumulation: Material and Cultural Factors in the Evolution of the Sports/Media Complex." *Insurgent Sociologist* 12 (1984): 41–57.

"Jockbeat: Making Nike Sweat." *Village Voice*, February 14–20, 2001.

Jordan, Ellen, and Angela Cowan. "Warrior Narratives in the Kindergarten

Classroom: Renogotiating the Social Contract?" *Gender & Society* 9 (1995): 727–43.

Kane, Mary Jo. "Resistance/Transformation of the Oppositional Binary: Exposing Sport as a Continuum." *Journal of Sport and Social Issues* 19 (1995): 191–218.

———. "Media Coverage of the Post–Title IX Female Athlete: A Feminist Analysis of Sport, Gender, and Power." *Duke Journal of Gender Law and Policy* 3 (1996): 95–127.

Kane, Mary Jo, and Lisa J. Disch. "Sexual Violence and the Reproduction of Male Power in the Locker Room: The 'Lisa Olsen Incident.'" *Sociology of Sport Journal* 10 (1993): 331–52.

Kane, Mary Jo, and Helen J. Lenskyj. "Media Treatment of Female Athletes: Issues of Gender and Sexualities." In *MediaSport*, ed. Lawrence A. Wenner, 186–201. London: Routledge, 1998.

Kantor, G., and M. Strauss. "The 'Drunken Bum' Theory of Wife Beating." *Social Problems* 34 (1987): 213–30.

Kaufman, Michael. "The Construction of Masculinity and the Triad of Men's Violence." In *Beyond Patriarchy: Essays by Men on Pleasure, Power, and Change*, ed. Michael Kaufman, 1–29. Toronto: Oxford University Press, 1987.

Kessler, Suzanne J., and Wendy McKenna. *Gender: An Ethnomethodological Approach*. New York: Wiley, 1978.

Kidd, Bruce. "The Men's Cultural Centre: Sports and the Dynamic of Women's Oppression/Men's Repression." In *Sport, Men and the Gender Order: Critical Feminist Perspectives*, ed. Michael A. Messner and Donald F. Sabo, 31–44. Champaign, Ill.: Human Kinetics Books, 1990.

Kilbourne, Jean. *Can't Buy My Love: How Advertising Changes the Way We Think and Feel*. New York: Touchstone, 1999.

Kimmel, Michael S. "Baseball and the Reconstitution of American Masculinity: 1880–1920." In *Sport, Men and the Gender Order: Critical Feminist Perspectives*, ed. Michael A. Messner and Donald F. Sabo, 55–66. Champaign, Ill.: Human Kinetics Books, 1990.

Kinder, Marsha, ed. *Kids' Media Culture*. Durham, N.C.: Duke University Press, 1999.

King, C. Richard, and Charles Fruehling Springwood. *Beyond the Cheers: Race as Spectacle in College Sport*. Albany: State University of New York Press, 2001.

Klein, Alan. "Dueling Machos: Masculinity and Sport in Mexican Baseball." In *Masculinities, Gender Relations, and Sport*, ed. Jim McKay, Michael A. Messner, and Donald F. Sabo, 67–85. Thousand Oaks, Calif.: Sage Publications, 2000.

Klein, Melissa. "Duality and Redefinition: Young Feminism and the Alternative Music Community." In *Third Wave Agenda: Being Feminist, Doing Feminism*, ed. Leslie Heywood and Jennifer Drake, 207–25. Minneapolis: University of Minnesota Press, 1997.

Koss, Mary, and J. Gaines. "The Prediction of Sexual Aggression by Alcohol Use, Athletic Participation and Fraternity Affiliation." *Journal of Interpersonal Violence* 8 (1993): 94–108.

Kupers, Terry A. "Rape and the Prison Code." In *Prison Masculinities*, ed. Don Sabo, Terry A. Kupers, and Willie London, 111–17. Philadelphia: Temple University Press, 2001.

Kusz, Kyle. "BMX, Extreme Sports, and the White Male Backlash." In *To the Extreme: Alternative Sport, Inside and Out*, ed. Robert E. Rinehart and Synthia Sydnor. Albany: State University of New York Press, forthcoming.

Kuypers, Joseph A. *Man's Will to Hurt: Investigating the Causes, Supports, and Varieties of His Violence*. Halifax, Nova Scotia: Fernwood Publishing, 1992.

Laberge, Suzanne, and Mathieu Albert. "Conceptions of Masculinity and Gender Transgressions in Sport among Adolescent Boys: Hegemony, Contestation, and the Social Class Dynamic." In *Masculinities, Gender Relations, and Sport*, ed. Jim McKay, Michael A. Messner, and Donald F. Sabo, 195–221. Thousand Oaks, Calif.: Sage Publications, 2000.

Lasn, Kalle. *Culture Jam: How to Reverse America's Suicidal Consumer Binge—and Why We Must*. New York: HarperCollins, 2000.

Lefkowitz, Bernard. *Our Guys*. New York: Vintage, 1997.

Leichliter, J. S., P. W. Meilman, C. P. Presley, and J. R. Cashin. "Alcohol Use and Related Consequences among Students with Varying Levels of Involvement in College Athletics." *Journal of American College Health* 46 (1998): 257–62.

Lenskyj, Helen. *Out of Bounds: Women, Sport and Sexuality*. Toronto: Women's Press, 1986.

———. "Sexuality and Femininity in Sport Contexts: Issues and Alternatives." *Journal of Sport and Social Issues* 18 (1994): 356–75.

———. "'Inside Sport' or 'On the Margins'? Australian Women and the Sport Media." *International Review for the Sociology of Sport* 34 (1998): 19–32.

———. *Inside the Olympic Industry: Power, Politics and Activism*. Albany: State University of New York Press, 2000.

Lorber, Judith. *Paradoxes of Gender*. New Haven, Conn.: Yale University Press, 1994.

Lyman, Peter. "The Fraternal Bond as a Joking Relationship: A Case Study of Sexist Jokes in Male Group Bonding." In *Changing Men: New Directions in Research on Men and Masculinity*, ed. Michael S. Kimmel, 148–63. Newbury Park, Calif.: Sage Publications, 1987.

Maccoby, E. E., and C. N. Jacklin. *The Psychology of Sex Differences*. Stanford, Calif.: Stanford University Press, 1975.

McDaniel, Stephen R., and Christopher B. Sullivan. "Extending the Sports Experience: Mediations in Cyberspace." In *MediaSport*, ed. Lawrence A. Wenner, 266–81. London: Routledge, 1998.

McDonald, Mary G. "Unnecessary Roughness: Gender and Racial Politics in Domestic Violence Media Events." *Sociology of Sport Journal* 16 (1999): 111–33.

———. "The Marketing of the Women's National Basketball Association and the Making of Postfeminism." *International Review for the Sociology of Sport* 35 (2000): 35–46.

McGuffy, C. Shawn, and B. Lindsay Rich. "Playing in the Gender Transgression Zone: Race, Class and Hegemonic Masculinity in Middle Childhood." *Gender & Society* 13 (1999): 608–27.

MacInnes, John. *The End of Masculinity*. Buckingham, England: Open University Press, 1998.

MacIntosh, Peggy. "White Privilege: Unpacking the Invisible Knapsack." In *Gender through the Prism of Difference*, ed. Maxine Baca Zinn, Pierrette Hondagneu-Sotelo, and Michael A. Messner, 247–50. 2d ed. Boston: Allyn and Bacon, 2000.

McKabe, Gail. "Jocks and Puck Bunnies: Intimate Relations, Cultural Negotiations and Sport Subjectivities." Paper presented at the American Sociological Association meetings, San Francisco, August 1998.

McKay, Jim. "'Marked Men' and 'Wanton Women': The Politics of Naming Sexual 'Deviance' in Sport." *Journal of Men's Studies* 2 (1993): 69–87.

————. *Managing Gender: Affirmative Action and Organizational Power in Australian, Canadian, and New Zealand Sport.* Albany: State University of New York Press, 1997.

————. "Teaching against the Grain: A Learner-Centered, Media-Based, and Profeminist Approach to Gender and Non-violence in Sport." In *Paradoxes of Youth and Sport*, ed. Margaret Gatz, Sandra Ball Rokeach, and Michael A. Messner, 103–18. Albany: State University of New York Press, 2002.

————. "Enlightened Racism and Celebrity Feminism in Contemporary Sports Advertisements." In *Sport, Culture and Advertising: Identities, Commodities, and the Politics of Representation*, ed. S. Jackson and D. Andrews. Greenwood, Conn.: Greenwood Press, forthcoming.

McKay, Jim, Michael A. Messner, and Don Sabo, eds. *Masculinities, Gender Relations, and Sport.* Thousand Oaks, Calif.: Sage Publications, 2000.

McPherson, Donald G. "Sport, Youth, Violence and the Media: An Activist Athlete's Perspective." In *Paradoxes of Youth and Sport*, ed. Margaret Gatz, Sandra Ball Rokeach, and Michael A. Messner, 241–48. Albany: State University of New York Press, 2002.

Malszecki, Greg, and Tomislava Cavar. "Men, Masculinities, War, and Sport." In *Feminist Issues: Race, Class, and Sexuality*, ed. Nancy Mandell, 166–92. 3d ed. Toronto: Pearson Education Canada, 2001.

Messerschmidt, James W. "Becoming 'Real Men': Adolescent Masculinity Challenges and Sexual Violence." *Men and Masculinities* 2 (2000): 286–307.

————. *Nine Lives: Adolescent Masculinities, the Body, and Violence.* Boulder, Colo.: Westview Press, 2000.

Messner, Michael A. "Sports and Male Domination: The Female Athlete as Contested Ideological Terrain." *Sociology of Sport Journal* 5 (1988): 197–211.

————. *Power at Play: Sports and the Problem of Masculinity.* Boston: Beacon Press, 1992.

————. "Indignities: A Short Story." In Michael A. Messner and Donald F. Sabo, *Sex, Violence and Power in Sports: Rethinking Masculinity*, 16–27. Freedom, Calif.: Crossing Press, 1994.

————. "Riding with the Spur Posse." In Michael A. Messner and Donald F. Sabo, *Sex, Violence and Power in Sports: Rethinking Masculinity*, 66–70. Freedom, Calif.: Crossing Press, 1994.

————. "Why Rocky III?" In Michael A. Messner and Donald F. Sabo, *Sex,*

Violence and Power in Sports: Rethinking Masculinity, 74–81. Freedom, Calif.: Crossing Press, 1994.

———. "Barbie Girls vs. Sea Monsters: Children Constructing Gender." *Gender & Society* 14 (2000): 765–84.

Messner, Michael A., and Donald F. Sabo. "Toward a Critical Feminist Reappraisal of Sport, Men, and the Gender Order." In *Sport, Men and the Gender Order: Critical Feminist Perspectives*, ed. Michael A. Messner and Donald F. Sabo, 1–15. Champaign, Ill.: Human Kinetics Books, 1990.

———, eds. *Sport, Men and the Gender Order: Critical Feminist Perspectives*. Champaign, Ill.: Human Kinetics Books, 1990.

Messner, Michael A., and William S. Solomon. "Outside the Frame: Newspaper Coverage of the Sugar Ray Leonard Wife Abuse Story." *Sociology of Sport Journal* 10 (1993): 119–34.

Messner, Michael A., and Mark Stevens. "Scoring without Consent: Confronting Male Athletes' Sexual Violence against Women." In *Paradoxes of Youth and Sport*, ed. Margaret Gatz, Sandra Ball Rokeach, and Michael A. Messner, 225–40. Albany: State University of New York Press, 2002.

Messner, Michael A., Michele Dunbar, and Darnell Hunt. "The Televised Sports Manhood Formula." *Journal of Sport and Social Issues* 24 (2000): 380–94.

Messner, Michael A., Margaret Carlisle Duncan, and Cheryl Cooky. "Silence, Sports Bras, and Wrestling Porn: The Treatment of Women in Televised Sports News and Highlights." *Journal of Sport and Social Issues* (forthcoming).

Messner, Michael A., Margaret Carlisle Duncan, and Kerry Jensen. "Separating the Men from the Girls: The Gendered Language of Televised Sports." *Gender & Society* 7 (1993): 121–37.

Messner, Michael A., Margaret Carlisle Duncan, and Faye Linda Wachs. "The Gender of Audience-Building: Televised Coverage of Men's and Women's NCAA Basketball." *Sociological Inquiry* 66 (1996): 422–39.

Messner, Michael A., Darnell Hunt, and Michele Dunbar. *Boys to Men: Sports Media Messages about Masculinity*. Oakland, Calif.: Children Now, 1999.

Mikosza, J., and M. Phillips. "Gender, Sport and the Body Politic: The Framing of Femininity in the *Golden Girls of Sport Calendar* and *The Atlanta Dream*." *International Review for the Sociology of Sport* 34 (1999): 5–16.

Miller, Kathleen E., Donald F. Sabo, Merrill J. Melnick, Michael P. Farrell, and Grace M. Barnes. *The Women's Sports Foundation Report: Health Risks and the Teen Athlete*. East Meadow, N.Y.: Women's Sports Foundation, 2000.

Miller, Toby, Jim McKay, G. Lawrence, and David Rowe. *Globalization and Sport: Playing the World*. Thousand Oaks, Calif.: Sage Publications, 2001.

National Federation of State High School Associations. "2000–2001 Athletics Participation Summary." http://www.nfhs.org/participation/SportsPart01.htm.

National Women's Law Center. "The Battle For Gender Equity in Athletics in Elementary and Secondary Schools." http://www.nwlc.org, 2001.

———. "Title IX and Men's Minor Sports: A False Conflict." http://www.nwlc.org, 2001.

Naughton, Jim. "Judge Approves Settlement of Brown U.'s Title IX Case." *Chronicle of Higher Education*, July 3, 1998.

Nelson, Mariah Burton. *The Stronger Women Get, the More Men Love Football*. New York: Harcourt, Brace and Co., 1994.

Nixon, Howard L., II. "Gender, Sport, and Aggressive Behavior outside Sport." *Journal of Sport and Social Issues* 21 (1997): 379–91.

"Now You Know: Star Search." *Los Angeles Times*, February 21, 2001, D-2.

Pierce, Chester M., and Wesley E. Profit. "Racial Group Dynamics: Implications for Rearing Black Males." In *The American Black Male*, ed. R. G. Majors and J. U. Gordon, 167–77. Chicago: Nelson-Hall, 1994.

Pollack, William. *Real Boys: Rescuing Our Sons from the Myths of Boyhood*. New York: Henry Holt, 1998.

Pope, Harrison G., Jr., Roberto Olivarda, Amanda Gruber, and John Borowiecki. "Evolving Ideals of Male Body Image as Seen through Action Toys." *International Journal of Eating Disorders* 26 (1999): 65–72.

Pratt, Mary. "The All-American Girls' Professional Baseball League." In *Women in Sport: Issues and Controversies*, ed. Greta L. Cohen, 49–58. 1st ed. Newbury Park, Calif.: Sage Publications, 1993.

Pronger, Brian. "Outta My Endzone: Sport and the Territorial Anus." *Journal of Sport and Social Issues* 23 (1999): 373–89.

———. "Homosexuality and Sport: Who's Winning?" In *Masculinities, Gender Relations, and Sport*, ed. Jim McKay, Michael A. Messner, and Donald F. Sabo, 222–44. Thousand Oaks, Calif.: Sage Publications, 2000.

"Quotebook." *Los Angeles Times*, May 11, 2000, D-2.

Raag, Tarja, and Christine L. Rackliff. "Preschoolers' Awareness of Social Expectations of Gender: Relationships to Toy Choices." *Sex Roles* 38 (1998): 685–700.

Rail, Geneviève. "Seismography of the Postmodern Condition: Three Theses on the Implosion of Sport." In *Sport and Postmodern Times*, ed. Geneviève Rail, 143–61. Albany: State University of New York Press, 1998.

Rand, Erica. "Older Heads on Younger Bodies." In *The Children's Culture Reader*, ed. Henry Jenkins, 382–93. New York: New York University Press, 1998.

Real, Michael R. "MediaSport: Technology and the Commodification of Postmodern Sport." In *MediaSport*, ed. Lawrence A. Wenner, 14–26. London: Routledge, 1998.

Reskin, Barbara F., and Patricia A. Roos. *Job Queues, Gender Queues: Explaining Women's Inroads into Male Occupations*. Philadelphia: Temple University Press, 1990.

Rigauer, B. *Sport and Work*. New York: Columbia University Press, 1981.

Rinehart, Robert. "Inside of the Outside: Pecking Orders within Alternative Sport at ESPN's 1995 'The eXtreme Games.'" *Journal of Sport and Social Issues* 22 (1998): 398–415.

———. *Players All: Performances in Contemporary Sport*. Bloomington: Indiana University Press, 1998.

———. "Dropping into Sight: Commodification and Co-optation of In-Line Skating." In *To the Extreme: Alternative Sport, Inside and Out*, ed. Robert E. Rinehart and Synthia Sydnor. Albany: State University of New York Press, forthcoming.

Risman, Barbara. *Gender Vertigo: American Families in Transition*. New Haven, Conn.: Yale University Press, 1998.

Robinson, C. C., and J. T. Morris. "The Gender-Stereotyped Nature of Christmas Toys Received by 36-, 48-, and 60-Month-Old Children: A Comparison between Nonrequested vs. Requested Toys." *Sex Roles* 15 (1986): 21–32.

Robinson, Laura. *Crossing the Line: Violence and Sexual Assault in Canada's National Sport*. Toronto: McClelland and Stewart, 1998.

Rogers, Mary F. *Barbie Culture*. Thousand Oaks, Calif.: Sage Publications, 1999.

Rowe, David. "Accommodating Bodies: Celebrity, Sexuality and 'Tragic Magic.'" *Journal of Sport and Social Issues* 18 (1994): 6–26.

———. *Sport, Culture and the Media: The Unruly Trinity*. Buckingham, England: Open University Press, 1999.

Rowe, David, and Jim McKay. "Fields of Soap: Rupert versus Kerry as Masculine Melodrama." In *SportCult*, ed. R. Martin and Toby Miller, 191–210. Minneapolis: University of Minnesota Press, 1999.

Rowe, David, Jim McKay, and Toby Miller. "Come Together: Sport, National-ism, and the Media Image." In *MediaSport*, ed. Lawrence A. Wenner, 119–33. London: Routledge, 1998.

Ryan, Joan. *Little Girls in Pretty Boxes: The Making and Breaking of Elite Gymnasts and Figure Skaters*. New York: Doubleday, 1995.

Sabo, Don. "Different Stakes: Men's Support of Gender Equity in Sport." In Michael A. Messner and Donald F. Sabo, *Sex, Violence and Power in Sport: Rethinking Masculinity*, 202–13. Freedom, Calif.: Crossing Press, 1994.

———. "The Myth of the Sexual Athlete." In Michael A. Messner and Donald F. Sabo, *Sex, Violence and Power in Sport: Rethinking Masculinity*, 36–41. Freedom, Calif.: Crossing Press, 1994.

———. "Pigskin, Patriarchy and Pain." In Michael A. Messner and Donald F. Sabo, *Sex, Violence and Power in Sport: Rethinking Masculinity*, 82–88. Free-dom, Calif.: Crossing Press, 1994.

———. *The Women's Sports Foundation Gender Equity Report Card: A Survey of Athletic Participation in American Higher Education*. East Meadow, N.Y.: Women's Sports Foundation, 1997.

Sabo, Don, and Sue Curry Jansen. "Seen but Not Heard: Images of Black Men in Sports Media." In Michael A. Messner and Donald F. Sabo, *Sex, Vio-lence and Power in Sports: Rethinking Masculinity*, 150–60. Freedom, Calif.: Crossing Press, 1994.

Sabo, Donald, and David F. Gordon, eds. *Men's Health and Illness: Gender, Power, and the Body*. Thousand Oaks, Calif.: Sage Publications, 1995.

Sabo, Don, Phil Gray, and Linda Moore. "Domestic Violence and Televised Athletic Events: 'It's A Man Thing.'" In *Masculinities, Gender Relations, and Sport*, ed. Jim McKay, Michael A. Messner, and Donald F. Sabo, 127–46. Thousand Oaks, Calif.: Sage Publications, 2000.

Sabo, Don, Merrill J. Melnick, and Beth Vanfossen. "Corporate-Sponsored Sport Research: A Holy or Unholy Marriage?" In *Applied Sociology of Sport*, ed. A. Yiannakis and S. L. Greendorfer, 219–31. Champaign, Ill.: Human Kinetics Books, 1992.

Sage, George. "Justice Do It! The Nike Transnational Advocacy Network: Orga-nization, Collective Actions, and Outcomes." *Sociology of Sport Journal* 16 (1999): 206–35.

Sanday, Peggy. *Female Power and Male Dominance: On the Origins of Sexual Inequality*. New York: Cambridge University Press, 1981.

————. *Fraternity Gang Rape: Sex, Brotherhood and Privilege on Campus*. New York: New York University Press, 1990.

Segrave, Jeffrey, Claude Moreau, and Douglas N. Hastad. "An Investigation into the Relationship between Ice Hockey Participation and Delinquency." *Sociology of Sport Journal* 2 (1985): 281–98.

Seiter, Ellen. *Sold Separately: Parents and Children in Consumer Culture*. New Brunswick, N.J.: Rutgers University Press, 1995.

Shakib, Sohaila. "Male and Female High School Basketball Players' Perceptions of Gender and Athleticism: An Analysis of the Familial and Peer Group Context and Institutional Structures of Opportunity." Ph.D. dissertation, Department of Sociology, University of Southern California, 1999.

Silver, Michael. "Dirty Dogs." *Sports Illustrated*, October 26, 1998.

"Six Football Players Arrested for Hazing." *High Desert Star*, November 13, 2000. http://www.hidesertstar.com/display/inn_news/news1.txt.

Spain, Daphne. "The Spatial Foundations of Men's Friendships and Men's Power." In *Men's Friendships*, ed. Peter Nardi, 59–73. Newbury Park, Calif.: Sage Publications, 1992.

Spencer, Nancy. "Reading between the Lines: A Discursive Analysis of the Billie Jean King vs. Bobby Riggs 'Battle of the Sexes.'" *Sociology of Sport Journal* 17 (2000): 386–402.

Sperber, Murray. *Beer and Circus: How Big-Time Sports is Crippling Undergraduate Education*. New York: Henry Holt, 2000.

Spigel, Lynn. "Barbies without Ken: Femininity, Feminism, and the Art-Culture System." In Lynn Spigel, *Welcome to the Dreamhouse: Popular Media and Postwar Suburbs*, 310–53. Durham, N.C.: Duke University Press, 2001.

Spindel, Carol. *Dancing at Halftime: Sports and the Controversy over American Indian Mascots*. New York: New York University Press, 2000.

Staples, Robert. *Black Masculinity: The Black Male's Role in American Society*. San Francisco: Black Scholar Press, 1982.

————. "Health among African American Males." In *Men's Health and Illness: Gender, Power, and the Body*, ed. Donald Sabo and David F. Gordon, 121–39. Thousand Oaks, Calif.: Sage Publications, 1995.

Staurowsky, Ellen J. "The Cleveland 'Indians': A Case Study in American Indian Cultural Dispossession." *Sociology of Sport Journal* 17 (2000): 307–30.

Stewart, Larry. "X Marks the Spot." *Los Angeles Times*, February 4, 2001, D4.

Strate, Lance. "Beer Commercials: A Manual on Masculinity." In *Men, Masculinity, and the Media*, ed. Steve Craig, 78–92. Newbury Park, Calif.: Sage Publications, 1992.

Suggs, Welch. "2 Appeals Courts Uphold Right of Universities to Reduce Number of Male Athletes." *Chronicle of Higher Education*, January 7, 2000.

———. "Uneven Progress for Women's Sport." *Chronicle of Higher Education*, April 7, 2000.

———. "Poll Finds Strong Public Backing for Gender Equity in College Athletics." *Chronicle of Higher Education*, July 7, 2000.

———. "Supreme Court Won't Hear Title IX Lawsuit." *Chronicle of Higher Education*, July 14, 2000.

———. "Will Female Kicker's Legal Victory Reshape Gender Roles in Athletics?" *Chronicle of Higher Education*, October 27, 2000.

———. "U. of Kansas to Drop Men's Swimming and Tennis." *Chronicle of Higher Education*, March 6, 2001.

———. "Female Athletes Thrive, but Budget Pressures Loom." *Chronicle of Higher Education*, May 18, 2001, A45–48.

Summerfield, Karen, and Anita White. "Korfball: A Model of Egalitarianism?" *Sociology of Sport Journal* 6 (1989): 144–51.

Take Action for Girls. "The Two Faces of Nike." *Take Action for Girls Newsletter* 1, no. 2, November 1996, 2.

Theberge, Nancy. "Sport and Women's Empowerment." *Women's Studies International Forum* 10 (1987): 387–93.

———. "Women Athletes and the Myth of Female Frailty." In *Women: A Feminist Perspective*, ed. Jo Freeman, 507–22. 4th ed. Mountain View, Calif.: Mayfield, 1989.

———. *Higher Goals: Women's Ice Hockey and the Politics of Gender.* Albany: State University of New York Press, 2000.

"They Said It: Kobe Bryant." *Sports Illustrated*, February 21, 2000, 26.

Thompson, Shona. *Mother's Taxi: Sport and Women's Labor.* Albany: State University of New York Press, 1999.

Thorne, Barrie. *Gender Play: Girls and Boys in School.* New Brunswick, N.J.: Rutgers University Press, 1993.

Totten, Mark D. *Guys, Gangs, and Girlfriend Abuse.* Peterborough, Canada: Broadview Press, 2000.

Trujillo, Nick. "Machines, Missiles, and Men: Images of the Male Body on ABC's *Monday Night Football*." *Sociology of Sport Journal* 12 (1995): 403–23.

Twin, Stephanie. *Out of the Bleachers: Writings on Women and Sport*. Old Westbury, N.Y.: Feminist Press, 1979.

Vander Werf, Martin. "Anti-Sweatshop Group Finds Abuses at Korean Factory That Produced College Apparel." *Chronicle of Higher Education*, January 26, 2001.

Vieira, K. G., and W. H. Miller. "Avoidance of Sex-Atypical Toys by Five- and Ten-Year-Old Children." *Psychological Reports* 43 (1978): 543–46.

Wachs, Faye Linda. "Leveling the Playing Field: Negotiating Gendered Rules in Coed Softball." *Journal of Sport and Social Issues* (forthcoming).

Waldron, Ingrid. "Contributions of Changing Gender Differences in Behavior and Social Roles to Changing Gender Differences in Mortality." In *Men's Health and Illness: Gender, Power, and the Body*, ed. Donald F. Sabo and Frederick Gordon, 22–45. Thousand Oaks, Calif.: Sage Publications, 1995.

Walters, Suzanna Danuta. "Sex, Text, and Context: (In) Between Feminism and Cultural Studies." In *Revisioning Gender*, ed. Myra Marx Ferree, Judith Lorber, and Beth B. Hess, 222–57. Thousand Oaks, Calif.: Sage Publications, 1999.

Watkins, Craig S. "Bad Boyz: The Black Body, Spectacle, and Basketball in American Culture." Paper presented at the Olympia's Daughters: Gender, Sport, and the New Millennium Conference, University of Texas, Austin, November 4, 2000.

Weidman, Lisa, and Becky Beal. "Authenticity in the Skateboarding World." In *To the Extreme: Alternative Sport, Inside and Out*, ed. Robert E. Rinehart and Synthia Sydnor. Albany: State University of New York Press, forthcoming.

Weistart, John. "Title IX and Intercollegiate Sports: Equal Opportunity?" In *Sport in Contemporary Society*, ed. D. Stanley Eitzen, 295–301. 6th ed. New York: Worth, 2001.

Welch, Michael. "Violence against Women by Professional Football Players: A Gender Analysis of Hypermasculinity, Positional Status, Narcissism, and Entitlement." *Journal of Sport and Social Issues* 21 (1997): 392–411.

Wenner, Lawrence A. "In Search of the Sports Bar: Masculinity, Alcohol, Sports, and the Mediation of Public Space." In *Sport and Postmodern Times*, ed. Geneviève Rail, 303–32. Albany: State University of New York Press, 1998.

————. "The Sports Violence Profile." In *Paradoxes of Youth and Sport*, ed. Margaret Gatz, Sandra Ball Rokeach, and Michael A. Messner, 119–22. Albany: State University of New York Press, 2002.

————, ed. *MediaSport*. London: Routledge, 1998.

Wenner, Lawrence A., and Walter Gantz. "Watching Sports on Television: Audience Experience, Gender, and Marriage." In *MediaSport*, ed. Lawrence A. Wenner, 233–51. London: Routledge, 1998.

West, Candace, and Don Zimmerman. "Doing Gender." *Gender & Society* 1 (1987): 125–51.

Whalley, Syd, and Brady M. Bustany. "Gender Equity in Youth Team Sports by the Department of Recreation and Parks in the City of Los Angeles." Unpublished paper, UCLA School of Law, April 28, 2001.

Whannel, Gary. "Reading the Sports Media Audience." In *MediaSport*, ed. Lawrence A. Wenner, 221–32. London: Routledge, 1998.

Wheaton, Belinda. "'Just Do It': Consumption, Commitment, and Identity in the Windsurfing Subculture." *Sociology of Sport Journal* 17 (2000): 254–74.

Wheaton, Belinda, and Alan Tomlinson. "The Changing Gender Order in Sport? The Case of Windsurfing Subcultures." *Journal of Sport and Social Issues* 22 (1998): 252–74.

White, Philip G., Kevin Young, and William G. McTeer, "Sport, Masculinity, and the Injured Body." In *Men's Health and Illness: Gender, Power, and the Body*, ed. Donald F. Sabo and David F. Gordon, 158–82. Thousand Oaks, Calif.: Sage Publications, 1995.

Whitson, David. "Circuits of Promotion: Media, Marketing and the Globalization of Sport." In *MediaSport*, ed. Lawrence A. Wenner, 57–72. London: Routledge, 1998.

Williams, Christine. "Psychoanalytic Theory and the Sociology of Gender." In *Theory on Gender, Gender on Theory*, ed. Paula England, 131–49. New York: Aldine de Gruyter, 1993.

Willis, Paul. "Women in Sport in Ideology." In *Sport, Culture and Ideology*, ed. Jennifer Hargreaves, 117–35. London: Routledge and Kegan Paul, 1983.

Women's Sports Foundation. *The Wilson Report: Moms, Dads, Daughters and Sports*. East Meadow, N.Y.: Women's Sports Foundation, 1988.

Wood, Julian. "Groping toward Sexism: Boys' Sex Talk." In *Gender and Generation*, ed. Angela McRobbie and Mica Nava, 54–84. London: Macmillan, 1984.

Young, Iris M. "Throwing Like a Girl: A Phenomenology of Feminine Body Comportment, Motility, and Spatiality." *Human Studies* 3 (1980): 137–56.

Young, Kevin, and Philip White. "Researching Sports Injury: Reconstructing Dangerous Masculinities." In *Masculinities, Gender Relations, and Sport*, ed. Jim McKay, Michael A. Messner, and Donald F. Sabo, 108–26. Thousand Oaks, Calif.: Sage Publications, 2000.

Young, Steve. "Young at Heart." *Sports Illustrated*, June 19, 2000, 55–61.

Zimbalist, Andrew. *Unpaid Professionals: Commercialism and Conflict in Big-Time College Sports*. Princeton, N.J.: Princeton University Press, 1999.

Zones, Jane Sprague. "Beauty Myths and Realities and Their Impact on Women's Health." In *Gender through the Prism of Difference*, ed. Maxine Baca Zinn, Pierrette Hondagneu-Sotelo, and Michael A. Messner, 87–103. 2d ed. Boston: Allyn and Bacon, 2000.

Index

Michael A. Messner is professor of sociology and gender studies at the University of Southern California. His previous books include *Power at Play: Sports and the Problem of Masculinity* and *Politics of Masculinities: Men in Movements*. He has conducted several studies of gender in sport media for the Amateur Athletic Foundation of Los Angeles and for Children Now, and he speaks frequently on sex equity and violence in sports to teachers' organizations and coaches' and athletic directors' associations.